THE RISK IN BEING ALIVE

ONE MAN'S ADVENTURES ACROSS THE PLANET

BRIAN HANCOCK

a division of nomad communications

Nomad Press
A division of Nomad Communications
10 9 8 7 6 5 4 3 2 1
Copyright © 2003 Nomad Press

All rights reserved.

No part of this book may be reproduced in any form without permission in writing from the publisher, except by a reviewer who may quote brief passages in a review.

The trademark "Nomad Press" and the Nomad Press logo are trademarks of Nomad Communications, Inc. Printed in the United States.

ISBN 0-9659258-8-9

Questions regarding the ordering of this book should be addressed to
Independent Publishers Group
814 N. Franklin St.
Chicago, IL 60610

Cover artwork by David Morin
Design and interior illustrations by Bruce Leasure
Edited by Susan Hale and Eric Goldwarg

Nomad Press, PO Box 875, Norwich, VT 05055

"There is always a certain risk in being alive, and if you are more alive, there is more risk."

—*Henrik Ibsen*

For Tomas—I hope this book inspires you to have some adventures of your own.

FOREWORD
By Skip Novak

In the summer of 1979 I was due to skipper the sixty-five-foot ketch *Independent Endeavour* on a commemorative race from Plymouth, England, to Fremantle, Western Australia, with a stop in Cape Town. I had found most of the crew by July, most of whom I had sailed with before. We were all in our twenties and about to embark on a great adventure. We were still lacking a sailmaker for the trip, and I was trawling the waterfront for candidates.

"Anybody around?" I asked a trusted Kiwi skipper who had just crossed the Atlantic.

"Yeah, try Brian Hancock, he's a South African, still wet behind the ears, a smartass, but a good shipmate. We picked him up in the Caribbean, just up from Cape Town. That's him on the dock there repairing a sail cover." I walked over.

"Interested in sailing to Australia via South Africa in September?" I asked, as he cranked away on a manual sewing machine. He looked like a kid.

"Sure, what's the deal?" he answered with a confidence that belied his age.

"It's the Parmelia Race. As usual there is no deal. You can join us next week."

"Why not, I'll be there," was his quick reply.

Brian Hancock, or Mugsy, as he was known then, was twenty-one years old. He had just signed on for a three-month voyage after a five-minute conversation. No pay or other prospects were forthcoming, but that was the way it was done back then, in what I call the "Golden Age" of ocean racing.

Things were generally casual, sometimes haphazard, at times reckless. In short, it was all about youth.

So began a twenty-year friendship that, among other things, has put over seventy thousand miles of blue water under a common keel. We sailed together on *Alaska Eagle* in the Whitbread Race in 1981–82, and again on *Drum* in 1985–86. We also raced to Uruguay with the Soviets on *Fazisi* in the 1989–90 Whitbread. There were many other minor voyages, as well.

We hit if off from the start—both ironic, able to laugh at people's misfortunes, and appreciative of the differences in race and nationality with a benign sense of humor which today is considered very "politically incorrect." We both came from disenfranchised backgrounds. If you have traveling in your blood from the beginning, Chicago, where I grew up, is just as restrictive as Pietermaritzburg, where Brian grew up. When other twenty-year olds were contemplating careers as doctors or lawyers, or planning business empires, people like us, and god knows there were many, had one simple agenda—to see the world. In both our cases, sailing was our ticket out, Joseph Conrad the author of choice.

Those were the days when you lived from a sea bag and could move at twenty-four hours' notice—to anywhere on the planet. We were nomads. Those in the genre blew with a metaphorical wind taking the path of least resistance, while paradoxically searching for another epic challenge. We were opportunistic, certainly not for material gain, as there was little, and also not for reasons of climbing any ladder—no, we were instead hungry for the next bold move, the next lot of shipmates to laugh at or with, always anticipating riding that next wave.

For an ocean sailor, it is all about that moment of toughing it out in heavy weather with all hell breaking loose, and knowing that you're still in control. At other times it's more serene, simply being at the wheel while carving a long surf in the deep blue. Brian was one of the best I sailed with, having both an appreciation for the serenity and a competence for the storms. The many sensations you experience at sea focus your mind in order to rest your soul—this in turn gives you the energy to want to do it all over again. It's an addiction. It's risk. It's simplicity. We can't imagine a life without it.

Robert Service, in "The Men That Don't Fit" wrote, "it's the steady, quiet, plodding ones who win the lifelong race." I'm sure he's right. Here we are in middle-age, landed, but not grounded. Brian is still scheming and planning the next move. In fact he called me this morning to discuss plans he has for skippering a big catamaran in the Cape to Rio race. I am the same. Long-term commitment in the workplace is an anathema, freedom everything, or at least a sense of it. Our sea bags have, of course, grown. We now have houses to keep them in. E-mail is the secret to our subsistence. Somehow, with no foundation whatsoever, we just know that things will turn out alright.

Common experience in the field, that's the thing. The traveling by land or by sea is the thread that has kept us together. Frankly, I think I would rapidly tire of Brian in a "drawing room" relationship, and he of me. So we keep voyaging, both tied to our separate helms, reaching hard with a driving spray in our face. We wouldn't have it any other way.

I hope you enjoy his book—it's a good read, written from the heart and told by a master storyteller.

TRUE TALES

"Listen attentively, and above all remember that true tales are meant to be transmitted; to keep them to oneself is to betray them."
—*Baal-Schem-Tov*

Writing a book is a self-indulgent exercise. Expecting someone else to take the time to read it requires a lot of nerve. Asking that person to pay good money for the privilege surely places writers among the most ego-driven individuals on earth, yet there are millions of books written each year, and most of them are read. I hope that you will read this one. I hope that you will take a moment to leave your day behind, and join me on a trip around the world.

These are true stories with a bit of poetic license tossed in. They were started for my daughter, who grew up with a father who was always away someplace on some adventure. I wanted to leave her a record of what I had done, hoping perhaps that she might be inspired to have adventures of her own. They have evolved into a book.

This is my take on life, especially life at sea. In all, it's a biographical look at the last twenty years. I am too young to be writing an autobiography, so take this for what it is. Stories of love and laughter, travel, adventure, and a little bit of soul searching. Take your time reading. Pass the book around, and when you are done, head off on an adventure of your own. Live a full, fun life. You only get one chance. But be warned: there is no going back. Once you have tasted the open road and seen the fresh dew on a new day, you will be hooked, and as I have found out, there is no antidote.

CHAPTER 1
UNDER AFRICAN SKIES

"I learned what every dreaming child needs to know—that no horizon is so far you cannot get above it or beyond it."

—*Beryl Markham*

I grew up at the bottom of Africa in a small town with a big name, a juxtaposition of the names of the two men who first settled there. The men were called Piet Retief and Gert Maritz and they named their settlement Pietermaritzburg.

The town is nestled among the rolling hills of the Natal Province of South Africa, midway between the Drakensberg Mountains and the Indian Ocean. It used to be an orderly town with soft edges, but the soft edges are gone now, eroded by time and the turbulent changes that swept the country over the past two decades. Where the hillsides were once green and covered with wild flowers, they are now red mud, laid bare from too many people living on too little land. Even the smell is different. The fragrance of jacaranda blossoms has given way to car exhaust fumes and cooking fires. It's an area steeped in history, the nearby hills once the scene of furious battles between the Boers and the Zulus and the soil to this day remains stained with the blood of thousands of men who died for the love of their country. Great struggles with descriptive names like the Battle of Blood River and the Battle of Isandhlwana took place where cows now graze peacefully in the shade of acacia trees, and the Ncome River, once red with blood, gurgles peacefully in the hot afternoon sun. The Zulus were beaten into submission only to rise again with political power to reclaim their land, and the air of British colonialism that permeated all parts of life is long since gone, replaced by the rough and tumble of a struggling Third World city.

It wasn't always that way, it never is. When I was small, the streets were safe and the town claimed the unofficial title of being the last outpost of the British Empire. At times it seemed more English than England, as expatriates clung to traditions long since given up back home, but treasured as fond memories in Africa. During the summer we dressed in white and played cricket, while our parents also dressed in white and went lawn bowling. In the winter it was rugby, whether we liked it or not, and I did not. I was too small to be of any use on the field, and not much of a team player. I was more interested in boats. I longed for the weekends when I could go sailing. I longed to leave the routine of school and work and slip away to the familiar surroundings of the waterfront. The smell and sound of the lake immediately erased all the muddle and mess and stress of growing up. The moment I set sail it was washed away, replaced by the slap, slap of clear water on the hull. I knew from an early age that my life would be tied to the water, and early seeds of adventure were planted in my resolve.

My earliest memory is of a short flight. I was six. I remember the take off, and I remember the landing. The bit in-between has gone, but then it was a very short flight—less than a second, actually. I launched myself off the verandah wall with a vague belief that a positive attitude and a bit of luck would see me safely down. I had makeshift wings strapped to my arms. The second my feet left the wall I discovered the undeniable effects of gravity, and dropped like a stone. Young bones are supposed to bend and mine did at first, but everything has a breaking point as my left leg discovered a split second after making contact with the hard earth. I don't remember much beyond the landing. I recall the sterile smell of disinfectant burning my nostrils while I waited for the cast to be molded, and I remember being given the heel-guard to keep as a souvenir when the cast was cut off three weeks later. I had healed quickly and was sent back into the world to see what new damage I could inflict upon myself. It didn't take long.

During the winter we would visit my grandmother for Sunday lunch. You could smell the roast beef from the parking lot outside her small flat. With ice cream and chocolate sauce for dessert, it was worth getting dressed in our best clothes and sitting through a few hours of adult conversation. One Sunday, not long after I had regained full use of my broken leg, I ran headlong into the back of my father's car using the top of my head as a brake. I do not remember much beyond the initial impact. I do know that I ruined my best clothes and lunch at grandma's, and recall that increasingly familiar smell of disinfectant.

Some time passed before I inflicted more damage. Like most middle-class families, we did not own a swimming pool and instead would visit the public pool. One day I decided that diving was going to be my forte, and spent the morning perfecting my somersaults and belly-flops. By lunchtime I had them mastered, and decided to seek out a new challenge. A simple back-flip. The dive would stun my group of admirers and I would be able to claim my station as the diving expert of the pool. I positioned myself on the edge facing away from the water, and shuffled backwards until my toes were clinging to the lip. My heels hung over the water and I balanced for a moment building up courage. I teetered for a second, and then with peer pressure coaxing me on, I leapt into the air. The moment my feet left the ground I knew that it was going to be the dive to beat all dives. I sprung upwards, arched my back perfectly and crash-landed right where my feet had been. For a split second I teetered on the edge, my head flattened against the hard cement, and then in slow motion collapsed into the pool in a bloody heap. I remember looking back into the water and seeing a pool of crimson slowly mingling with the turquoise water. There was that all too familiar smell of disinfectant in the emergency room and the return trip to remove the stitches two weeks later. The best part of that disaster was being given a hokey-pokey ice cream. I was told that ice cream slowed bleeding and was not about to argue.

I survived my early years, albeit with a few scars, and when I turned seven I was scrubbed and polished and sent to school. I joined the ranks of other scrubbed and polished children all being sent to school to be taught by scrubbed and polished teachers. The schools in South Africa in the 1960s were segregated, not only along racial lines, but along gender and language lines, as well. I received a pasteurized education, while attending an English-speaking, whites-only, all-boys school. It seemed perfectly normal to me at the time. Children accept their parents' ways without questioning the logic until later in life. It took me twenty years before I figured there might be a better way. Each day, as I rode my bicycle to school, I passed black children heading in the other direction to their schools in the country. They were all walking, most of them barefoot, and it never occurred to me that there was anything out of place. They had their schools, we had ours, and that was that. My biggest concern was not being late.

I would arrive at the school gate promptly at 8 a.m. and wheel my bicycle to park it neatly alongside the other bikes. Morning assembly began at 8:01. Attendance was compulsory. The entire school would assemble for morning prayer recited in Latin, while our Latin teacher beamed down on the assembly. He was the only one that had any idea what was being said. His name was Joe Harding, but we referred to him simply as "Spud." Sitting alongside "Spud" in the teachers' gallery, was "Meatball," our aptly-named geography teacher who never anticipated that I would put his lessons to such good use. Neither did "Howie," our English teacher who glided from class to class like a sailboat with a list.

"You must read more books," he constantly admonished. "Books are the source of all knowledge." I took his advice to heart and read them by the dozen, mostly about travel and adventure. They planted a restless wanderlust in my blood.

The vice-principal was simply known as "Max"—that was his real name, although it might well have been short for

"Mad Max." It was rumored that he had a steel plate in his head, the result of an accident received during the second of the big wars. On hot days the plate would expand, causing headaches that immediately translated into a bad temper. Only the headmaster and vice-principal were allowed to cane students and we prayed for cool weather if "Max" was handing out punishment. Many of us paid a visit to his office at least once; in my case it was many times.

Morning assembly was a boring affair with the headmaster interspersing his comments between the unintelligible prayer and hymns sung out-of-key by an overanxious choir. The only change in routine was on Monday mornings when the sports results were read—and the mood on campus was set for the week by how well the teams had done. The headmaster's usual routine was to stride purposefully into the hall after everyone was seated, turn and glare down at us from behind his podium, glance towards the singing teacher who would strike up the choir, and then seat himself front and center to conduct the proceedings. One particular morning, sabotage took place. During the night someone sawed most of the way through the back legs of his chair, and as he took his seat, they gave way. Those that laughed were later singled out for a good caning. The headmaster meanwhile found a new chair and continued without comment. The choir seemed more off-key than ever. An inquisition was held, but they never found the culprit or the tool used in the crime. We were all made to stand on the rugby field in the blazing sun until someone either owned up or forwarded incriminating evidence. I had no idea who did the sawing, but he remains a hero in my mind three decades later. It takes nerve, cunning, and careful planning to pull off sabotage, and I envied his skills.

During high school, someone suggested a feat that, if performed, could earn you a "Victoria Cross." The highest award for bravery on the battlefield was to be our reward if we accomplished the task. It wouldn't be easy. You had to run naked from our school, along a main road for over a mile, to the all-girls school at the other end. When you got there you had to climb to the top of the high diving board, jump into the pool, swim twenty-five yards across, and then run back to our school. Get caught and there was no VC. It seemed like a perfect challenge and I was among the first group to go for it.

Five of us gathered behind the changing rooms at our school. The evening air was tepid and damp; it was a perfect night for a run, but each of us was hoping that one of the others would call the whole thing off. It had seemed like a good idea during the light of day, but darkness exposed hidden doubts. There had to be some reason for bailing out, but everyone was silent. No one was going to be the first to chicken out and peer pressure has forced worse judgment calls. Two students had already been dispatched. They would be waiting for us at the girls' school to ensure that we carried out that end of the deal. Another two acted as witnesses for the start, and hopefully, the finish. It was a little after 9 p.m. I would have preferred to run at midnight when there would be less traffic on the road, but there was no way I would be able to be out after midnight on a school night. As it was, I had to make up some story about doing homework over at a friend's house. The changing rooms were locked, but it didn't matter. We did not need the privacy they offered when our task was to spend the next hour running naked in public.

We slipped our clothes off, feeling vulnerable in the moonlight and awkward in our puberty. The first obstacle would be the night watchman. We had to pass his post to get through the school gates, and he would surely blow the whistle if he saw us. We crept from bush to bush hiding from the shadows that instantly took on the form of a teacher. In a few minutes we made it to the gate and peered out into the street. No sign of the watchman. There was a single car coming towards us; after that it was all clear. We waited for the car to pass before making our move. We would run the main road, one of Pietermaritzburg's more busy streets, even after dark. The problem was that there were few bushes along the way where we could hide. The trick was going to be finding one when we needed it, especially a bush that could shelter five naked boys.

The car passed with the driver oblivious to the moving shadows. My heart was pounding. Getting caught would mean a severe caning by the headmaster, and perhaps even expulsion from school. Still, what was a VC worth if there was no risk involved? We were about to start running when another car appeared.

"Wait," I said to the others. "Just let this one go by and then we'll make a run for it." The car slowed as it approached the gates, and then suddenly it turned onto the school grounds. We shrank into the shadows keeping very still. The car stopped and I was certain that we had been seen.

"No one move," someone whispered. I felt the urge to run for it. They would never know it was me. I could get back to the changing rooms, grab my clothes and be out of there in seconds, but peer pressure kept me frozen to the spot. I heard the car's engine rev, and it pulled forward slowly. As it slid by our hiding place we could make out the familiar outline of one of our teachers. He was not looking our way.

"OK guys, let's make a run for it." The pent-up adrenaline squirted directly into my bloodstream, and I sprinted as fast as I could out into the street and up the road. My legs were a blur as I tried to make as much distance as I could before the next car appeared, but the others were much faster, and I was quickly left behind. That was the last thing that I needed. Running in a pack was one thing. You had the security of others to hide behind. Running all alone was a frightening experience. I felt very exposed and very naked. The first driver didn't see us and we chased the flickering tail lights up the street.

Less than a quarter of the way along another car appeared. We scrambled for a bush and waited until it had passed. The road was dark again except for the dim glow of the street lights. Another couple of cars appeared and we crouched lower, attempting to be as inconspicuous as possible. The street seemed busier than it had all day. We hid in silence hoping that the collective thumping of our hearts would not give us away. The cars passed, the drivers unaware of the activity taking place just feet from them. Once again the street was dark and empty, and we ran on.

The worst part was running beneath the street lights, where we were instantly bathed in light. What if we were caught? How would I explain this to my parents? Too late now. We found the fence surrounding the girls' school, scrambled through a hole and melted into the shadows. Laughter spilled out nervously.

"We made it this far. There's no going back now," I blurted, quickly regretting that I had spoken. It came out sounding as if turning back was something I had been contemplating, and even though it was, there was no way I wanted to admit it.

"The school is all dark," someone noted. Through the trees we could make out the buildings and they all appeared to be unlit. The swimming pool was on the near side of the school, but it was close to one of the girls' dormitories, and we would still have to make our way past a few other buildings before getting there.

"Shit, what's that over there?" Someone pointed in the direction of the nearest building. "It looks like a person." We all squinted, but could see nothing.

"Don't be a fool. There's no one there." I was certain that he was seeing things, but kept on staring into the darkness. All the trees started to look like teachers and night watchmen swaying their way towards us. My heart lurched as one of the shadows moved.

"Christ, guys, we're going to get caught," I said.

"Shhh, keep still," someone whispered, and then, "oh fuck, there is someone there." The shadow moved again, and this time we could all see a person clearly outlined against the building. Another shadow appeared alongside the first.

"They're coming this way." My breath caught and my throat felt dry and ached. Perspiration drenched my palms, and for a second time that night I fought the urge to run for it. The shadows moved slowly in our direction. We shrunk back in desperation.

"Hey, you pussies, what are you doing just standing there? You are supposed to be swimming." It was the two witnesses that had been dispatched earlier to make sure that we did the jump and the swim. I took a breath and relaxed a little.

"Christ, you bastards scared us," I said.

"It's okay. There's no one about. We've checked out everything for you. The night watchman is on the other side of the school, probably locking up class rooms and turning off lights." They looked awkward standing fully clothed beside us. There is nothing like safety in numbers, even when you're the one who's naked.

"What time are the girls supposed to have the lights out?"

"Nine-thirty and it's past that now. Anyway, the place has been dark since we got here." We made our way slowly past the outer buildings. The girls' dormitory was dark and silent. It was on the far side of the swimming pool. I wondered if they would hear the splashing as we jumped into the water. By the time they heard the noise we would be across the pool, out the other end and well on our way. We crept forward. In a moment we would be completely exposed standing on the diving board, but for now we were still in the shadows. I looked up, hoping for a cloud to pass in front of the moon, but it was a clear African night. We would just have to go for it.

"Okay, guys this is it," I whispered. We climbed onto the ladder and quickly made it to the top, pausing to catch our breath before jumping. All of a sudden the lights went on and we were bathed in floodlight. From the girls' dorm shrieks of laughter and cheering erupted. We could not see beyond the glare and stood frozen like rabbits caught in a car's headlight.

"Let's see what you've got," a voice called out from behind the glare. "Show us your dicks!" We were busted and naked in front of two hundred laughing girls. I jumped, and so did the others. We hit the water with a collective splash and struck out for the shallow end. I hoped like hell that I would not be recognized. My dick had shrunk into itself from the cold and nerves, and there was no way I wanted anyone to see that there was so little there. There wouldn't be any chance to explain that it was much bigger on a warm day. By the time I made it across the pool, the others, all being faster swimmers, were out and had run for the shadows. A huge cheer went up as I scrambled out of the water and then I heard a voice call out at the top of her lungs.

"It's Brian Hancock. Hey, everybody, it's Hancock." I fled for the safety of the shadows, laughter ringing in my ears. I found the others huddled by the hole in the fence. The witnesses were with them, laughing harder than the rest.

"You bastards," I said, "you tipped them off, didn't you?" We were the only ones that didn't know it, but the school had been tipped off earlier in the afternoon, and by the time we were on the diving board, the dorm was practically bursting with anticipation. We scrambled through the fence and set off down the main road. This time we were much more cavalier. We jogged together and didn't attempt to hide when the first car drove by. The driver honked his horn and waved; we felt like kings who'd conquered the enemy.

Our clothes were where we had left them, and we dressed breathlessly. We had made it. No one mentioned that we could still get caught if word of our antics spread from the girls' school to ours. If questioned, we would deny everything and the rest of our class would stand with us, just as many had done for the saboteur who had cut the chair legs.

That night I had my first wet dream.

I gained some stature among my classmates after running for the VC, and there was no fallout from the girls' school over my size, or lack thereof. As far as I knew no one ever found out about the run and we were spared a caning and the possibility of expulsion.

The following summer I managed to push the boundaries once again, only this time I was to feel not only the full impact of being on the wrong side of "the establishment," but the bite of the rod, as well.

We held a sit-in over school regulations that restricted the length of our hair. The protest was led by a fellow VC holder, and regardless of how I felt about hair length, I was in with him on the protest. On the morning in question a few of us assembled on the rugby field and spread the word that we would not be going to morning assembly until our complaints were heard by the headmaster. Word soon spread and our ranks swelled, but the protest barely caused a ripple and the headmaster made no mention of it in his morning remarks. I had no firm views on hair length, and when the sit-in fizzled we capitulated, thinking that was the end of it. The headmaster had other ideas.

His sources exposed the ringleader and inner circle, and we received a summons. Being called to the headmaster's office was not good news. He was the head of "the establishment," and knew how to use his power very effectively. His office was at the end of a long corridor. To get there we had to pass the administrative offices, the secretaries' desks, the teachers' lunch room, his personal secretary, and finally, his door. Portraits of past headmasters stared sternly at us from gilded frames. Four of us had been singled out as troublemakers and we were under no illusion that we had been summoned to discuss our demands for longer hair.

We knocked, but there was no answer. From within we could hear muffled voices. We knocked again, but still no acknowledgment. We waited. Keeping us waiting was part of the strategy. My palms were dripping sweat. Suddenly the door flew open and a red-faced headmaster filled the space. He looked much bigger up close than he did from a distance.

"Ah," he said, "please come in." His manner seemed friendly, and for a fleeting moment I thought that we had been wrong to jump to conclusions. Maybe this *was* about easing hair restrictions. His office smelled of leather and perspiration, and was dominated by a huge walnut desk situated in the far corner. We stepped into the room and closed the door behind us.

"Please take a seat," he said waving us to a bench against the wall. We shuffled towards it and sat down. Out of the corner of my eye I could see the rack of bamboo canes mounted on the wall. I tried not to look at them, but they held my gaze.

"Hancock, I see that you are admiring my display case," the headmaster said, piercing me with his eyes.

"Oh no, sir."

"Don't worry," he said, "you will soon have the opportunity for a closer look." My heart skipped. I knew for sure that we were not there to discuss new hair regulations.

"Do any of you have anything to say?" he demanded from behind his desk where once again he looked his normal size.

"No, sir," we replied in unison. He made some notes on a pad and then picked up the phone to make a call. We sat in silence while he discussed lunch plans with his wife. The bench was hard and I realized that the smell of perspiration was coming from me, and not from the room.

"Well, then," he said, having allowed us to sweat for another few minutes, "I sentence you each to four of the best. Except you, Bassett. You will get six for being the ringleader." It was not an appropriate time to say anything. We just hoped that we could get it over with as quickly as possible. Now that we knew what we were in for, waiting for the caning would be unbearable.

"You will all report to my office tomorrow morning at 8:30." With that he dismissed us and with a wave of his hand sent us scurrying for the door. The hallway seemed to laugh at us as we ran past the secretaries and out into the fresh air.

"Fuck," said Bassett, "I don't want to wait until tomorrow. It's the waiting that's the worst." We all agreed, but we also knew that it was part of our punishment. The system had the power and the headmaster knew how to use it.

That night I kept waking up and looking at the clock, but time dragged. My mind scrambled for a way to cushion the caning. I'd heard of a student who had sewed soft leather onto the inside of the back of his shorts to add an extra layer of protection, but I did not have any leather. I thought perhaps I could stick something down my pants, but was worried about it being spotted and getting me into more trouble. By the time the soft light of dawn cast shadows on my bedroom wall I had given up on the idea and decided to face the caning like a man. That was how I felt at dawn. It would likely not be the same at 8 a.m.

It was a crisp, beautiful morning, but I felt like a prisoner about to face the gallows. Getting four of the best was a lot. Two was considered reasonable punishment. Six was the most you could get and I wondered how Bassett was feeling.

I was early for assembly for the first time in my school life. Everyone crowded around anxious to hear what we were going to do, but there was nothing we could do. Just sit through the assembly and hope for the best. At 8:29 a.m. we made the long walk back down the hallway to the office at the end. We were let in right away. The headmaster seemed to be enjoying our discomfort and asked us if we had anything to say. We shook our heads in unison.

"All right," he said. "All of you wait outside except Bassett." The door closed behind us and we could hear muffled voices coming from within the office. After a moment it went quiet, and then suddenly, "thwack." We heard the whip of the cane as it came down, and the sharp biting sound of bamboo against cotton-covered flesh. Then again, "thwack." Again, "thwack." It seemed to take forever to get through all six, especially the last two, and then as suddenly as it had started, the noise stopped. There was the sound of muffled voices and a moment later Bassett came through the door, his face red, but with a huge grin across it. He had survived.

"You next," he said, pointing to me. "He wants you next."

"Shit." I felt my stomach flip and all thoughts of facing the music like a man quickly evaporated. I opened the door and the headmaster was standing behind his desk waiting for me.

"Mr. Hancock," he said, "come on in and make yourself comfortable." I could smell leather again. "I know that you did not have much to do with this incident. You were just there to support Bassett were you not?"

I nodded. "Yes sir."

"Well then, perhaps I should be lenient on you, shouldn't I?" I nodded again.

"Yes, sir." He should be lenient on me. I was only doing it to support my friend and after all, wasn't that what they tried to teach us at school? I wondered if I might be let off.

"I am being lenient on you, Hancock. That is why you are only getting four instead of six. Now, pick your pleasure," he said, pointing towards the rack on the wall. "You were admiring them only yesterday." I walked over to the wall and opened the case. Seven bamboo canes were neatly displayed. They looked like instruments of torture. I tried to remember what others had said about which cane was the worst. I had not expected to be given a choice. Was it the thick one? It looked the meanest. Perhaps the thin cane was the best. It would not weigh as much as the thick one, but then I remembered someone telling me that the thin one was the worst. The cane was so light that it did not seem to hurt at first, but the end whipped around and caught you on your side. I wondered if it would be worse with the long cane rather than the short one. In the end I just grabbed one and handed the flimsy piece of bamboo to the headmaster.

"Ah, good choice," he said. "This one doesn't often draw

blood." I couldn't tell if he was joking or not, but nothing seemed very funny. My palms were sweating and my heart felt too large for my chest. Perspiration drowned out the smell of leather.

"Mr. Hancock," he said. "Did you enjoy your evening run last year?" I looked at him in surprise, wondering what he was getting at. His eyes were smiling though his face was serious.

"I don't know what you mean, sir."

"Ah, perhaps I should shine a little light on the matter," he said. I knew right away what he was getting at. He did know after all. The headmaster knows everything.

"No," he said, as if reading my mind. "We do not know everything. I still do not know who used the saw on my chair. Do you have any ideas?" I shook my head.

"So you are the proud holder of a Victoria Cross then. And what do you plan to do with this achievement once you leave school?" I knew that the game was up.

"N . . . nothing, sir, we just did it for fun," I stammered.

"Don't worry, Mr. Hancock, we will let sleeping dogs lie. You were all getting good grades at the time and I thought there was no need to disrupt matters. I heard your dive was splendid." He waved the cane at me. "Well, enough of that. Face the wall and bend over." I turned away from him. "And," he added as an afterthought, "do not forget to say thank you after each one. This is for your benefit, not mine."

"Yes, sir."

I faced the wall and bent over slightly.

"Over more and pull your pants tight. I do not want any baggy pants. Touch your hands to your shins." I bent further and waited. He was enjoying his little game. He knew that there was more punishment in the waiting than there was in the actual caning. A moment later I heard the whoosh of the cane as it whipped down, and then I heard, rather than felt, the whack. There was no pain at first, but suddenly the end of the cane caught me. It whipped around and caught me on my side where there was no protection from my underpants. I jumped with fright since I had not expected it. The pain burned, but I bent down again, grabbed my shins and waited for the second blow. I waited, but nothing came.

"Mr. Hancock, haven't you forgotten something?" I heard the voice from behind me.

"Yes sir, sorry sir, thank you sir," I said. I immediately heard the cane and felt its sting. "Thank you, sir," I said. There was another whoosh followed by a sharp sting, and then the last one came. "Thank you, sir," I said, and stood up. I was dying to rub my backside.

"Well, Mr. Hancock, that wasn't too bad was it?" I nodded, not trusting myself to speak. I wanted out of there, but he kept on talking. "You don't really care about the length of your hair, do you?"

"No, sir," I said. "I like short hair." I knew what his game was. He was keeping me talking so that I couldn't rub. I could feel my backside throbbing and knew that he had got me good.

"Tell the next one to come in please," he said. "You choose."

"Yes sir, thank you sir." I left the room in a hurry. "You're next," I said, pointing to my friend, and bolted down the hallway. All the other students were in class. I headed straight for the changing rooms. Bassett was already there with his pants down. He had been splashing cold water on his backside and was laughing as I ran in.

"How was it?" he asked.

"Not too bad," I replied, dropping my pants to inspect the damage. There were four thick welts across my backside, raised up and bright purple. The marks on my side had all merged into one. There were small flecks of blood on it and it hurt like hell, but I knew that for the next few weeks the marks would serve as a badge of honor. Everyone in the school would want to see them. My stature amongst my fellow students was raised a further notch. I splashed cold water on the marks, and waited for the others to show up.

Before I give the impression that I was always in trouble let me point out that I spent most of my time trying to avoid trouble, but it seemed to follow me. The same held true later in life when I set off to sail around the world, but by then I was expecting it and was ready for it. What I did not expect was for my best friend to turn against me, and worse yet, for him to challenge me to a fight. Barry Sefton and I had formed a bond that was based on stature. We were both small and because of it we stuck together. I thought, as kids do, that our friendship would last a lifetime. Clearly, Sefton had other ideas.

It started in the school toilets where many of these things begin. Somehow we bumped into each other and before long there was a bit of pushing and shoving. That should have been it, but within seconds a crowd had gathered and to my horror I realized that there was no going back. The crowd wanted to see a fight. I wanted out of there, but Sefton had other intentions. He came at me with fists flying and in seconds I was skidding around in the urinal trying to fend him off.

Fortunately the school bell came to my rescue. Its piercing ring signaled the end of lunch and the crowd started back for class. Again that should have been the end of it, but Sefton, buoyed by his early success, wanted more and so did the crowds.

"Meet me under the scoreboards at three o'clock," he snarled, referring to the usual venue for settling such matters. "If you're not there the school will know that you're a chicken." With that he turned and walked out of the toilets. My small crowd of supporters helped clean me up.

"What are you going to do?" they asked. What could I do? I had no interest in fighting Sefton, but having everyone know me as a chicken was a fate worse than death (to a 14-year-old kid at least). I was going to have to fight. The afternoon classes were a blur and the 2:30 school bell seemed to taunt me. I was already starting to feel sore from the two minutes of fighting at lunch and I was horrified by the idea of picking up where we left off. I walked slowly to my bike and pedaled up the hill to the rugby field where the fight would take place.

In the two hours since lunch, word had spread and a large crowd had gathered. The scoreboard was near a wall of the stadium where even a large crowd would be hidden from anyone driving by. Sefton was already there and had rolled up his sleeves. He could smell victory and along with his "new" friends, started to taunt me. He had every right to feel confident. My legs were barely strong enough to support me and the blood had drained from my face leaving me light-headed and a bit nauseous. All he had to do was blow and I would fall down. Worse yet, I didn't even hate him. You need hate to fight, at least if you want to win. Hours earlier he had been my best friend and I could not find a single reason why I wanted to fight him. I would have been happy to forgive him for his earlier transgression and move on, but before I could extend the olive branch he came at me with fists flying. His first punch connected on the side of my face. The indignity of the smack hurt more than the actual knuckle against bone, but it was all I needed to get into the fight. I lunged at Sefton, but he side stepped and hit me from behind knocking me to the ground. In a second he was on top of me. The crowds roared their approval while I tasted grass and dirt as he shoved my face into the freshly mown lawn. I felt his fists pummel my head, but there was no pain. I was wondering how it was all going to end. I was surely going to lose, but I had no idea how to get it over with before he really hurt me.

We stood up again and circled, fists in front of faces, staring at each other. I wanted to say I was sorry, but I knew a comment like that would only set the crowds off. We circled a bit longer and then I landed a lucky punch. I knew it was a lucky punch because it surprised me as much as it did him. I felt my knuckles snap as my fist connected with his face, and he dropped to the ground. I jumped onto him, but he rolled out of the way and in seconds was back on top of me, making me chew grass once more. The crowd wanted blood, but for a second time, thankfully, Sefton let me get up. I hit him with another lucky punch and he went down again, only this time he was up against the wall and had no where to roll. I landed on top of him and had his head in a fierce lock. I didn't want to hurt him, but at the same time I was afraid that if I let him go, he would hurt me.

Then I saw my opportunity. Because of the way we were entangled, I could knee him in the head, and to make it worse, his head was up against the wall so he couldn't move. This was my chance to finish him off and he knew it. I felt he was going to say something as I readied myself to smack his head, but he kept his mouth closed and his eyes shut waiting for my knee. I had a perfect opportunity, but I couldn't do it. The guy was my best friend after all, and I still could not find reason to hate him enough to crack his head open. We lay like that for a few minutes while the crowd jeered, and then suddenly everyone started to run.

"Quick, let's get the hell out of here, a teacher's coming," I heard someone say. I let Sefton go, ran for my bag and bike, and along with the rest of the crowd, sped off towards home. There was blood from my nose dripping onto the handlebars and for the first time I felt the pain, but the fight was over and I had saved face. That was the best outcome I could have hoped for.

Friendships come and go easily as a teenager, and after the fight, Barry and I fell into different groups in school. We were never friends again.

※ ✦ ※

Growing up was also a time for girls, and the Royal Show, an annual agricultural fair, was just the place to meet them. The Royal Show was a big part of my childhood. My grandmother worked for the organizers and each year, a week before the show began, she produced tickets. The tickets were good for multiple entries and we wore them like a badge of honor. When we were really small my grandmother would accompany us and she showed us off to all her co-workers, but later we were happy to go alone. Granny would not have approved of the things we did there, like climbing under the flaps of the beer tent and sipping the dregs out of glasses left on the floor.

Just after my fifteenth birthday I went to the show with my "new" best friend, a good guy by the name of Mart Krige. Mart had a blind date and he asked me to accompany him. His date was bringing a friend. Since that's what best friends are for, I had no problem, but when we met the girls, Mart was horrified by his date and wanted to make a run for it. I agreed and we let the girls lead us into one of the exhibits. As soon as they were through the door Mart bolted, but I was not quick enough and got caught trying to make my escape.

It turned out to be one of the luckiest unlucky events of my adolescence. Mart's date's best friend was a thirteen-year-old named Liz and she was not too bad looking. We spent the rest of the afternoon watching cattle being judged and visiting the pig pens, and it soon became obvious that there was mutual interest. We left the show around 5 p.m. with a plan to meet up later that evening. The only real drawback was that Liz was the same height as me, but it seemed I was the only one who noticed. Mart had some high heel boots and he loaned them to me for the evening.

I arrived at Liz's house feeling nervous about meeting her parents. I had not dated much, but it's a rite of passage for all kids and this was my time. I knocked on the door and Liz appeared. She looked better than I remembered; in fact, she looked downright beautiful.

"Come in," she said. "Come and meet my Mum and Dad." Her home was nicely decorated and spotlessly clean. My heart was thumping as I stood in the hallway looking at the freshly vacuumed white carpet that stood between me and the kitchen where I heard voices and presumed the parents were waiting to take stock of me. I followed Liz towards the kitchen and was just about across the carpet when I had a sinking feeling. I looked back over my shoulder and there was a trail of black, muddy footprints leading from the front door to the bottom of my feet. Ruining the carpet was the least of my problems; getting found out that I had high-heeled shoes on was more humiliating than anything I could imagine. Fortunately Liz and her parents made as if they didn't notice and our friendship, and eventually relationship, built from that incident to span seven years. It only fell apart once I started to travel, but the memory is still sweet.

By the mid 1970s, as I approached the end of high school, the vulnerable edges of apartheid were beginning to show. Black people put their tribal differences aside and banded together as one in a struggle that was becoming too huge to ignore. All through my childhood the obscenity of segregation had been neatly swept under the carpet; out of sight was out of mind, but things started to change. Although Nelson Mandela had been in prison for most of my life, his reach was beginning to be felt outside the walls of his cell on Robben Island and revolution was in the air. The Soweto riots galvanized a disenfranchised population. Each unjust slaying of an innocent person or manipulative move by the whites-only government chipped away at the status quo and it became obvious that change would be inevitable. For some, the change would be good; for others, their lives would be forever altered, and not necessarily for the better. School children do not think much about the problems of the world, and I was no different. Adolescence had its own set of problems and we took it one day at a time, growing strong and healthy with a broad sense that Africa was a fine place to grow up.

A few miles from my family home there is a small concrete memorial on the side of the road. I had passed the plaque many times, but never thought to stop and read what it said. It took until I was in my early forties before I pulled over to read the words cast in cement. The plaque marked the place where Mandela was arrested by security police in 1962. At the time it was routine for black men to be randomly grabbed and shoved into the back of a police wagon and taken away.

While I gazed at the plaque what struck me about the place was the serene beauty that belied the historical turn of events that had occurred on that spot—events that had such an effect on the future of South Africa. A lot of living has taken place since I was a child growing up in Pietermaritzburg, some of which will be recounted in this book, but on that particular day when I had taken the time to stop my car, the world was turning a little slower. Green fields gave way to small rocky outcroppings, while weaver birds collected straw for their nests among the rushes. The air was warm and still and for a short time, those very same hills where the bloody Zulu wars had taken place were bathed in sunlight and the country was at peace.

CHAPTER 2
A GUEST OF
THE GOVERNMENT

"Enjoy yourself to the brim and remember that whenever you get into trouble, trouble is only temporary."

—*Shelly Barron*

High school graduation marks a turning point in the lives of most young people, but if you were white, male, and graduating in the mid 1970s in South Africa, two years of hell stood between you and freedom. There were no patriotic posters urging you to join up; instead, an official letter arrived in the mail with your posting. I was summoned to report to the train station in Pietermaritzburg at a specific time to join my fellow recruits for a two-year stint as a guest of the South African Defense Force. Failure to appear would result in dire consequences, or so the posting paper threatened. I was to be stationed in Bloemfontein, a bleak, Afrikaans-dominated town in the middle of the Orange Free State, which to someone from Natal Province might as well have been the middle of nowhere.

Throughout most of the 1970s and early 1980s, South Africa fought a guerrilla war on the western front of its northern border against the Cuban-backed Angolan army, and on the eastern end against Mozambique. All young males were good fodder and there were no exceptions. If you were missing a leg, you were assigned a desk job. If you were missing a brain, you were promoted to corporal. There would be basic training for three months, specialized training for nine, and for a year thereafter you were posted to the border to defend your country. We were all pawns in a flawed war that claimed thousands of lives on both sides. Not one of us knew why we were there, nor did we know what the ultimate objective was. The conflict finally ended when all sides ran out of money.

My hair had barely grown long enough to touch my ears when it was time to report to the train station for recruitment. My mother offered to drop me off. Neither of us spoke on the way, although I know that there was a lot we both wanted to say to each other. Sons leaving home are a burden mothers accept with quiet dignity, and this was not the first time that she had made the trip to the station. There are four boys in our family. The platform was packed with baby-faced kids saying goodbye and relishing the feeling of being a civilian for the last time. The whistle blew and we boarded the train. As it chugged out of the station I leaned out of the window and looked for my mother's face in the crowd. She had moved away from the tracks and was waving—I could see a tear trickle down her cheek. She looked so young and beautiful. It was the last time I would see her looking well; she died soon after I finished basic training, and with her death I rolled reluctantly into adulthood.

There was no point trying to sleep on the train. Everyone was getting drunk. We swayed and clattered our way through the night singing rugby songs and putting on brave faces. Occasionally someone would lean out of the window and puke into the darkness. For the next three months beer would not be on the menu, and we would be cut off from the rest of the world. Our hours of freedom were waning. When the train pulled into Bloemfontein station we were a sorry lot—unwashed, exhausted, and hung over. The train smelled of stale beer and vomit, and the army was waiting for us.

They say that there are two ranks in the army that wield the power. The corporal and the general. For the next few months we would face the wrath of the corporals, and it started as soon as the train stopped.

"Get your sorry arses off the train right now and 'sak for fifty!'" We quickly found out what "sak for fifty" meant. Stop everything, drop everything, and do fifty pushups. Do them properly, and do not look up. Most importantly, do not look at the corporal.

"Now, Manne," the corporals yelled in Afrikaans, "do you see that tree over there? Fok weg. Get going." Around the tree we went, and then again and again until the first ones fell and started to puke.

"Kyk jou maatjies. Look at your friends," they yelled. "Hulle slaap nog al. They have gone to sleep." We were sent to pick them up and drag them back to the train. This running, dragging, and puking carried on until late in the day. We weren't even signed in yet, and life had become hell. Bloemfontein is hot, dry, and dusty, and the heat was taking its toll. The medic trucks hauled away the first batch, while the rest of us struggled in the dirt. As the shadows lengthened we were marched through the gates of the camp, and with a symbolic clang, they were closed behind us. The camp had ten-foot walls around it topped with barbed wire. They were there to keep us in, not the enemy out.

Later that night, after we had been signed in, hosed down with a fire hose, and issued army fatigues, we were shown to our tents. Sixteen cots jammed into a small tent was to be our home for the next year. We ate at the mess and returned quickly to the sanctuary of our new home. The lights went out automatically at 9 p.m. I fell into a deep sleep on my first night this far away from home.

At 11 p.m. the sirens went off. The lights came on and the corporals arrived.

"What the fuck do you think you are doing sleeping in your beds?" they screamed. "The beds are for inspection only. You sleep on the floor." And so for the next year we would spend hours making our beds until they were perfect, and then sleep alongside them on the cold gravel floor. The beds had to be absolutely square, and the sheets starched, ironed, and folded back a bayonet length. The edge had to be crisp as a blade and a perfect right-angle. We learned how to get them exact. If you marked out precisely where you wanted the edge to be and then rubbed a soft soap along the underside, you could use two books to crease the fabric to a perfect right-angle. By day seven we knew how to bone shoes, clean a rifle, make a bed that would pass the spirit-level test, and polish everything in sight to a deep shine. We were tired and homesick, hating the food and the corporals, and only had one year, eleven months, and twenty-four days to go. Counting down the days would become a way of life.

Basic training is meant to be hell. The premise is to break your spirit, and then rebuild you in the mold of a soldier. Initially it was a premise that I cautiously resisted, but I was quickly singled out and worked over until I threw up and begged for mercy. After that, compliance seemed to be an easier course, so comply I did. For our efforts we were paid one Rand and five cents a day, or the equivalent, at that time, of one US dollar, out of which, each month, they deducted three Rand for haircuts, two Rand for mess fees and seventy-five cents for church donations, regardless of your faith.

The corporals' imaginations knew no limits when it came to creating a miserable environment. They were masters at it. One of their favorite creations was the piss-parade. Once or twice a week we were roused from our makeshift bunks in the middle of the night and made to stand half naked on the parade ground until we peed. Peeing with an audience is difficult at the best of times, and almost impossible in the middle of winter with frost on the ground and three hundred people watching. No one was allowed to leave until the last person had peed. Sometimes we would anticipate the piss-parades and drink gallons of water before going to bed, only to wake up in the middle of the night with a bladder about to blow. So we got up and went, only to return to the warmth of the cot in time to be roused for a piss-parade. There were times when we stood in the cold for hours waiting for the last person to splash before we were all allowed to go back to bed. Some mornings we had just made it back when the 5 a.m. siren blasted, followed by a nasal voice over the loudspeaker.

"Opstaan manne. Hands off your cocks and onto your socks. You are in the army now."

In the pre-dawn light, streams of sleepy men made their way to the showers for an ice cold wash. Hot water would only be allowed after basic training. The ablution block was an oblong shed with a row of showers running the length of one side, and a wooden bench along the other side. The bench had holes cut every three feet partitioned by low walls, and served as toilets. No doors. A trough filled with water ran under the bench and every minute a tank at one end would flush, washing everyone's business down the trough into a long-drop well at the end.

One morning a friend and I situated ourselves at the end nearest the tank. We crumpled up newspaper, and just before the flush came, we lighted it and dropped it into the trough. The flush came on cue, carrying the burning paper down the trough, roasting bare arses as it went. The corporals found out and we were marched around the parade ground for five hours, but the image of a dozen arses on fire made the time fly by. A strong sense of humor was needed to get through each day.

Guard duty was the responsibility of new recruits, and until a fresh crop arrived after six months, we would stand twice a week. We were issued live ammunition, but told not to use it under any circumstances. The watch system was two hours in the tower, and then two hours back in the guard tent trying to get some rest, and so on through the night. It made for an unpleasant night, but the only real danger was getting caught sleeping. It was here that I first perfected the art of sleeping standing up.

We were almost through our basic training when Solly shot himself. He was standing guard in one of the towers and used the field radio to summon the corporal in charge.

"I am going to kill myself," he announced. The corporal arrived in his jeep with reinforcements and a megaphone.

"Solly, you sorry excuse for a soldier, you get down here and let me kick your lily-white arse," the corporal announced with all the tact of a steamroller. "You have disturbed my sleep and you are going to pay for it." Solly said nothing. He was sitting on the floor of the tower staring at the cold cement walls. He slipped the catch off his rifle and put it up to his mouth.

"Solly, I am going to kick the shit out of you if you do not come down from there and explain yourself," the corporal continued, his nasal voice sounding more menacing through the megaphone. "You're going to be sorry that you disturbed my sleep, you lowest form of life." Solly stood up and was caught in the glare of the corporal's spotlight. His eyes were wide with fear.

"Solly, you stupid shit. If you waste any ammunition you will be sent to detention," the corporal continued, missing the irony of his comment.

Solly blinked back at him, shoved the end of the rifle into his mouth, and without saying a word, blew his head off. The shot rang out across camp. I had been hot-bunking with Solly that night, and heard the shot from the guard tent. It was my bad luck that I was next on duty, and was slated to stand guard in the same tower. The military police dragged both Solly and the corporal away, and sent for me.

"Meneer Hancock, you are on watch. Get up there and make the place shine." I was given a bucket and mop and told that it would be inspected in the morning. I was terrified. I had never come across death before. I climbed slowly up the ladder into the tower and shone my flashlight around. Someone had already made an attempt at cleaning, but there was still blood and bits of brain splattered on the walls. I shone my light on the roof and saw the hole where the bullet had continued its trajectory after exiting through the top of Solly's head. It was a small, neat hole through the tin roof. My stomach lurched, and I threw up on the floor, adding to the mess. I felt sick and scared. Life had suddenly become too real for me. I was not ready to grow up.

A special meeting was called the next day. We were marched onto the parade ground and left standing in the hot sun. After two hours the colonel in charge of the camp appeared and threatened that there would be real trouble if any of us attempted to do anything as stupid as Solly had done. He shook his finger and glared at us as if we were somehow responsible for Solly's death. It was a tough lesson to learn, but he made it clear; there was no place for pity in the army. No personal counseling sessions. No comforting social workers. It was back to basic training and on with life.

※ ✦ ※

As our three months of basic training was drawing to an end, we were told that we would be given a weekend pass to visit our families. We had become skeptical of good news, and sure enough this bit of information was followed by a caveat. We first had a week-long maneuver in the bush, and only those who survived would be granted a pass. Once again we were marched onto the parade ground and made to stand in a long line. At the far end of the parade ground was a pile of tins glinting in the sunlight. From where we stood we could see that all the labels had been removed.

"Right, Manne," the corporals announced. "That pile over there is your food for a week. One tin, per man, per day. Now, fok weg. Get out of here." We bolted across the parade ground with the big guys elbowing their way to the front. By the time I arrived at the pile all the big tins were gone. A few small cans lay strewn about, which I gathered and stuffed into my backpack. I approached a big Afrikaner and asked if he would swap a big tin for one of my small ones.

"You blerrie crazy," he said leaving me in no doubt that he was not interested, and I didn't blame him. Even a big tin would not provide enough sustenance. It was going to be a long, hungry week. We piled into trucks and headed north out of town to a swampy area where our maneuver was to take place. Later that night, sitting around the camp fire, I discovered that there was indeed someone above looking out for me. The Afrikaner ended up with seven tins of jam; I had oysters.

We slept with our boots on and spent the days crawling through mud and slime. It was hell week and everyone puked and passed out at least once. The full moon had the corporals in a creative state. By week's end we were certain that they had exhausted all of their draconian fantasies, but they had kept the best for last and sent us on a twenty-mile march through swampy terrain without water bottles. Before we departed, a half-dozen sheep were ceremoniously slaughtered and there was a promise of a feast upon our return. The spits were being assembled and the fires were ready to be lit. There was even a rumor cold beer would be served.

About five miles from the end of our march we were told to start collecting wood for the fire and to carry it back to camp. I was tired and sick of the army and did not see any point in carrying wood five miles when there was plenty to be found right at the camp. This was just another corporals' sadistic fantasy, and I was not about to fulfill it. I was not alone. A dozen of us felt the same, but I should have remembered high school and the caning. They had the power and we were the pawns.

As we approached camp, the delicious smell of roasting meat wafted towards us. We had stopped halfway and drunk tepid water from a stream, but the effect had long since worn off and I was dying of thirst. I dared to imagine a cold beer in my hand. It had been three months since I last tasted one and memories of the train ride and too much beer had long since faded. I was ready for a good meal and a cold drink. We came out of the trees into the clearing that had become our camp. In the center, the sheep were hoisted onto huge spits and were roasting slowly over beds of hot coals. Tables had been erected and kegs of beer were placed all around. It looked like an oasis, but first the corporals had something to say to us.

"Manne, manne, manne." The corporals shook their head in mock disbelief. "You blerrie bastards have been here almost three months and not learned a thing." We stared back wondering what they were up to. Just then I was grabbed from behind and dragged off to the side. All the others without wood were singled out.

"Manne, manne. Look at these soldiers. Too blerrie smart to carry wood," the corporals sneered. "Your maatjies will drink beer tonight and eat until they can't move. You will be crawling through the mud again." My heart sank. I looked around hoping for some wood to miraculously appear in my hands, but it was too late. I was busted and feeling more tired than ever. We were marched off into the woods and crawled and sweated late into the night while the smell of roast lamb and the sound of laughter wafted over to torment us. The next day we were issued our first weekend pass. Back in Bloemfontein we were hosed down, issued step-out clothes, given army regulation haircuts, and set free for the first time in three months.

My father loaned me two hundred Rand and found an old Volkswagen Beetle for me to buy. It was turquoise blue, a little rusted, and had a sun roof that leaked, but I treasured the car. It was a tight fit, but with a little persuasion it could carry five people and all our luggage. The car was my freedom and a way to get back home. In the beginning I would head home on weekend passes, but as time passed it became less important. The tug of life in the big world was pulling me away from the security of family. The tug would grow stronger as my army training progressed, and after my mother died, returning home was traded for visits to Liz, who was still my girlfriend. She had moved with her parents to Johannesburg and I spent the weekends at their house.

In the late 1970s there was petrol rationing around the world and South Africa was no exception. The government lowered the speed limit and forbade the sale of petrol on Sundays, making it difficult to get back to camp after a weekend at home. I needed more than two full tanks of gas for the four-hundred-mile trip. Adversity breeds creativity, so I made arrangements to stop halfway at a friend's house, and siphon petrol from his mother's car. To make the final part of the trip, I kept a small jerry can of petrol under the back seat alongside the battery. This was illegal and the police routinely stopped cars to search for containers of petrol, but they never thought to look under the back seat of my car.

A few months after our first weekend pass I had an experience that might have saved my life. Using my ration of cigarettes, I traded a corporal for his parking privileges. New recruits were not allowed to park at the camp, but cigarettes could buy you just about anything, and for a while I was allowed to park my car outside the camp gates. Occasionally a few of us would slip out on AWOL and head into town for the night. We had civilian clothes stashed in the car and getting past the guard post was easy, but the road to town ran along the perimeter of the camp, and there was always a chance of being seen. AWOL was punishable by a minimum of a week in detention, and army detention was much worse than civilian jail.

One evening three of us slipped past the guards and took off for a night on the town. The old Volkswagen had coiled springs and some kind of straw stuffing for the seats. Unfortunately, the battery cover had rusted through, and each time we went over a bump one of the springs shorted the battery connections. I drove as fast as I could, but not so fast that it would attract attention, and we had almost made it all the way around the perimeter when I smelled smoke. Puffs wafted up from under the back seat—and then suddenly we were on fire. I slammed on the brakes and we jumped out of the car, grabbed our civilian clothes from the trunk and tried to douse the flames. It only served to fan the fire. Just then another car approached. It pulled up alongside us and the window rolled down to reveal a stern-faced colonel.

"And what seems to be the problem here?" he asked. My heart was in my throat. I managed to squeak out a reply that we needed a fire extinguisher. We were suddenly in deep trouble and the flaming back seat was the least of our problems. The colonel produced a small fire extinguisher and passed it to me. I pointed it at the base of the flames and filled my car with foam. The fire subsided immediately. I handed the extinguisher back to the colonel, bracing myself for what was sure to come, but he just looked amused and said, "Have a good day, soldiers," and he drove off without another word. He never did realize that we were AWOL. All I could think of was what would have happened if we had had a jerry can of petrol under the seat.

The first year passed quickly enough, and the sign pinned to the back of the tent door read, "365 days to go." Our status rose from being "the lowest forms of life," to "ou Manne," old men. We now had some of the power. I graduated at the top of my platoon. The top twenty were selected to be part of the elite tank division. The rest were sent off to train in armored cars. We would spend our days out on the shooting range lobbing shells at targets three miles away. It was a pathetic waste of money. We gunned down cactuses, and any bird that had the temerity to fly close by was instantly blown out of the sky. In fact, anything that moved that wasn't human was mowed down. We were kids and we were bored. The armored car divisions were sent up to the border to fight the war against the Angolans. Because the terrain was thick bush it was no place for a tank, and so we were left behind to sit in the sun, polish the brightwork, and change the oil.

The boredom was somewhat relieved when a fresh crop of recruits pulled into camp. We were now in a position to make their lives miserable. We had been well taught and it was time to pass along some of our hard-won knowledge. We conducted inspections every morning, running our fingers along the tops of the tin cupboards, knowing full well that we would find dust—moments after you clean it, dust settles again.

"So, manne," we would say. "You are a bunch of pigs. You live like savages." The new recruits would tremble and stare at the ground while we did our best to suppress a laugh. It was all so ridiculous.

"So, manne, you know what pigs can do if you train them properly?" They knew the answer. They had heard it many times before.

"Pigs can fly," we would say with dramatic emphasis. "So, pigs, it's time to fly." The recruits would hand us their steel helmets and climb up on top of their cupboards. We would remove the soft inner-lining and pass the helmets back. They stood on the cupboards, helmets on, strap unbuckled, arms outstretched and when we said fly, they jumped. For a moment they were airborne and then they landed softly on the gravel floor. A split second later five pounds of steel helmet landed on their heads, knocking most of them to the ground, and in some cases, knocking them clean out. It was great fun now that we were the instigators, but I'm afraid generations of soft-headed South Africans were created this way.

Each morning we marked off another day on the calendar and pinned the result on the back of the tent door. Slowly, the magic number decreased. When it read "one hundred days to go," we had a huge party and then went back to polishing our tanks. Bloemfontein had become home, and despite the dust and the heat I discovered that it wasn't such a bad place. We fought boredom and watched the days go slowly by. With just forty days remaining, I was called to the colonel's office.

"Meneer Hancock," he said, "you are a sailor, are you not?" he commanded rather than asked.

"Ya, colonel," I replied.

"Well then, meneer, you take a train to Cape Town and you represent this camp in the Defense Force Championships. They are racing a regatta and you make blerrie sure that you win."

"Ya, colonel," I replied, and took off to the purser's office to get a cash advance. He handed me a train ticket and the following day I reported at Simonstown Naval Base. The navy appeared to be a much more relaxed place than the army. I was given a private room and a boat to sail. We would race in False Bay in clunky old dinghies. The wind howled down the back of Table Mountain, and the regatta turned into a survival of the fittest. I won all six races, beating the best of the army, navy, and airforce, and was awarded a trophy that became my ticket out of the army.

I took the train back to Bloemfontein while the trophy was flown on an airforce jet; it went first class, while I was still traveling third. The train rumbled across the dusty Karoo, and as I watched the scenery pass, I thought about how much I had changed since my first train ride to camp almost two years earlier. I had grown up. The army was not a place I would have chosen to spend two years of my life, but the training and discipline had been good. I had the rest of my life to look forward to. Sailing for a living was a lifestyle that I was slowly daring to dream about. As night fell, the landscape faded through hues of oranges and reds, until finally it all turned black. I made up my mind to leave South Africa and look for work in Europe. In less than a month I would be free to do anything I wanted, and I decided to travel the world looking for sailing regattas.

When I arrived back at camp, I was met at the gate by the Military Police. They seemed friendly, but my first instinct was suspicion. I tried to think what I might have done wrong.

"This way, meneer Hancock," they commanded, and led me to my tent. "Pack your stuff and make sure that your rifle is clean. We will be back in twenty minutes to get you. And," they added as an afterthought, "stay in your step-out clothes." In a moment they were gone and I sat on my bunk wondering what was going on. The tents were deserted. In the distance I could hear a corporal drilling new recruits on the parade ground. His voice carried through the empty camp. I sighted down the barrel of my rifle, saw that it was clean and tossed it onto my bunk. I emptied out my tin cupboard and stuffed everything into a duffel bag wondering where they were transferring me. The Military Police returned and took me to the quartermaster's tent where he took the rifle and checked the contents of the duffel. They then marched me out to the parade ground.

As we came around the corner I saw the whole regiment assembled. A stage had been set up and the top company brass were all seated. On a table front and center stood the trophy. I could not believe my eyes. After two years of being "that fooking Englishman," I was being recognized with a parade. The band struck up, and when they stopped the colonel stood and made a short speech in Afrikaans. He then summoned me to the stage and presented me with the trophy.

"Meneer Hancock," he said, "you have brought honor to our camp." I stared at him, not quite believing what was happening, and shook his hand. "You are fooking lucky you did not lose the blerrie races. I have something for you." He handed me an envelope. "You are finished with the army. These are your get-out papers. You may go home now." I stared at the envelope. "You may go now," he said. I saluted him, turned around, and as I walked off the parade ground I heard him call out behind me. "Jus' make sure you make something of your life, hey. It's too short to waste." The amount of compassion in his voice took me by surprise. The colonel was not known for sentiment. The parade ground looked different as I walked away. It was no longer a place to fear. I stepped onto the grassy verge and ran down the slope towards my tent. After more than seven hundred days I was finally a free man.

I turned in my step-out clothes, signed out at the guard hut, and walked to my car with the few possessions I had managed to accumulate over the past two years. It was not much to show for all the grime, sweat, and tears, but I had arrived there as a boy and was leaving a man.

I had hair on my chin to prove it.

CHAPTER 3
A SERENDIPITOUS PISS

"In time, and with water, everything changes."
—Leonardo da Vinci

Bahia, Brazil is a city that throbs. There is no better word to describe it. The tropical heat and clinging humidity mingle with the sweat of lovers who stroll the beaches and boardwalks by night, while samba music filters through palm fronds. Rhythm hangs heavy in the air. Occasionally a cool breeze wafts in from the ocean and blows the laden air onto the plains, but mostly it just sits there like a pregnant woman; uncomfortable and hot. The city can be intoxicating. The stagnant warmth stirs feelings long since latent. It awakens primal urges. Bahia is a city with a soul, and when you step ashore it wraps around you, hugs you tight, and reminds you that you will never be the same. When you leave, a small piece of Brazil leaves with you.

I first visited Bahia in the summer of 1979 while sailing between Uruguay and the Caribbean. The only way I could get out of South Africa with no money was to sail out, and so I did. I left a few months after finishing my stint in the army, joining a South African yacht by the name of *Dabulamanzi*, which is a Zulu word meaning "sweet water." I signed on as their sailmaker for a race from Cape Town to Uruguay. Halfway across the South Atlantic I decided that I wasn't going back. What had started as an idea while traveling through the Karoo was becoming a reality. I was already planning to sail around the world. It was a perfect way to avoid the realities and responsibilities of life, and a great way to meet girls. What was not to like? It was on the passage north to the Caribbean that we saw the loom of land and altered course for Bahia. Up to that point the trip had been a tedious slog into a strong northerly headwind, and the boat and crew were getting tired of the grind. We were ready for a few days of fresh food and a firm footing.

A little after noon we passed the harbor wall and sailed smack into the embrace of tepid air. The water changed from a deep blue to milky brown, and smelled of runoff and rotting vegetation. A small armada of local crafts jostled for position, hawking produce and trinkets. They escorted us to an anchorage. As the hook went down I stood on the bow drinking in the sights and sounds of land, longing for some time ashore. My hormones were cranking and a night on the town was on my mind. The back alleys with their forbidden fruit beckoned. I decided I would slip ashore later that night to see what I could find. I had no idea that my life would almost end in the next few hours.

There is a huge public elevator that transports passengers from the dock area up to the main part of the city. You leave the quiet squalor of the docks to land among the hum and bustle of the old city where street vendors air their wares, and buskers tap out a rhythm that echoes on the walls of the old buildings. Open fires burn on the sidewalks with strange pieces of meat grilling over low coals. The fatty morsels are sold to the passing trade. Thick smoke hangs in the air, blurring the lights, adding to the heady feeling of being in a foreign country.

While riding the elevator I studied the character lines on the face of an old woman standing next to me. She clutched her basket closer to her breast and eyed me sharply. I smiled at her, and saw her shoulders drop and the furrows on her brow smooth in response. She shuffled her feet and smiled back. If wrinkles were anything to go by, she had lived a full life. A wide-eyed kid with a snotty nose stared at me without blinking. His round face glowed with innocence, yet to be marked by the passage of time. Behind him a businessman gazed at the floor with a bored look. I felt bad for him. He looked uncomfortable in his conforming dress. Patches of sweat marked his suit. The elevator was hot and stuffy and I was glad when it came to a halt. I slipped the kid a few cruzeiros and headed into town.

It was still early, and the streets were empty, but as I ambled towards the central part of town I felt the city come alive. Street vendors hawked everything from live parrots to dead rabbits. The street urchins were out in force and I patted the back of my trousers, checking for my wallet.

"Mister, Mister," they yelled at me. "Mister, Mister, come and look." I smiled and kept moving while shoving my wallet deeper into my pocket. A group of kids had set up drums and were banging away to some inner beat, their faces transfixed by the rhythm. A crowd had gathered to watch, and now and then someone would toss a few cruzeiros into a hat. The takings were meager, but the evening was still young. As the sun disappeared an occasional rumble of thunder rolled in from the plains. The light on the old buildings changed, throwing shadows across the square, softening the hard edges.

Looking out across the bay I could make out our boat at anchor. A shadowed figure on the foredeck was rigging the anchor light. A dim glow emanated from the portholes reflecting on the still water. I thought of the crew sitting below preparing dinner, drinking beer and red wine. None of them had wanted to come ashore, opting instead for an early night. I was glad to be alone. I was an anonymous stranger, a refugee from another world, privileged to catch a glimpse of life in Brazil.

I kept moving, drinking in the sights and smells, feeling the beat of the city resonate in my gut. Soon I was beyond the main square, into the back alleys where the streets narrowed. While Bahia can hardly be described as a city for tourists, the central area accommodates commercialism much better than the alleys. Some of them were unlit, most of them filthy. I was searching for a hole-in-the-wall restaurant, and knew that the farther from the square I went, the better my chances would be of finding something in my price range. I glanced into a couple of restaurants but they were deserted. Brazilians seldom venture out for dinner before midnight. Bored waiters hung around the doorways, chatting amongst themselves and commenting loudly on the passing crowd. Macho men swaggered, chain-smoking unfiltered cigarettes, most sporting a forest of coarse hair protruding from their open vests. Girls in tight jeans swung their hips and pouted their over-painted lips in response. Not a soul paid me heed. Not that I blended in very well with my blond hair and blue eyes, but no one seemed to mind my presence.

I stopped at an old cathedral, went in and sat in the cool darkness watching people come and go. The confessional was doing a brisk trade. An old priest came in through a side door and nodded to me as he passed. I smiled at him and watched as he lit candles around the alter. I could hear the kids banging their drums, though the sound was muffled by thick walls. A young girl sat next to me and showed me her rosary, but she left when she realized that I could not speak Portuguese. I wished I could. There was something sublime about the old building. The stained-glass windows had been there for hundreds of years, and the pews had provided sanctuary for many weary travelers. I was only the latest, not the last. It was an oasis away from the bustle of life on the streets, and open to all. I enjoyed the quiet for a moment, but the pull of the street was strong, and I was dying for a cold beer, so I headed back out the way I had come in. Out into the heat and humidity.

By 10:30 p.m. the bars had started to fill, and elderly couples were nursing drinks in some of the more well-lit restaurants. I found a narrow bar down a side street, and slid in for some refreshment. Cigarette smoke hung thick, engulfing the piles of sausages and salamis that were strung from the ceiling. I wondered how much of the curing process took place in cigarette smoke. The bartender nodded as I took a seat by the door, and an icy Brahma Choppe appeared in front of me. My eyes smarted from the acrid air, while my throat gratefully accepted the beer.

At first glance the place looked to be full of men only, but then I noticed a couple of women sitting by themselves in the corner. Hookers? Perhaps, not that it mattered. They were keeping to themselves and seemed to be surveying the scene as much as I was. The crowd was relaxed and laughter pealed out from all corners. The beer was good, but I wasn't sure how much of the smoke I could take, so I signaled the bartender. Did he have any suggestions for a good restaurant? "Something where locals eat, preferably locals that do not have much money yet enjoy a decent meal every once in a while."

"Sim," he beamed, "Sim, Sim. Tudo bem." Yes, no problem. He had a brother that liked to eat. He rubbed his stomach vigorously to emphasize the point. "I like to drink," he said, clutching a glass for effect. Two blocks away. A good meat place. It sounded fine, so I drained my beer and headed out into the warm night. The throbbing had started. Bahia was coming alive.

"Psst, Mister, you wanna watch?" A kid no older than ten tugged at my sleeve. "Wanna watch?"

"Watch what?" I asked.

"No, Mister, I gots watches, all kinds." He pulled his jacket back to reveal an array of the latest sports watches tacked to the lining of his grubby coat.

"No, thanks," I said and kept walking, checking my back pocket for its familiar lump.

"Mister, Mister you wan' smoke?" he persisted, "I gots American cigarettes."

"Nope, I don't smoke," I replied. I removed my wallet from my back pocket and slid it inside the front of my trousers.

"I see you later, Mister. I bring nice girl." With that he disappeared into the crowd.

A few blocks away I came across the restaurant. On display in the front window was a small lamb splayed on a spit, roasting slowly over hot coals. The juices dripped onto the ashes, quickly igniting and sending puffs of pungent smoke into the air. The restaurant was crowded. Smoke filled the place, although this time it was the greasy kind from the fire pit at the back of the restaurant. The waiter had looked askance when I asked for a table for one, but said nothing and showed me to a small setting alongside the bathroom. I guessed that eating alone was considered bad form.

The entire back of the restaurant was an open fire pit with logs piled on top of each other. They were held up against the wall by a sturdy wire grate. The chef threw new logs over the top of the grate to feed the fire, and extracted red hot coals from the bottom to cook the meat. I watched him use a stubby rake to spread the embers over the length of the grill, piling coals where heat was needed. Thick slabs of meat sizzled on the racks. Off to the side an assistant attacked a carcass with a cleaver. A loud "thwack" resulted in a portion of the carcass being dismembered in a splattering of blood and bone chips. It was shoved aside for grilling. On the table in front of the chef lay a pile of intestines ready for separating and grilling. Nothing would be wasted. I noticed that some of the beef still had skin attached. It was separated from the meat by a layer of yellow glutinous fat. Special cuts for those willing to pay extra. These pieces are slow grilled over low coals, skin side down. The heat permeates through the hide, heating the fat which sizzles and splutters, slowly roasting the meat. I ordered a slab with a green salad side and fried potatoes dripping in oil— guaranteed to clog the arteries, but so good. A jug of house red came with the meal. It was served in a terra-cotta carafe and poured into a heavy glass.

I separated the meat from the fat, and set the hide aside. It was tender and tasty and more than made up for the discomfort of sharing my plate with the singed waste. The beef melted in my mouth, and the red wine had just enough bite to cut through the grease. The fries were salty and crisp, and the salad was fresh, with a smattering of palm hearts.

It was well after midnight when I paid the bill and dragged myself out onto the sidewalk. The night air had cooled considerably, and a fresh breeze blew in from the ocean. The clinging humidity of the early evening was gone. Thunder rumbled and occasional sheet lightning danced off the buildings, throwing a stark light onto the faces of the crowds that were still out in force.

"Mister, Mister," I heard a now-familiar voice alongside me. "Mister, Mister you need come meet my sister. She's a birgin, look like movie star." The ten-year old had changed hats. He was no longer hawking merchandise, but was offering his family. I shook my head.

"You no like girls, Mister? You wan' boy?"

"No thanks," I said, hoping he would quit his sales pitch and leave me alone. I felt guilty having just gorged myself while I knew the kid was only looking to make enough so that his family could eat.

"Let me see those watches," I said. "Maybe I will buy one." I was immediately surrounded by a dozen kids, all hawking watches.

"Mister, Mister, look here Mister. I gots better deal, Mister. You buy watch my sister go home wit' you. She's a birgin. Very beautiful." A woolly-headed kid looked up at me with pleading eyes. My mood changed from heady exhilaration from a night on the town, to a disconsolate pity for the kids of the street. I wanted to run. I wanted to give them something, but I had nothing to give. My mind was whirling, and while my jumbled thoughts tried vainly to think of a way out, the gang dispersed.

"Tomorrow, Mister, tomorrow I bring my sister. You see how great she looks and then you decide." An optimistic final sales pitch rang out and hung in the air.

"Tomorrow, Mister."

I was determined not to let the incident ruin my evening. My own financial status could hardly be called flush, and there must have been tens of thousands of street kids roaming the back alleys of Bahia. Buying a watch or accepting the offer of their sister would hardly have helped, but for those living on the edge, every bit counts. They were gone, for now, swallowed up by the crowds. I had a night cap on my mind.

I made my way back to the smoky bar and eased through the doorway, clutching my stomach for the amusement of the bartender. The place was packed and the noise level had increased significantly. There was hardly elbow room. The girls had slipped from their perches and were working the crowd, their heavy caked-on makeup and lipstick straining to remain intact. They were already showing signs of a rough evening. I ordered a shot of black coffee and a glass of house cognac. Any residual grease from the meal would not stand a chance against the combination. The coffee and cognac worked against each other with a delightful effect. The coffee threatened to send my pulse rate up through the roof, while the cognac eased into my system, slowly entering my bloodstream, attempting to shut the system down. I felt the tug-of-war in my belly and forgot about the street kids. Someone produced a concertina and the place erupted into song following a scratchy, offbeat tune. I didn't recognize the melody and had no idea what the words were, but the anonymity of a back-alley bar brings out the Pavarotti in all of us. I belted out a few songs, reluctantly acknowledging that the cognac was winning the tug-of-war. My eyes smarted and my head thumped. It was time to get back to the boat.

I made my way back through Pelourinho Square, which was thronged with people and buzzing loudly. Young mothers were pushing infants despite the late hour. The thunder was closer and lightning flashes more frequent. The harbor was dark except for the anchor lights that hung suspended above the water like glowworms. I couldn't make out which light belonged to our boat, until lightning flash-framed the image for a microsecond. The harbor was bathed in brilliant light, and then plunged back into darkness. We were anchored the farthest offshore.

The elevator was empty for the ride down, and I was preoccupied with getting back out to the boat. I needed to find the dinghy, which I hoped was still tied to the dock where I had left it. I had disconnected the fuel line and removed the safety catch, about as much precaution as you can take to discourage theft. The sand was cool and soft, and I slipped my shoes off, enjoying the walk down the beach. Part way along I stumbled over two bodies entwined in the shadows, and heard a low curse emanate from the fleshy folds. My presence did not seem to deter them—a Bahia night has that sort of effect on everyone.

The dinghy bobbed a gentle greeting, and then, suddenly, a loud clap of thunder rolled across the harbor and the air turned cold and damp. Rain could not be far off. I fumbled for the safety key and connected it to the outboard. The end of the fuel line was lying in the water, so I banged it against the side of the dinghy, hoping to dislodge any moisture, and then dried it carefully on my shirt. My luck with engines has never been good, but this one had yet to let me down. It started on the first pull. I cast off and headed out.

The inner-harbor was littered with crab pots, and I threaded through them hoping I would not snag one on the propeller. I fought the urge to gun the engine and roar out to the boat. Rain was imminent and I wanted to stay dry. I would be lucky to make it without getting wet, but wasn't worried. The red wine and cognac had left me in a contented frame of mind, and a bit of rain would not be a problem. I motored slowly through the pots until I was well clear of them, and then gently opened the throttle. The engine chugged in response. A brisk offshore wind whipped up an occasional wave, which lapped into the dinghy. I could either gun the engine and take a soaking from the waves, or slow down and chance not beating the rain. I decided to gun it; once up on a plane the waves would not be a problem. I opened the throttle—the engine roared, the boat surged forward, and then the engine quit.

The sudden silence was replaced by the sound of wind whipping through the rigging of a nearby boat. I pulled the starter—nothing. I pulled again. Still nothing. I choked the engine and pulled again. Not even a sputter. The wind had really picked up and it was pushing the dinghy out to sea. I pulled a few more times, putting all my effort into it, still without success. I could smell fuel and guessed the engine must be flooded. The only thing to do was wait. The night had become black, with heavy clouds hanging low. A low fog blurred the lights of the city, and their glow barely illuminated the harbor area. The dinghy started to drift away from land. Beyond the boats out to sea, it was a black night.

The thunder now rumbled continually, and in the lightning flashes I could make out the lay of the land and the boats at anchor. *Dabulamanzi* was a quarter of a mile abeam of me, and in the darkness I could see her anchor light bouncing in the wind. I found the small dinghy anchor and chucked it overboard. It touched the bottom, then skipped along. We kept drifting. I was starting to feel the first pricks of apprehension. What if the engine didn't start? There were no oars in the dinghy. I had left them on the deck of the boat. I jumped up with renewed vigor and pulled at the starter cord. Still nothing. No sign of life. Not even a spark. I yelled out to the boat, but the wind whipped my words and flung them out to sea like spindrift.

Things were not looking good. The mellow afterglow of a good evening was rapidly being replaced by panic. I yelled again, but to no avail. It was no use. I sat cursing the engine and tugged at the starter cord out of frustration, but still no luck. I was in trouble. Our boat was now almost half a mile dead upwind. And downwind? It was a long way away, but Africa was over the horizon. I cursed and kicked and tugged at the starter, and then cursed some more, all without effect. The wind whipped the tops off the waves and flung them into the air. Lightning flashed constantly, followed by loud cracks of thunder directly overhead, and then darkness.

"Fuck!" I yelled into the night. "Someone help me, please," but my words were lost in the wind. I slumped onto the bottom of the boat and stared at the rubber sides. I was in big trouble and I knew it. By morning I would be miles out to sea. Damn, what an idiot. What a stupid idiot. What a dumb, stupid, stinking thing to have happen. I could taste the frustration in my throat, and feel the sting of salt in my eyes. The dinghy kept drifting.

It was dark and I was scared. I kicked the engine out of desperation, and then yanked the starter cord one last time. No sign of life. Nothing. I slumped back down, resting my head on my knees and wondered what I would do.

I looked out to sea, and thought I saw something, but it was only my eyes playing tricks. Another flash of lightning and I thought I saw it again. Maybe there was something there. What could it be? I waited for the lightening to flash again, but it had stopped.

"Come on, man," I moaned. "Give me a break." It was pitch dark, and then suddenly another flash of lightning. Sure enough there was something directly downwind of me. I could barely make out a low platform, and then I remembered what it was. When we sailed into Bahia earlier in the day, I had noticed some fishing boats tied to a platform. It was anchored offshore and the fishermen were using it to gut and clean their catch. I distinctly remembered the smell of rotting fish guts. I hung over the bow of the dinghy, and with both arms paddled as hard as I could. I could not afford to miss it. Between flashes it was pitch dark, and I could only guess where to paddle. Closer now, and then suddenly I smelled it. I was right on target for a perfect landing. I jumped onto the platform and fastened the painter to a metal ring. At least I was no longer heading for Africa. My heart was beating wildly. I could no longer see the lights of the city, or any of the anchor lights in the harbor. My boat, with its crew tucked safely into their bunks, was about a mile away, dead upwind. I sat on the platform and stared into the night, shivering from the cold, and hugging my knees under me.

After the initial euphoria of a safe landing, I took time to assess the situation. It was not good. The platform was covered with fish guts, and the gulls had been by, leaving their calling cards. It was a slippery mess, certainly no place to spend the night. I thought about sleeping in the dinghy, but then things got worse. The skies opened up and rain started to fall. It came down cold and steady, drenching me. I had to stand to avoid the rivulets of fish guts that ran along the cracks. Visibility was down to zero as the rain hammered on the platform and turned the water white. The good news was that the wind had subsided, but this did little to comfort me. I decided I had only one option. I was going to have to swim for it. It was not a great thought, but I had no choice. I was not going to stay on the platform, so I removed my shoes and jeans, and slid into the water. It felt warm after the cold wind and rain. I took one last look in the direction of land, let go of the platform, and started swimming.

I am a reasonable swimmer, but not cut out for long distances. At school I had tried hard to avoid swimming lessons, preferring to be on top of the water, rather than in it. The rain had smoothed the surface, and with the wind down I swam easily, saving my energy. On a calm day in the middle of summer I would have had difficulty covering the distance, but this time was different. I had to make it.

I felt the adrenaline race into my bloodstream. I guessed where the boat was, and swam in that direction. Salt water splashed my face, choking me, but there was nothing I could do except push towards my invisible goal. I settled into an easy rhythm and let my mind wander. I thought about the street kids and wondered where they would take shelter from the rain; about the hookers in the smoky bar and wondered how much they made on a good night. I thought about the priest in the old cathedral, the glow of the candles around the altar, and of the little girl with her rosary. My mind drifted back to my childhood and I thought of my family back home in South Africa. How I wished I had never left. I cursed myself for eating too much dinner, and wondered what effect the cognac and wine would have on my stamina.

The platform and dinghy were no longer in sight. It was black all around. Most of the town was asleep, and any lights would be blanketed by rain and fog. I was enveloped by darkness, and felt the first fingers of panic starting to rise again. My gut constricted. I felt my body tighten with tension.

"Cool it," I told myself. "Don't panic." I knew that if I panicked it would be all over. There were no landmarks for bearings—only the direction of the wind. I was certain that the boat was upwind, or at least I assumed it was, so I kept swimming into the waves, fighting to keep panic under control.

I had been swimming for over an hour when the rain suddenly stopped, and the visibility improved. I could see lights ahead, but had no way of knowing if they were anchor lights, or something on land. At least I knew that I had been swimming in the right direction. My legs felt heavy, and my arms burned with each stroke. I strained to see the anchor light again. I needed something to work towards, a beacon of hope. Anything to keep me going. But it only got worse. The wind picked up again, and it blew straight into my face. The waves increased, and an occasional rogue swamped me. I choked and gagged and tried to keep swimming. There was nothing else to do. With only an occasional flash of lightning, I had no means of figuring out which direction I was heading.

I swam and spat water, and swam some more until I felt a numbness seeping in. I felt like quitting, and wondered if I would die. I stopped to tread water, and thought about drowning. Would it happen quickly? Would it hurt? Would they ever find my body? I felt overwhelmed and terrified. I was going to drown. My heart raced and my breathing got shallow and uneven. I was going to drown all alone in a black sea on a cold night. I wept tears of frustration and sadness.

And then I thought of my stint in the army and how the corporals had made us grovel. How they pushed us until we bled. How they humiliated us and tried to break our spirit. How they wanted us to quit. I thought of the piss-parades and the hours spent standing in the cold on the parade ground waiting for the last person to go before we could get back to our bunks. I resented the humiliation and vowed I would never be broken. I learned that there is such a thing as mind over matter. I learned to never give up. I never let them see me sweat. Never quit. Don't quit, don't quit, don't quit, don't quit, don't quit. The words became my mantra and I started swimming again. I pushed on towards the boat. Don't quit, don't quit, don't quit. For a moment I thought I could see the anchor light, but it was only my eyes playing tricks. Don't quit, don't quit. I couldn't stop—stopping would mean drowning. I had to keep pushing. There was that anchor light again, this time I was sure of it. It wasn't my imagination. It had to be the boat.

My arms burned and my legs floated behind me. I had no

more strength. Waves kept breaking into my face, and I coughed, and spewed, and choked, and cried. It had to be the boat because I couldn't go any further. "Don't quit," I yelled into the night, "don't quit," but I started to sink, and a warm wonderful feeling came over me. The pain seeped from my arms and legs, and was replaced by a floating feeling, a wonderful floating sensation. "Don't quit," I repeated silently, willing my body to keep going. The pain rushed back, and I ached from the effort. I longed for the floating feeling, but my mantra kept me going. Don't quit, don't quit. The wind howled and the waves swamped me. I kept swimming.

Then out of the howling I heard a different sound. A familiar sound. The sound of halyards clanging against a mast. And then I saw the light again. This time I was sure that it was a light and not my imagination. It was an anchor light. It had to be. The dark outline of a hull loomed in front of me. Don't quit, don't quit, my mantra chanted. Never give in. Never give up. I could just make out features on the deck. Keep going for few a more yards. Don't give up. Don't give up. Please don't give up. Don't quit, don't quit. I longed for the painless floating feeling, but the light was getting stronger.

I was almost there when I remembered that the deck was five feet above slippery and sheer topsides. How was I going to get on board? I tried yelling, but my voice was only a feeble groan.

"Please, someone help me," I begged. I swam the last few yards and noticed a line hanging over the side. Something to hang onto. Something to pull myself on board with. Maybe I was going to make it after all. With a final desperate push I made it to the boat and clung to the rope. It was all I could do to hang there.

"Someone, please," I croaked. "Someone, please." The

wind swallowed my words and spat them far into the black night. I felt my arms weakening. I tried to pull myself up, but they were too weak and started to shake from the effort. I lunged at the side of the boat, kicking with my feet, hoping to wake the crew, but the noise was absorbed by all the gear in the lazarette. There was no way I was going to wake anyone, and no way that I could hang onto the rope all night. I felt myself slipping and cried bitter tears.

"Why now?" I cried. "Why after getting this far? Why can't I get on board? Someone, please." I felt a welcoming warmth and relaxation seep slowly up my legs, gently caressing my lower body. Maybe if I rested a while I would be okay. The warmth was soothing, and I slipped back into the water. Perhaps it was too much for me. Perhaps I should let go. My arms were being caressed. They felt warm. My neck was being gently massaged. My whole body felt warm and limp. I closed my eyes and wondered why things had to come to an end in Brazil. Why now? Why here? I had no answer. I felt the warmth reach my brain and it felt good. Warm and spongy and gentle and very relaxing. My hand slipped on the rope, and I started to float.

It had been a raucous night on board—so much for everyone getting to bed early. They had started with caiparinos, a Brazilian staple with a bittersweet taste and a kick guaranteed to flatten the most seasoned drinkers. A case of Brahma Choppes had been drunk, as had a couple of bottles of wine. Pete had stuck with beer and had finished his fair share, but a six-pack leaves very little room in your bladder. Long after you go to sleep the residual beer continues to filter down, and it was the persistent pressure that woke him at 4 a.m. He lay in bed for a while listening to the wind rattling the rigging, and felt the boat tugging at the anchor. Someone had forgotten to lash the halyards, and one of them was banging against the mast. He tried to ignore the noise, and the load in his bladder, but it was no use. The monotonous clanging was keeping him awake. He would have to get up and tie off the halyard.

The cabin was dark as he made his way through the saloon and out the companionway. He hung under the dodger for a few moments, waking up slowly and taking in the night. It had turned cold and he shivered in the damp air. First the halyard. He dashed onto the foredeck grabbing a sail-tie as he went, and lashed the halyard away from the mast. It was suddenly much quieter. And now for a quick pee before hopping back into the warm bunk. He wandered aft to the transom to relieve himself. The deck was wet. It had been raining and the night was very dark. The town was asleep, and out to sea there were low thunderclouds scudding across the water. "We probably won't be leaving until the weather clears," he thought. "I wonder where the dinghy is? Must be tied up on the other side of the boat."

Pete noticed a line hanging in the water, but didn't bother with it. "That's funny," he thought. "No dinghy." He checked both sides and decided that I must have stayed ashore for the night. Probably too wet to make it out to the boat, or perhaps I had found love in one of the bars and was sleeping ashore. It was much quieter now without the incessant banging. But what was that other noise? Something faint and far away like a gull wheeling on the strong night winds. He knew that gulls land during bad weather, and wondered what the sound could be, but the lure of the bunk was too much for him. Pete slid down the companionway and padded back to his cabin. His sleeping bag was still warm and he pulled it up around his neck. "What could that sound have been?" he wondered. There was something disturbing about it. He wondered if he should take another quick look around the deck, but didn't feel like getting up. Pete lay there for a while listening to the night noises. Sleep didn't come. The sound had disturbed him. He would have to get up and take a look outside.

On deck the wind still whipped through the rigging, but above the sound there was another noise. A plaintive cry for help. He dashed aft to the transom, and in the water could make out a shape. A human shape. Pete is a big guy. He reached down into the water and grabbed me by the scruff of my neck, dragging me through the lifelines.

"What the hell do you think you're doing?" he yelled. "This is no time for a swim." I looked up into his big, soft, brown eyes, and wondered if all the angels in heaven spoke with a South African accent.

CHAPTER 4
MEETING NANDO

"Men play at tragedy because they do not believe in the reality of the tragedy which is actually being staged in the civilized world."
—*Jose Ortega y Gassett*

Memories fade with time, and if it had not been for some clear-air turbulence over Brazil I might have forgotten my long swim in Bahia. I had shoved it to the back of my mind and left it there. A decade and a half later I was flying back to South America on a business trip, and heard the captain tap back on the engines as we hit the first bump. The seatbelt light flicked on and some of the passengers stirred, but it was three in the morning and most of them dozed off again. I glanced at the television monitors. The screen showed our current position, with a thin red line snaking back across the Caribbean Sea and up the eastern seaboard of the US, all the way to New York. The monitor paged to the next screen and zoomed into a close-up of our location. We were directly over Bahia. I lifted the window shade enough to see the lights flickering below, and the memory of the swim came back with a rush.

South America does indeed have a distinct throb. It is the pulse of the people and it connects where you expect it would: right under your diaphragm. The moment we landed in Argentina I felt its familiar tug. The bustle of the airport was distinctly Third World, with a haze of cigarette smoke permeating every sense. The seemingly chaotic immigration procedure resolved itself, and I was ushered into the transit lounge awaiting my connection to Uruguay. It was still early, but the bar was crowded with old men sipping strong black coffee and drinking brandy. I believe in the old "when in Rome . . ." adage, and joined them.

"Uno café solo con Cognac," was the extent of my Spanish. It was sufficient to impress the bartender, and he placed a shot of rich black coffee in front of me, poured a tumbler full of brandy, and placed the bottle where I could refill at will.

I propped myself on a stool at the far end of the counter and pulled my laptop from my backpack. The conversation lulled momentarily at the sight of it. The familiar tug-of-war between coffee and brandy took over and the sights and smells of South America surrounded me. It was a good place to write. The bartender was amused and refilled my snifter. I felt like Hemmingway.

An extraordinary thing happens as soon as the first sentences are set down. Memories that had long since faded into the recess of the subconscious are suddenly reawakened as thoughts hit the page. The words act like keys, and the little boxes where memories are stored start opening. I was well into recounting the atmosphere of Pelourinho Square when my flight to Montevideo was called, so I packed up my laptop, paid the bill, and made for the gate. We landed in Uruguay a half-hour later.

I love the bus ride from the airport in Montevideo to Punta del Este, a wealthy resort on the east coast. It reminds me of Africa. Goats and chickens scatter as the bus passes through small towns and winds along the waterfront, until the bright, modern buildings of Punta come into view. The big flashy homes and trendy boutiques contrast starkly with the surrounding poverty. Faded billboards hawk American dreams with a Colgate smile. The gap between rich and poor is made more apparent when the two standards coexist side by side. The poor appear poorer, the rich richer, and the middle class nonexistent.

Ten miles before arriving in Punta, I passed Casa Pueblo, a sprawling mansion built into the hillside overlooking the ocean. Owned by Carlos Paez Vilaro, Uruguay's most famous artist, he has made the home his life work. The hundred rooms are interconnected by tunnels, bridges, and an occasional walkway, and the result is a magnificent, if somewhat eccentric, edifice.

Since my first visit to Uruguay aboard *Dabulamanzi* I had returned many times, often by air, but it was that first visit that I remember the most. Our crew was invited to a cocktail party at Casa Pueblo to meet "some interesting people." Finding the front door was not easy, but once we managed to locate it we were met by our hostess and taken through a maze of rooms and tunnels until suddenly we were on a balcony overlooking the bay. It was one of the most beautiful sights I have ever seen. The whitewashed features of the house accentuated the graceful architectural lines, and contrasted with the blues of the water and the faded green of the surrounding countryside. There was a light wind blowing off the water cooling the evening air. The other invited guests were a mixture of Punta socialites and transient sailors, making for some interesting conversation. Cocktail parties generally bore me, but this one promised to be different.

I noticed a good-looking man sitting apart from the crowd. He was wearing riding chaps and a thoughtful expression. I watched him sip his wine and followed his gaze out towards the horizon. There was an old tramp steamer heading up the Rio de la Plata towards Montevideo. I picked up my drink and sauntered over to talk to him. At first he did not seem to want company, and I was about to leave when he asked me to stay.

"Those old steamers remind me of a bygone time," he said. "I think I would like to have lived back then." His English was perfect, but laced with a rich, South American drawl. There was a wistful expression on his face, and a faraway look in his eyes.

"I'm sorry," he said, extending his hand. "My name is Nando Parrado." I took it and felt his strong handshake. There was something familiar about his name, but I couldn't place it. "Still I am not complaining," he continued. "I have been very lucky in this life."

"How so?" I asked. He looked me in the eye and told me it was a long story, but didn't offer to elaborate, so I moved on to other topics. His name was very familiar, and I wondered if we had met before. He asked me about sailing. He asked what it was like out on the ocean and asked if I was ever scared. I had just turned twenty-one and was naively invincible. I told him that the ocean did not scare me. He smiled at the comment. His questions were probing and I was enjoying the conversation, all the while feeling sure that we had met somewhere before. I knew it was unlikely, but his name was so familiar. Nando Parrado. Nando Parrado, I thought to myself, and then I remembered. The Uruguayan soccer team whose plane had crashed in the Andes mountains. The survivors ate the dead, and they were eventually rescued months later after one of the group walked out and found help. That man was Nando Parrado. I suddenly wished I hadn't told him that the ocean didn't scare me.

Nando knew instinctively that I had recognized him, and he waved his hand at the house in an expansive gesture and said, "All this wealth, and there are times when even money is not enough." The owner of the house had put up huge sums of money for a search and rescue effort, but they had failed to find even a trace of the plane. His own son had been on the flight.

During our stay in Uruguay I got to know Nando. He came sailing with us aboard *Dabulamanzi*, and took me horseback riding along a stretch of deserted beach. I learned from him the importance of living life to its fullest, and I learned about the strength of the human spirit and its natural instinct for self preservation. He told me about never giving up hope and that if I ever found myself in a crisis situation to always look at the immediate picture and not at the big picture.

"The big picture can overwhelm you," he said. "You need small victories to nurture your spirit and to give you the strength the go the distance. It's the exact opposite of life, where you need to concentrate on the big picture, where small details can trip you up."

He also gave me some advice that I hope I never have to use. I was surprised to hear him talk about it. He told me that if I was ever in a similar life and death situation, that I should not hesitate to eat the dead. Those among them who had waited until all their rations were gone before eating human flesh had died of protein poisoning. It seems that human flesh is very rich in protein, and when supplemented with other foods can be a useful source of nutrition. When eaten alone on an empty stomach, however, it can be deadly.

A few weeks after leaving Uruguay we stopped in Bahia. Nando's words helped me survive the long swim back to the boat. "Always look at the immediate picture and not at the big picture," he had said. "The big picture can overwhelm you." I might have not made it if I had considered the big picture. It was just too far to swim.

CHAPTER 5
THE ROO
IN THE REFRIGERATOR

"And we catch a sound of a fairy's song, as the wind goes whipping by, or a scent like incense drifts along from the herbage ripe and dry, or the dust storms dance on their ballroom floor, where the bones of the cattle lie."

—*Banjo Patterson*

After my swim in Brazil we sailed to the Caribbean and on to England with a brief stop in the Azores. Later that summer I crewed in the disastrous Fastnet Race where several people died after a severe gale swept through the fleet, wreaking havoc on the smaller boats. We were lucky and ended up in Cork on the south coast of Ireland. It was soon after returning to England that I met ocean racer Skip Novak, and he invited me to join his crew for the Parmelia Race aboard *Independent Endeavour*.

Other than sheep, Western Australia is famous for gold and that is how the owner of *Independent Endeavour* had made his fortune. He and his partner, a man by the name of Hancock, had staked their claim to vast gold reserves in the

Kalgoorlie area and mined them in the early 1900s. The gold wealth had been turned into political power through the newspaper business and it was the *Sunday Independent*, the boat owner's newspaper, that sponsored our trip to Fremantle. The race was to celebrate the 150th anniversary of the discovery of Western Australia by the ship *Parmelia*, and the event was named the Parmelia Race.

The race had two classes, our racing class and a cruising class. The cruisers had more fun. They had to pick their own start date in England, stay for a minimum of a week in Cape Town, and arrive as close to 10 a.m. on the morning of November 22 as possible to win the $20,000 in prize money. The time and date were significant because it was the exact time and date 150 years earlier that the ship *Parmelia* had landed on those shores. While we pushed our boat across the Southern Ocean, the cruising boats took their time, all of them having allowed more than enough time to make the passage. They knew that they could burn off days or hours at the end if they had to.

On the eve of November 22, six boats were in sight of the finish in Fremantle, cruising up and down the coast, burning off hours until ten o'clock the following morning when they could claim their prize money. It seems as if one of the French boats decided to take the opportunity to finish their red wine reserves and drank long and hard into the night. It was blustery and clear and someone should have been paying attention, but the wine had taken over and sometime in the early morning they ran hard aground on Rottnest Island. Twelve thousand miles behind them, with less than a dozen to go, and their race was over. They ended up taking a ferry to Fremantle and were there at the finish when the five other yachts sailed across the line, all within seconds of the 10 a.m. deadline. They shared the prize money and in a grand gesture included the French boat in the rewards.

After the race, I set off hitchhiking to see Australia, and after a succession of short rides from farmers, I was left stranded in the Outback. I was beginning to think that I might have to spend the night on the side of the road. It had been almost an hour since the last car passed and daylight was coming to an end. I did not want to be hitching once darkness came. The cars, what there were of them, flew by and it would be dangerous to be sticking out my thumb once night fell. I had been pacing the same dry patch of grass for almost six hours and did not relish the prospect of no dinner and a night on the hard ground, but there was no other option. I was more than two hundred miles from Perth with another two hundred to go to Kalgoorlie, the nearest town. It had already taken me two days to get this far and I was beginning to think about turning back. The air ticket price had seemed unreasonable when I stopped by the travel agent in Fremantle, but compared to hitchhiking it was beginning to look positively cheap.

At least the heat of the day had passed and I was grateful for the cool breeze that picked up. Unfortunately it kicked up the dust, but it was a worthwhile trade for some relief from the scorching temperatures. Earlier in the day it had been over 100 degrees in the shade and my throat was parched and caked with dust. The Australian Outback was no place for the meek and I was starting to feel on the meek side of brave. What had seemed like a good idea in Perth was quickly becoming a trip of nightmare proportions, and to make it worse, I had emptied my water bottle. Talk about setting off across a continent on a wing and a prayer. After three months at sea with nothing but water to look at, I had been relishing the thought of some time on dry land, but had not counted on the heat and so few cars. Sydney seemed like a lifetime away.

As the sun crept closer to the horizon the sky changed from harsh and bright to a softer, less intense light, and the earth took on a red glow. The sunset was spectacular, and as soon as the sun dropped below the horizon I felt the first nip of cold air. I was on the edge of the Great Victoria Desert that occupies a large part of southern Australia, and despite the heat of the day I knew the night was going to be cold. I paced a while longer, kicking at a stone, and then decided it was time to find a place to sleep. The embankment sloped away from the road towards a dry gully and beyond to a low hill. The hill was quite far from the road and I was not sure if I would be safer in the ditch, or up on the rise. The movie, *A Cry in the Dark*, was foremost in my mind and I couldn't help but think of the scene where the dingo snatched the child and made off with it. Other than a few kangaroos I had not seen any wildlife since Perth, but who knew what lurked in the shadows at night? The darkness brings out creatures and I was sure that Australia had its share of sharp-teethed animals. Fortunately I had some matches and an old magazine and I would be able to make a fire for warmth and protection. It was going to be a long night and the sooner I got settled, the better. There were no cars anyway.

I grabbed my pack and walked slowly towards the hill, gathering firewood as I went. Darkness was quickly approaching; I had forgotten how rapidly the day turns to night in this part of the world. By the time I had gathered enough wood and found a bare spot to throw my sleeping bag, it was pitch black. I struck a match and lit the fire, the dry wood immediately taking and flaring up. The warmth felt good despite my having spent the day wishing for something cool. I rested against a rock and contemplated the night ahead. I might have run out of water and had no food, but I did have a small bottle of good cognac stashed in my pack, and after climbing into my sleeping bag I took a long swig. The brandy burnt my throat as it went down, but it took the dust and dirt from a long day of traveling and washed it away.

Moments later I felt a warm glow and despite my lousy predicament, I felt content. I had left home looking for adventure and here I was in the Australian Outback miles from anywhere on an adventure of my own. In the distance I heard the whine of a truck, the first in hours, and saw the headlights as small dots near the horizon. "Typical," I thought. "Nothing during the day and now they come." I watched as the lights came closer, snaking their way along the narrow road, and soon the roar of the engine filled the night air. With a whoosh the truck flew by and for twenty minutes I watched the red tail lights flicker and fade into the night. The silence was filled with the sounds of night creatures coming out. I heard an owl hoot and a far-off cry of what must have been a dingo. I threw more wood on the fire, took another long swallow out of the bottle and fell asleep under a big night sky.

Sometime before dawn I woke feeling stiff and cold. The fire was down to a few smoldering embers and my mouth tasted like a spent cartridge. The brandy had been a good sleeping pill, but the alcohol had only added to my dehydration. I got out of the sleeping bag and stretched, feeling like I had been on the road for months, not just a couple of days. There were a few small pieces of wood left over and I threw them into the embers, blew on the fire and warmed my hands. I needed to get back to the side of the road and be ready for the first car that came my way. The dawn brought a cold light, but I knew that in a few short hours I was going to be baking in hundred-degree heat so I tried to make the most of the cool temperatures. It was not quite light when the first vehicle approached. I could hear it long before it came into view and by the time it got close to where I was standing I could hear the driver applying the air brakes. My ride had arrived. I wondered how far it would take me.

As the truck pulled alongside a weathered face peered out the window, a bush hat pulled low over the eyes. The man grinned and signaled to me to hop in. From behind I could smell the distinctive smell of sheep heading for slaughter. It was as if they could sense their fate and instead of giving off a nice farmyard smell, there was a whiff of death in the air. I climbed into the cab and shook the farmer's huge hand. It was calloused and scarred from years of hard work. He ran a sheep ranch 30 miles up the road and was heading for Kalgoorlie to take his lambs to slaughter. I was grateful for the ride, and even more grateful to share his thermos of hot tea and a ham sandwich. As the truck picked up speed I watched the bush pass by and listened to stories of a life working the land. The farmer had never seen the ocean and could not believe that I had sailed all the way from England. He shook his head in disbelief when I told him about the big waves and cold temperatures of the Southern Ocean, and laughed when I told him that we had won the race—beating Rolly Tasker, Fremantle's most famous offshore sailor. "Good on yer, matey," he said, and I felt happy and proud. Four hours later we rolled into Kalgoorlie.

The farmer dropped me on the far side of Kalgoorlie after we had sunk a few beers in the local pub, and I fell asleep in the shade of a tree. The heat was unbearable and flies buzzed around my head. I had attached corks dangling from thin line to the brim of my hat in an effort to keep the flies away from my face. It worked well when I was standing up and the corks were moving, but the second I sat still they managed to get past the cork barrier and landed on my face, getting into my ears and licking at the damp areas around my eyes. Several cars passed by, but since I was still close to a town none of the drivers took pity on me. By mid afternoon I was thinking of getting a room in Kalgoorlie when a small sports car pulled up.

The driver was an attractive blonde with a soft accent and I spent a very enjoyable hour trying to look down her blouse as the wind blew her shirt open and her long hair all over the place. Unfortunately, she was not heading for Sydney and she dropped me alongside the road fifty miles from Kalgoorlie, promising to pick me up and take me back to the town if I was still there the following morning. I almost hoped that I would not get a ride, but as luck would have it the first truck picked me up. It was an old Bedford, faded orange, with three young guys from Sydney. They were musicians who had moved to Perth seeking fame and fortune, but found neither, and, somewhat disgruntled, they were heading home. If I was lucky this would be my final ride across the Nullabor Plain, still 2,800 miles to go to Sydney. "Hop in," the driver said, "and help yourself to a beer. The esky (cooler) in the back is full." I climbed into the van, found a place to sit, and cracked the top on a cold Fosters. Sydney might be a long way away, but at least we were going to ride in style.

We drove through the night, swapping stories and drinking more beer until I fell asleep. I kept feeling the van sway from side to side and I knew that the driver was having a hard time staying awake. The road across the Nullabor is straight and flat, the landscape featureless. We swayed our way through the night and it was just after dawn when we hit our first kangaroo.

Since leaving Perth I had seen a number of dead kangaroos on the side of the road. It seems that the average roo does not have any fear of cars or trucks, and they do not seem to understand that if they hit one they will come off second-best. Fortunately car owners know this and all vehicles that make the trip across Australia are equipped with a roo bar, a metal bar across the front of their vehicle designed to protect the car from errant kangaroos. The roo bar is triangular in shape with one of the pointy ends sticking out ahead, and it effectively deflects any kangaroo that crosses too close in front of the car.

Our kangaroo had been pacing us from afar, hopping like mad to keep up, when all of a sudden it had an urge to cross the road. Without warning it veered in front of the truck and connected with our roo bar. The bang reverberated through the truck, the music instruments in the back clattering as the driver slammed on the brakes. It was in vain. We pulled over and jumped out to inspect the kangaroo, but it was dead before we got back to it. We took the still-warm creature by its huge hind legs and dragged it off the road onto the sandy shoulder. The night animals would make a good meal of it and the heat would take care of the rest. For my fellow travelers the roo incident was cause for another beer and the day started with dry cereal and cold Fosters.

It may have been a coincidence, but shortly after hitting the kangaroo the van started to have engine trouble. Before the incident we had been able to keep a top speed of 50 miles an hour, but now the truck would barely make 40 and that was only after a lot of coercing and coaxing. We all looked under the hood, picking and pulling at bits of the engine, but none of us was a mechanic and it was obvious that we had no idea what we were doing. We were going to have to find a mechanic. The nearest town of Loongana was still 300 miles away so we piled back into the van and opened another beer to commiserate. At least we were not going to go thirsty.

The Nullabor Plain is a vast area south of the Great Victoria Desert. The name Nullabor comes from the Latin word meaning "no trees," and it's true to its name. It's a flat, featureless landscape dotted with low scrub. The road that crosses the plain is tarred; a few years earlier large sections were still dirt and the locals laughed when I mentioned the dust. "You should have seen the dust before the road was tarred," they would say, and I believed them. There is a section of road that doesn't curve, dip or elevate for more than a hundred miles. It is dead straight and flat, and with no geographic features alongside from which to gauge distance, it felt as if we were standing still. The heat started to turn on full power around noon and we roasted in the back of the truck. That air ticket was looking more like a bargain with each mile traveled. We rotated shifts at the wheel while the pile of empty cans grew larger until finally, around midnight, we drove into the town of Loongana, or what there was of it.

On the road across the Nullabor there had been gas stations every 200 miles where we could fill up and buy ice. The gas station owner lived in a small house attached to the station and pumped gas for each car that came by. It was too far to go to the next station so you had to stop at each one. I asked one of the station owners about his life and he was philosophical. "I like it out here in the bush," he said. "It gets a bit lonely, but when I want some fun, I go into town." The town he was referring to was Loongana, 200 miles away, and as we drove along the main street I could not see anything about the place that I would consider fun. There were only a handful of buildings along a single street, with some scattered houses making up a small suburb. On closer inspection I noticed that most of the buildings on the main street were pubs. I did not see a hotel or a restaurant, but I guess for a man used to living alone in the middle of the Australian Outback, it must have been an oasis.

We drove up and down the main street hoping to find an open pub. Most looked closed for the night and we were about to give up when we heard a loud noise coming from behind one of the buildings. We stopped the van and climbed out, making our way to the back of the building. Sure enough there was a pub, and it was open. As we went inside the place grew silent. It was obvious that a lot of drinking had been going on that night and it was also obvious that few strangers ever stopped in for a beer. Moments later we were being "shouted" a round by a burly man with a stained hat pushed back on his head. "Where you from then, matey?" he asked, detecting a foreign accent. When I told him South Africa, the place erupted. The South African rugby team had recently beaten the Australians and for that I was instantly subject to a long round of good-natured ribbing. Schooners (small glasses) of beer were lined up on the counter and before we had time to discuss our common love of rugby we were downing beer after beer in a mad race to get as many down before the place closed for the night. We left having not spent a cent, but with new friends including a mechanic who promised to look at our truck in the morning.

The night air was cold and I shivered as we climbed back into the truck. It was hard getting used to the sudden changes in temperature. We drove a mile out of town, and while my traveling companions made themselves comfortable in the back of the truck, I wandered off to find a grassy patch to lay my sleeping bag. With a long day of drinking beer behind me it did not take much to pass out and with a carpet of stars above, I fell asleep. Morning would soon come; I did not know then that it would arrive with such a racket.

Through the fog of a mild hangover I heard a dog barking and then felt something hot and slimy land on my face. I opened my eyes and stared straight up the nostrils of a large hound. I dared not move. The dog started barking again and I could smell its breath and feel a light shower of dog spit spray my face. Fortunately I noticed that it was being held at bay by a chain, but unfortunately, standing at the other end of the chain, was a disheveled man with a scowl on his face. He yanked the chain, dragging the dog off me, and then whipped it with a stick. I heard the dog howl and then cower whimpering. Moments earlier I had been afraid of the dog, now I felt sorry for it. I was afraid of the man. I sat up and rubbed my eyes, wiping the drool off my face and wondering what I was in for.

"Who are ya, matey?" the man asked. "What's your business here?" His tone was neither friendly, nor unfriendly. I scrambled to my feet feeling stiff and sore, and started to explain about the car. My sudden movement set the dog off again and it started barking and straining at the chain trying to get at me. The man smiled, enjoying my discomfort, and then lashed the dog with a stick, beating it on the side of its head. I noticed open wounds with yellow puss oozing and as the stick hit them the puss splattered all over the place. The dog yelped in pain, immediately cowering submissively. I did not know what to say, but being in unfamiliar territory, decided to keep my mouth shut. It was still early and just getting light. I looked over at the Bedford hoping that one of the guys had heard the noise and would come to my rescue, but there was no movement. They were all sleeping off the beer.

"What's your business here?" the man asked again. "This is private property and you could get arrested for sleeping here." I looked around. There were no signs or fences. I was in the middle of the Outback and certainly did not know that I was on someone's property.

"The cops will be along in a minute and they will chuck you in the slammer if they find you here," he said. "They trawl for drunks every morning." I said nothing. My head was pounding and I felt as if I was aging by the day.

"They pick up all the drunks and throw them in the slammer until they've sobered up," he continued. "Are you a drunk?" I shook my head and began again to explain about the car, but my voice only set the dog off again.

"Shuddup yer bloody mutt," the man said, whacking the poor animal in the face. He turned to me and in a softer tone said. "Well, if you're not a drunk yer must be hungry. Do you want some breakfast?" Caught off guard I nodded politely and moments later found myself following him towards a pile of corrugated iron. The pile turned out to be the man's home. It was primitive by any measure, and as we got closer I noticed a number of old appliances laying in the grass. "I'm a handyman," he said. "I fix things for people." I looked at the rusted machines overgrown by grass and wondered when last he had worked on any of them, let alone fixed one.

The sun rose and immediately warmed the night air. Moments later I could feel its heat and knew that we were in for another long, hot day. I followed the man to the front section of his house and saw that there was some homemade furniture and a tattered carpet on the floor. "Sit, matey," the man said. "Anywhere you like." He waved at the only chair and I obediently sat down. The dog came and lay on the floor next to me, whimpering with each step. The sores on its face were laid open and it was obvious they were badly infected. I wanted to pat the dog, but didn't dare. I had already seen its teeth and knew that it would not hesitate to bite me.

The man left and went into a back room while I sat taking in my surroundings. It was clear that he had been living in the tin shack for many years. There was a well worn look to the place. I could feel the heat radiating from the metal sides and knew that in a few hours it would be impossible to be inside. Already flies were buzzing around my head and I could smell a faint odor of rotting meat.

After a while the man came back with a cup of tea and handed it to me. There were some strange objects floating on the surface, but I needed liquid and sipped the tea. It was surprisingly good. "Yer hungry, matey?" the man asked. I was, but said, "No thanks, I'm fine." The floaties in the tea were bad enough. I wondered what breakfast would be like. "When you get hungry we can whup up some grub," he said. I was not going to be able to escape without eating something. "There's plenty in the refrigerator," he said nodding towards an old fridge standing in the corner of the room. It was large and rusted, the motor chugging hard to keep the contents cool as the heat in the room started to build. "When you're hungry there's plenty to eat." The dog whimpered, resting its head on the floor, staring at me with sad eyes. We sat in silence. I was hoping that my traveling friends would not leave me and was thinking of using them as an excuse when the man said, "You must be hungry. Let's make breakfast."

"Sure," I replied. "Thanks." The fridge chugged in response and the dog stood as I got up.

"There's plenty of grub in the fridge," the man said and I took that to mean that he wanted me to choose what I wanted for breakfast. I walked over to the fridge and hesitated for only a second before opening the door. Inside, squatting on its haunches, staring at me through dull, glazed eyes, was a kangaroo. The shelves had been removed and the roo was the only thing in there. It had been skinned. The man had it propped up on its haunches with only its small face still covered with fur. The rest of the body was bright pink. I stared at the kangaroo for a few moments and then noticed that one of its forearms was missing. I heard a cackle from behind me and turned to see the man standing in the doorway. His face was scrunched into a smile and in his hand he was holding the severed arm.

For the first time I noticed a small meat grinder on the counter alongside him and with another cackle he thrust the forearm into the grinder and started turning the handle. Bits of meat and bone were being ground into what was going to become my breakfast pattie. The insanity of the situation suddenly hit me. The man was completely mad. I looked around for my sleeping bag, grabbed it as I ran out the door and heard a final, faint cackle as I ran towards the van. My friends had been looking for me and were anxious to get the car fixed and back on the road. None of them were more anxious than I.

We left Loongana later that day after another long session in the pub, and sometime in the night crossed over into South Australia. The road followed the curve of the Great Australian Bight and once we were clear of the Nullabor the vegetation turned greener. There were even some curves in the road. The old Bedford van kept on keeping on and we slowly made our way to New South Wales, stopping in Broken Hill for another long night drinking beer. This time I was more careful where I slept and woke to the sound of dingos howling in the hills.

We crossed the Darling River, stopping briefly for a wash, spent another full day in the back of the van, and then started a long, slow climb through the foothills of the Great Dividing Range. We were almost in Sydney. It was still hot, but not fry-an-egg-on-the-roof-of-the-car hot. Just pleasant summertime hot. The road wound through small, attractive villages as our truck struggled with the incline, and eventually we crested the Blue Mountains and looked down on a lush landscape with Sydney's tall buildings in the far distance. The van ticked off the last few miles cruising effortlessly downhill. My traveling companions and I finished off the last case of beer and vowed to keep in touch. Looking back on it, hitching across Australia had been a worthwhile adventure, and I was glad not to have taken that easy flight. In a few weeks I would be back at sea again, happy to be out on the open ocean and knowing better than to be polite to crazy old men.

CHAPTER 6
CAPE HORN CAPSIZE

"A great cape, for us, can't be expressed in longitude and latitude alone. A great cape has a soul, with very soft, very violent shadows and colors. A soul as smooth as a child's, as hard as a criminal's. And that is why we go."

—Isak Dineson

There are two places on this planet that consistently bring grown men to their knees. They are places where men drop equally from exhilaration, exhaustion, and frustration. The first is Mount Everest, the highest peak in the world. The other lies at the southernmost tip of South America: Cape Horn. Two words that have for centuries served to inspire and strike fear into the hearts of sailors, and for good reason. Cape Horn is the sailor's Everest, with its attendant risks and rewards, and many hundreds of sailors have perished in their quest to round what some refer to as the "uttermost cape." For me it has always been a beacon of inspiration, a place steeped in history and mystery.

Cape Horn is like no other sailing landfall. It's geographically remote, located below 56 degrees south, and it's visually striking, with steep cliffs constantly pounded by relentless Southern Ocean waves. The water has carved deep striations in the hard granite, forming giant organ pipes where seabirds nest and damp spray mingles with the souls of sailors who have lost their lives in those turbulent waters.

The whole Tierra del Fuego area fascinated me from a very early age. Geography lessons at school would have me flipping to the pages of South America, intrigued by the rugged west coast and its remote tip. The Andes mountains run the length of Chile, dipping briefly under the Southern Ocean before rising again in Antarctica. The land is fragmented; it appears to have been shattered by some giant prehistoric upheaval. The thousands of islands that make up the Chilean archipelago stretch from Cape Horn in the south, almost all the way to Santiago in the north. I imagined protected bays and anchorages waiting to be explored, and at times I would picture myself as a smuggler hauling goods ashore at night, protected from prying eyes by myriad islands. Other times I would see myself as an adventurer, scaling the Andes with a team of yaks; mostly, though, I would be aboard the clipper ships rounding Cape Horn in fierce gales, heading for the trading grounds of the Far East.

I had read all the books by the great sea captains, and knew the tales of dozens of Cape Horn roundings: graphic stories of men and ships beating into the teeth of strong westerly gales. It sometimes took weeks for them to clear the Horn. I wanted badly to be a part of it. In fact, after my experiences in the Uruguay and Parmelia races I wanted to be a part of extreme ocean racing no matter where it took me. But we should be careful what we wish for. Sometimes hopes and dreams have a way of coming to be.

I got my first chance at a Cape Horn rounding in 1981 during the Whitbread Round the World Race aboard an American yacht by the name of *Alaska Eagle*, and it was a memorable experience. The Whitbread, as it was commonly known (renamed the Volvo Ocean Race for the 2001–2002 edition), is an extreme sailing event by anyone's measure: a 30,000-mile circumnavigation of the globe by way of the five southern capes. The Whitbread grew from humble beginnings in 1973 when a rag-tag bunch of sailors gathered in England to compete in the first race, to a dynamic, professionally run, and professionally sailed event that attracts the elite in the sport. The course sends the fleet through the torrid heat of the equatorial regions to the blinding cold of the Southern Ocean, stopping along the way in Africa, Australia, the Americas, and Europe. It also treats the sailors to some of the most magnificent sailing conditions on the planet: long, nerve-wracking surfs on giant waves in the Southern Ocean where speeds consistently top 30 knots, to balmy tropical evenings where the boats sail on diamond-studded water with dolphins guiding the way.

Sailing a Whitbread is a tough way to make a living, but the rewards are huge. The pure sense of accomplishment at finishing the race rapidly outweighs the trials and tribulations, to say nothing of the discomfort, of making the trip. The cold, wet, windy days soon becoming distant memories, the misery quickly forgotten, replaced by a sense of achievement that stands foremost in your mind. Above everything else that happens along the way, rounding Cape Horn is the single most memorable part of the nine-month journey.

We had been trailing the twenty-nine-boat fleet in a slow boat. *Alaska Eagle* had not found her stride in the southern latitudes, and no amount of canvas and coaxing could help her. We had to sail the boat on the edge the whole time just to keep up, and would carry our spinnaker long after the rest of the fleet had doused theirs. Careening out of control down the face of massive Southern Ocean waves became a part of our every day.

Sixty miles west of Cape Horn we were suddenly becalmed. After days of thrashing across a vast and hostile ocean, freezing from blasts of polar air and hanging on for a fast ride, we were going nowhere. The sails slatted against the rigging as the boat lurched in leftover slop. The air was damp and heavy. My watch was called up from below to help coax some speed out of the boat, but it was no use. What little wind there was bounced out of the sails with each wave. After a while we gave up, dropped the headsail, centered the mainsail, and put the kettle on for tea. We might have been becalmed in an area known for gales, but the view was no less spectacular.

The water was a cold, steel gray, laced with streaks of white foam left over from a front that had passed through the day before. To our south, enormous clouds over Antarctica filled the sky. They were every shade of dark, and hung ominously, waiting for us to make a mistake. We were in dangerous waters where the wind could whip up at a moment's notice, and an errant wave would easily topple us. It had happened many times before. I lay in my bunk trying to sleep, but the noise of the sails banging back and forth jolted my nerves with each slat. I must have dozed off because I woke a while later to the sound of bubbles running along the hull. There was less than a quarter inch of aluminium separating me from the cold water. I felt the boat heel and heard footsteps running on deck. My bunk was under the main winch, and I could see the cogs spinning as the crew on deck trimmed the sails. The sound of the bubbles turned to a low whine, and the activity on deck became more frantic.

"We need some help up here." A voice called down the companionway. "The wind is picking up." I scrambled from my bunk and pulled on layers of damp, smelly thermals. We had been living in a wet world for weeks and salt sores chafed against the rough fabric. The thermals had been soft and warm when we left New Zealand, but they were now crusted with salt and filth. I grabbed my foul weather gear and headed for the hatch. The wind had picked up and we were surfing the edge of Antarctica's weather.

"Bring up the storm spinnaker with you," someone yelled. "We're going to need it." I found the sail in its bin and dragged it on deck. The air was cold and biting. It was blowing directly off the polar ice, and was laden with moisture. The sea had turned black, and spray whipped across the deck, saturating everything. I clipped my harness on to a safety line and dragged the sail forward. The on-watch had set up for a sail change, and were ready. All they needed was the new spinnaker. The foredeck hand was positioned at the end of the spinnaker pole with a spike in hand, ready to release the sail. He took the corner of the new sail, clipped it to a changing strop, and waited for a signal from the helmsman. I looked back and swallowed hard. Twelve thousand miles of Southern Ocean and I was still not used to the size of the waves. In a very short time the seas had picked up again, and huge swells rolled in from behind. The helmsman would wait until the boat was on a good long surf, and then signal to the foredeck that it was time to spike the spinnaker. Our forward speed would bleed off some of the wind's force, making it easier to get the sail down.

We waited with practiced ease, and then I felt the stern rise to a big sea. *Alaska Eagle* surged forward and white water streaked past the hull.

"Crack the spinnaker!" I heard the helmsman yell, and the foredeck hand spiked the shackle. The old sail snapped free, the man on the halyard dropped the sail while the rest of us gathered it under the boom. The nylon was cold and damp. We shoved it down the hatch and hooked up the new spinnaker. It was our secret weapon. We had the fabric custom woven for the race, and the three-ounce nylon was doubled up in places. There was a thin wire running down each edge of the sail to take the shock of a sudden collapse. By anyone's measure it was bullet-proof. It set with a loud bang, and the boat groaned under the load. The bow dropped away and we took off down a wave at 25 knots, plunging into the trough and sending spray flying across the deck. We were less than 40 miles from Cape Horn.

The radar was the first to pick up land. A small blip slowly turned to a larger mass of interference, and the island of Cape Horn could clearly be seen on the screen. We could not see anything from the deck. Spray wiped out all visibility. The air was chilled and I shivered despite the exertion. We were on the edge of control and the boat was veering from one wave crest to the next. I was riding shotgun, standing alongside the helmsman ready to assist if the load got too much for one person. Every fifteen seconds the boat would plunge down a wave and bury its bow in the trough ahead. "This is crazy," I thought. We had wanted to round the Horn with a spinnaker up, but this was beyond anything we had done before. The boat was groaning from the strain and shuddered as the bow lifted out of the water and shook the foredeck dry. No one said a word.

A cross sea lifted the stern and flung it sideways, beam to the waves, and the boat rounded up into the wind. I grabbed the wheel, and together with the helmsman we forced the bow down, but the damage was done. The spinnaker collapsed. It fluttered in the lee of the mainsail for a few seconds, and then started to fill. As it swung out of the dead air it refilled and exploded. Bits of tattered nylon fluttered to the water, and what was left hung from the masthead like a sorry pennant. We pulled the pieces down and readied the foredeck for a headsail. It had started to snow.

I looked up and saw a small black cloud directly above us. Horizontal snow swept the deck, dusting the crew and rigging. I turned my back to the wind and pulled my foul weather hood over my hat and snugged it tight. The Southern Ocean swirled around us. With fingers that were frozen and numb I checked to see that my safety-line was secure and held on for a wild ride.

"You should see land about ten miles ahead," the navigator yelled up from below. "I can see Cape Horn clearly on the radar." "The guy is nuts," I thought, "We can hardly see the bow." Heavy flakes of snow had reduced the visibility to fifty feet.

"This squall won't last for long. It's clear ahead, and behind." The navigator was monitoring his instruments, placing his faith squarely in the hands of technology. "We should try and get more sail up," he yelled. We dragged a small sail from below and hauled it onto the foredeck. It was hard work, made more difficult by the occasional wave that swamped the deck.

"Christ, I'm sick of this," someone yelled. "Let's get around the corner and out of the bloody Southern Ocean." Just then the corner appeared ahead of us. The squall passed through, the snow stopped, and dead ahead less than four miles away was Cape Horn. It crouched low in the water, looming ominously dark and brooding. A silver light shone through heavy clouds and brightened the water, which turned from dark black to silver gray.

"Cape Horn!" I yelled. "I see land." It was our first sight of something solid in three weeks, the last being the Kerguelen Islands, a remote archipelago in the southern Indian Ocean. The silhouette of Cape Horn was just as I had dreamed it would be: high, rugged, and windswept. The waves were getting steeper and closer together as the continental shelf slowed the flow of ocean. They were dangerously steep. We dragged the sail forward and yanked it onto the forestay. At times the bow dipped below the surface of the water, and we were swept aft by a rush of cold ocean. The wind, by now, was at full gale, blowing horizontal spray and reducing visibility. At times we lost sight of land, but then it would reappear again, right on the bow.

I made my way aft to the halyard winch and we started the slow grind of raising the headsail. The heavy Dacron snapped in the wind, but soon the sail was up and sheeted on hard. *Alaska Eagle* surged forward, also eager to make the corner and head north. It had been a tough three weeks, but first we had dreams to fulfill. Dreams of rounding Cape Horn under full sail. Dreams that had been born in the pages of dusty school books. Dreams that were about to become a reality. I was glad the wind was honking—I would not have wanted it any other way.

As we drew closer to the infamous Cape I could see birds nesting in crevices just below the rugged spires that gave the land its ominous outline. Southern Ocean rollers slammed into the headland, flinging spindrift high into the air before crashing back into the sea. We were in close—too close. I shouted down to the navigator who was peering intently at the radar screen.

"Roger, we're in too close. It doesn't look good up here."

"We're okay," he replied. "We're just under a mile off, but the water is plenty deep." The land loomed above us. The wind shrieked in the rigging. The boat surged down steep seas while we hung on. We had reefed the mainsail and I wished we had set our smallest jib rather than the one we had up. We were still carrying too much canvas. The steep seas were making it hard to control the boat. We cut a white swath across the ocean as *Alaska Eagle* surfed towards the corner. The clouds lifted, and for a brief moment there was blue sky above. In the distance I could see sun reflect off the snow-covered mountains in Chile. We were looking at Tierra del Fuego, a land that I had longed to visit since childhood. Cape Horn was hard abeam. The whole of South America was above us. The crew were yelling with excitement. And then it hit us.

I saw the cross sea a second before it slammed into the boat. The helmsman saw it too, and abandoned the wheel.

"Watch out!" he screamed. "Hang on." He cowered in the cockpit, bracing himself against the helmsman's seat while the wheel spun madly. The wave lifted the stern and shoved it sideways. We swung beam-on to the following sea, and the next roller broke right over the boat. I felt myself falling as the boat capsized and cold water hit me in the chest. I dropped until my safety line snugged tight and I felt it jerk me backwards. Cold water rushed by, and for a few seconds it was quiet. I realized that I was underwater. We had been knocked down and I was on the leeward side. Icy seawater found its way into my clothing, and the shock of it against my body jolted me. Almost immediately the boat came back upright again. We careened along the side of another swell, and then went over a second time. I felt another blast of cold water. The boat came back upright, and for a split second I saw Cape Horn dead ahead. We were lurching towards land in a mad dance.

The keel was forcing us back upright; the wind was filling the sails and knocking us over again. We went over a third time and I hung at the end of my safety harness. I could feel the boat groan under the load and heard a loud snap. "Christ," I thought. "We're going to lose the mast." My mind was clear. If we lost the rig we would be in deep trouble. We were too close to land. The boat came upright and I looked aloft. The mast was still there, but the sails were shredded. The mainsail had split in two and the headsail hung from the end of the spinnaker pole. It had ripped along the edge of the sail. The heavy Dacron fabric flogged in the wind.

"Watch out!" I heard the helmsman yell. I looked aft and saw that he was back behind the wheel. "I am going to bear off and gybe." I felt the boat shudder and then slowly come back onto course. Land was less than a half mile away. The craggy sides of Cape Horn were sharp and ominous. I could hear the boom of water hitting the rocks and surprisingly, I could hear the cry of birds. I thought for a moment that I was hearing the voices of departed sailors, but their cries were blown away by the shriek of wind ripping though ripped Dacron. *Alaska Eagle* lurched forward and surfed the crest of a short, steep swell. Even with torn sails we were doing 16 knots. The boat was back under control and a quick head-count confirmed that everyone was still on board. We looked like wet rats, soaked and shivering, but safe. For now.

I crawled forward and slipped the jib halyard off its winch. The sail dropped to the deck and dragged in the water, but it was soon gathered up and shoved into a bag. Someone had already grabbed the storm jib. We lowered the mainsail, gybed, and headed for deeper water. The boat swung around, and behind us Cape Horn loomed large. "Thank you," I muttered under my breath. "Thank you." I thought of all the sailors and ships that lay on the bottom directly below us, and thanked the gods for sparing us.

We did not deserve to go unpunished. We had been in too close with too much sail up. I vowed to return to Cape Horn in the future to pay my respects to the area. Sailors, by nature, are a superstitious lot. We don't tempt fate. My way of being thankful that we had not drowned was to promise a return.

Once we were past the Horn the wind died a little in the lee of the land, and the seas began to flatten out. The crew was shaken and for a long while it was quiet on board, each of us lost in our own thoughts. It was the first Cape Horn rounding for most of us and we were absorbing the experience. The Andes mountains provided a spectacular backdrop while albatross and sooty petrels wheeled in our wake. We were even visited by a pod of pilot whales. Later that evening we rode a fair tide through the Straits of Le Maire and pointed our bow towards England for the first time in five months. We still had 8,000 miles of sailing ahead of us, but the relief of heading home was palpable. We were out of the Southern Ocean, around the Horn with stories to tell, and best of all, we had survived. Dreams do come true.

CHAPTER 7
SAILING THE WINDS OF FREEDOM

"All men dream, but not equally. Those who dream by night in the dusty recesses of their mind awake in the day to find that it was vanity; but the dreamers of the day are dangerous men, for they may act upon their dreams with open eyes to make it possible."

—T.E. Lawrence

They say that it helps if your IQ is less than the length of your boat, especially if you plan to do more than one Whitbread, and while I am sure that there is some merit to that statement, I kept coming back to the event in the hope that I would get a chance to do the race properly at least once. "Properly" meant on a good boat, with good people, and well funded. The race committee cleverly spaces the event four years apart—it takes that long to forget the misery—and I had long since forgotten the cold and wet sailing aboard *Alaska Eagle*, to say nothing of the capsize, when I joined the crew of *Drum* in 1985 for my second go around. *Drum* became famous before the race even started when the keel broke off and the yacht capsized. The crew (I was not among them) was airlifted off, and the boat was eventually salvaged, refitted, and readied for the race. *Drum* also turned out to be a slow boat, but the guys were great, and the campaign had an added flair because of the celebrity status of the owners. Simon Le Bon, the lead singer in the rock group Duran Duran, along with the two managers of the band, footed the bill and sailed on board. We were greeted at each stopover by screaming Duran Duran fans. It was a teenage frenzy, but as one of the crew dryly pointed out, "It would have been better if the boat was sponsored by Julio Iglesias; at least his fans were of legal age."

By the time 1989 rolled around I had hung up my Whitbread boots and was living a quiet life on Cape Cod, dabbling in real estate and raising a daughter. I had not given any thought to another race around the world until Skip Novak called a couple of days before the race started. He had been hired to sail as co-skipper on *Fazisi*, the Soviet entry in the race, and he needed help.

"It should be fun," he said, "the guys are great, and the boat seems fast. You need to be here by tomorrow night," and so it was the following afternoon that I arrived at Ocean Village in Southampton on the south coast of England. I was jet-lagged and tired. The previous twenty-four hours had been a mad scramble to get ready for the race. I dragged my bags out of the taxi and made my way towards the marina where the Whitbread fleet had assembled. It was a damp English afternoon—the air smelled of rain, despite a bright forecast. I left my luggage with security, and was about to order a beer when I noticed a crowd gathered along the breakwall. I wondered what they were watching. As I elbowed my way to the front of the pack, I could see a sleek, low-slung yacht short-tacking up Southampton water. The Soviet flag snapped briskly in the wind as the crew maneuvered the yacht through a throng of spectator boats. White letters along the waterline announced that *Fazisi* was her name. My ride had arrived and all seemed well, but my sailing and communicating skills would soon be tested. This was not going to be an ordinary ocean crossing. I was about to become the "other" non-Soviet on board the Soviet Union's first-ever Whitbread entry.

I fought my way through the crowd on the dock, and scrambled on board while Skip did a quick introduction. He then departed for more pressing issues and I was left to my own resources. I nodded at the crew who were still not quite sure who I was or why I was there, and made my way down below. The crisp red and white paint job of the exterior contrasted sharply with the dull gray of the rough interior. The low-slung freeboard that gave the yacht its unique "watch out, here I come look," did nothing for the inside, and there was only a small crawl space between the rear of the yacht and the front. Headroom was minimal and reduced to nonexistent when the sails were dragged through the cabin. The comforts of home were going to be few.

I found my bunk jammed high in the aft end, nestled amongst the salamis. The cook was busy stowing food, and had a variety of sausages strung from the overhead. Later in the trip when the tropical sun beat down on the deck, the salamis would drip oil all over the sails, but for now they added a certain charm. I stowed my gear, wondered for a moment if

I had lost my mind, and then headed for the beer tent. There was nothing a few pints of warm pub beer couldn't cure. The Whitbread would start in less than eighteen hours.

Race day dawned bright, but my mood was dark—the effect of too much beer, too little sleep, and the news Skip had given me as we tossed the dock lines ashore.

"We've hardly sailed this boat," he said, "the crew have no clue what they are doing, they don't speak English, we've run out of money, and you're on the other watch." Skip delivered the news in the same cavalier manner to which I had become accustomed, but this time there was six thousand miles of open ocean ahead of us, and my heart sank. It dropped a notch farther when I noticed one of the crew spinning the winch to see which way it turned before he wound the line around. They really had no clue, no idea what they were getting themselves into, and no sense of the difficulties that lay ahead. I envied them.

When the start gun fired I was filled with a sense of elation and dread. It was an uneasy combination, but the dread was soon washed away by the excitement of the crowds and the unbridled enthusiasm of the crew. They were just happy to be anywhere but the Soviet Union. The recent odds handed down by the London bookies did nothing to deter their excitement. They had been betting 100:1 that the Soviet crew would not make the start, let alone the finish, and we had just proved them wrong. If victory comes in small packages, we had just opened our first one, and there would be many more. There would also be unwelcome packages, but for now we were Russians headed for fame and fortune, just as Jason and his Argonauts had done, two centuries before.

The Solent is a narrow strip of water between the Isle of Wight and the British mainland. On the day of the start it was churned from its usual dull gray into a foamy white, whipped up by a mass of spectator boats and twenty-three world-class yachts headed for Uruguay, six thousand miles away. Our low freeboard had us plowing through the slop and chop with the boat half submerged. By the grace of god and a dash of luck we had our sails up, and the boat pointing in the right direction when the start gun fired. *Steinlager*, the powerful ketch from New Zealand, was on our starboard hip, and the rest of the fleet were tucked well to leeward, and behind. It was the best showing *Fazisi* would ever have. I trimmed the genoa on the port side and fought the urge to throw up. The realization that I would be spending a month at sea on an untried yacht with an inexperienced crew had just hit me, and the thought sunk to the bottom of my gut like an unexploded depth charge. It would take many days of fair sailing in the Trade Winds before the feeling went away.

My first problem was reprogramming my mental rolodex to try to get a grip on the names of the crew. Common names are hard to remember. Uncommon names delivered in a strange tongue are nearly impossible. Igor and Viktor were easy, but Nodari and Gennadi were not. "Hey, you!" didn't cut it because of the language barrier, so I ended up remembering those with nicknames first, and gradually figured out the rest with time. The "Elephant" and the "Crocodile" were extroverts and became my immediate conduit to the rest of the crew. They understood more English than they let on, and had a good grip on sign language and universal gestures. Juki didn't speak a word of English, but was one of those rare individuals who is able to communicate perfectly with hand gestures and rich body language. Most of the others were going to take some time, but as we plowed out of the Solent and into the English Channel, I had other matters on my mind.

There was the immediate problem of sailing the boat. Maxi yachts are heavy and cumbersome, and dangerous to the inexperienced. The lines that control the sails are half-inch wire and when under load, they are strung bar tight. One mistake can cost you a finger, or worse, your life. To my surprise and delight *Fazisi* seemed to sail herself just fine. She was much lighter than her counterparts, and slipped through the water leaving barely a trace. A few bubbles in the wake were the only sign that we had passed by. The crew had (eventually) hoisted the spinnaker, and we carried the sail well into the Bay of Biscay, gybing occasionally, and changing to a lighter sail as the wind fluctuated. We plotted a route that would take us to the northwest corner of Spain, and then out into the Atlantic before crossing the equator and closing land again at the bulge of Brazil. It was a simple strategy. We were taking it a day at a time, adjusting our plan to suit the mood of the crew and the speed of the boat. We had no illusions about winning—finishing the leg in one piece would be a victory, and who knew what lay beyond the first finish line? The Soviets had run out of money, and Uruguay was hardly a Mecca for sponsorship dollars.

The *Fazisi* project was the brainchild of Vladislav Murnikov, a civil engineer from Moscow. He had read a copy of *Sail Magazine* and seen photos of an earlier Whitbread fleet. Undeterred by the practical impossibilities the Soviet Union presented, he decided to launch a Soviet effort. His country was flirting with change, and he reasoned that a high-profile worldwide sailboat race would be the ideal vehicle for promoting Soviet industry. The chairman of Fazis Company, an import-export business based in the Soviet province of Georgia, agreed, and the Golden Fleece Syndicate was born. They would build a high-tech yacht and go up against the world's top ocean racers, proving that there is no substitute for pure optimism, focused energy, and most important of all, blind faith.

The theme of their campaign would be the Greek legend of Jason and the Argonauts, and their search for the Golden Fleece. The legend has it that Jason and his Argonauts landed in Colchis (Soviet Georgia), where Jason surreptitiously rowed up the river Phasis and recovered the fleece hanging from a tree, where it was being guarded by a serpent. Metaphorically speaking, he who finds the fleece finds success, and for the Soviets their "golden fleece" was to be western sponsorship. What most people forget, and the Soviets chose not to remember, was that recovering the fleece was the easy part. The return trip was fraught with danger and problems. If anyone had dared to contemplate the tale in its entirety, they might have seen a warning of events to come.

The Soviets had appointed a co-skipper for the race. A bull of a man with a moon face and shallow chin, Alexei Gryshenko epitomized my stereotyped impression of all Russians. He was, in fact, from the Ukraine, but looked and played the part of "party leader." He shook my hand when I was introduced, grunted something I didn't understand, and barely acknowledged my presence on board for the duration of the trip. He sat apart and aloof from his crew, occasionally beckoning one of them to join him, like a lord to his serfs. I had no interest in crew politics and ignored Alexei for the most part—a choice I would later regret.

On our fourth day at sea I came on deck to see Alexei sitting alone at the back of the boat. He nodded to me and grunted a greeting. I wondered about his frame of mind. Building the boat in Georgia and finishing it in England on an insecure financial footing had taken a toll on all the crew, none more so than the co-skipper, but I figured a few days of sunshine and warm weather would sort him out. On the horizon ahead we could see two Whitbread boats, and behind us, a third. We were doing okay. The weather had been good and crew morale remained intact. I found time to figure out the deck lines and halyards, and learn some Russian. I had one of the crew translate "I need food," and "I need sleep," and I used the two phrases as often as I could. It seemed to amuse the guys, and got me what I wanted.

By the end of the first week I thought I had their names all figured, until one day I noticed a new crewmember joining us for dinner. I had not seen him on board before, and wondered how I could have missed him. He also showed up on my watch and I asked Skip if he had traded a guy from his watch, and taken Juri, who was missing from mine. Skip laughed and pointed to a razor and mirror in the bucket on the aft deck. Juri had shaved his expansive beard, and shed thirty pounds in the process. They were not making it easy for me.

They were not making it easy for Alexei either, or perhaps he was not making it easy for himself. He was slowly becoming more remote, and spent much of his time on deck alone with his thoughts. I had given up greeting him, and he had given up grunting at me. I wish I had made more of an effort.

As we approached the equator, the routine on board settled into a rhythm. We were languishing in last place, lagging way behind the second-last boat. The crew had slowly sorted themselves into a loose-knit team. Without the language I missed the conflicts and struggles that were being waged among them. To me, all appeared fine.

The team had been drawn from across the Soviet Union, and despite having grown up under a single Soviet decree, their cultural backgrounds were diverse and varied. The only constant was their lack of personal motivation and intuitive sailing ability. They waited to be told what to do, rather than getting on with the job at hand. Sailing a powerful maxi-boat like *Fazisi* required a lot of forethought and instinctive action, and Skip and I were doing our best to hammer some western themes into them. We appeared to be failing. It's hard to undo a lifetime of different thinking.

I did notice that the cook was being used as a political football, but then that's the lot of sailing cooks the world over. Good ones give what they get, and Alexei (the cook), was doing just fine. He was dishing up a combination of freeze-dried fare and Soviet specialties, handed out with a dash of abuse. He had a difficult job. With no standing headroom below, he was forced to sit down to cook. The galley was built under the cockpit, and was hot, cramped, and stuffy, but despite the squalid conditions, the food was passable.

Alexei had been recruited at the last minute and doubled as ship's doctor. His most recent assignment had been as a bush doctor in Afghanistan, and his bedside manner reflected it. It was nonexistent. So, too, were his cooking skills. His lack of culinary expertise was exaggerated by the fact that the food was freeze-dried. He had never seen western food, let alone western freeze-dried food, and he couldn't tell the difference between powdered egg, powdered milk, and mashed potatoes. Some mornings we would get mashed potatoes for breakfast, and powdered eggs in our coffee. Other mornings it was simply a plate full of chopped garlic and onions. The Soviets loved their garlic and onions.

"Good for the blood," they said. Out of self-defense, Skip and I followed their lead, and soon discovered their secret. Halfway though my first onion my throat turned numb and stayed that way for a week. It made the cook's cooking palatable. I was learning quickly.

We charged through the doldrum belt, seeking out rain squalls with our radar, and hooking onto the windy side of each one. The brain trusts on board the other boats were ensconced in front of computer screens, crunching numbers and analyzing weather data, but we had no sophisticated weather receiving equipment, and relied on the old-fashioned method—we looked out the window and dealt with what we had been given. By luck more than good judgment, this technique soon had us in fifth place, snapping at the heels of the leaders. In our enthusiasm we called our race headquarters in Moscow.

"Great news," we said. "We are no longer in last place. We're now in fifth."

"Ah, good, good," they replied. "Good news, but it makes no difference really. The Russian press has been reporting you in first place since the start, anyway!" It was my first lesson in the power of propaganda. We were guaranteed to win no matter how badly we finished— as long as we finished. Skip and I were quickly learning the Russian way, but they were not mastering ours. They were still waiting to be told what to do.

"Think for yourselves!" Skip would yell. "For Christ sake, don't wait to be told what to do. If someone falls overboard are you just going to sit there and wait for us to tell you that they're drowning?" The guys sat with blank expressions and waited for Skip to finish. It was not in their makeup. They looked sheepish, but said nothing. For the next few days one of the crew didn't come on deck. He spent his time at the nav station with a pencil and reams of graph paper working feverishly on some plan he was concocting. He reappeared with a triumphant look on his face.

"I have solution," he said, and handed each crew member a sheet of graph paper. In neat script he noted the time of day for the following week in half-hour increments. Across the top of the page were a list of duties that might need doing, such as grinding winches, helming the boat, trimming sails, or doing dishes. Penciled in were the duties of each member of each watch for each half hour of each day. At the time change they were to consult their sheet and move to their next duty; no questions, no comments. It was a beautiful piece of social dissertation, but doomed for failure. It never took into account what sails might be up, and fell flat when some of the crew realized that they were relegated to winding winches for most of the rest of the trip, while others would be doing all the driving. I buried my face in my hands and wondered why the West ever feared the Soviet Union.

For the most part I was keeping to myself. It was difficult to communicate with the crew, and with Skip on the other watch, there was no one else to talk to. We passed each other in the companionway at watch change. It was tiring work, and I usually headed for my bunk as soon as I could. Sometimes Skip would climb aft and sit on the sails and we would discuss the crew, the boat, and the trip in general, but mostly we would talk about life on land, passages past, and future projects. Skip had a lot vested in the success of the Soviet effort. His name was up there in the headlines, and if the project faltered, he would falter right along with it. I did not have much to lose. I was along for the ride. I knew that there would be some good stories to tell after the finish, and time at sea was always time well spent. I was enjoying life. The only thing that was getting on my nerves was the music. There was only one tape on board; a compilation of Russian folk songs. The tape player had an auto-rewind feature and the tape stuck in the machine soon after we left England. It auto-rewound itself all the way to Uruguay.

On day twenty we converged with land and passed close by Recife. A couple of days later we saw the loom of Bahia and I remembered my visit there a decade earlier. A day later we blasted through a maze of oil rigs off Cabo Frio, and saw the loom of Rio far to the west. The lights faded into the dawn, but the sight of land stirred memories, and we were starting to crave civilization. Three weeks of Alexei's cooking had us hungry for home-cooked meals.

We were still holding onto fifth place, but once the Trade Winds settled in, the powerful ketch, *The Card*, rolled us. She sailed abeam for a few hours, and then pulled ahead with her mizzen gear adding horsepower. It was time to get to Uruguay. The crew were restless and Skip and I were ready for a break. Our only concern was the well-being of the co-skipper. Alexei had become more distant and less communicative. I wondered if he was pleased or disappointed with our placing, but never thought to ask.

When we closed land again, it was the flat, featureless coast of Uruguay. White sandy beaches sparkled in the hot summer sunshine, and waves washed up on the shore. The sight was a feast for the crew, whose last look at land had been the coast of France almost a month earlier. Much had happened since. They had molded themselves into a team of sorts, and their English was improving. As they told me later when I asked why they were so keen to speak English, they said, "In port we need meet girl, we need speak English." It was the old universal motivator that had them studying the language, and what's more, it appeared to do the trick.

Many hard-won miles and a respectable placing should have left a deep sense of satisfaction among the crew, but I noticed some tension building as we neared the finish line and wondered what the stopover would bring. The rhythm of life at sea abruptly gives way to the hard reality of life on land, and I knew the stop in Punta del Este was not going to be easy. It was a clear, moonlit night when we powered across the finish line, four weeks to the day after leaving Southampton. The guys had come to accept me as part of their crew and acknowledged my input. It was all I could ask from them. My contract was up, and with a sea bag full of memories and some new friendships to count on, I headed to the airport. Ocean Village and the start of the race seemed a lifetime away.

I flew to England and took a train to Cornwall for a family vacation. The lush English countryside was all the more pleasant after a month at sea, and the village of St. Just-in-Roseland was a picture perfect place to ponder my future, far removed from the hustle and bustle of Punta del Este. Each morning I walked along the shore and looked out to sea. Cold fall weather had settled over the British Isles. Out in the Atlantic Ocean great sheets of rain gathered to drift slowly towards land, and wet weather drenched the coast. The Whitbread fleet had escaped to the Trade Winds in the nick of time.

On my way back from one of my walks I stopped in a café for tea. It was the only place in the area that sold newspapers and I bought a copy of the *Daily Telegraph* in the hope of gathering news about the remaining yachts finishing in Uruguay. I flipped to the sports section, and glanced at the bottom of the page. The headline sent me reeling:

RUSSIAN SKIPPER FOUND HANGED FROM TREE

I did not have to read further. I'd had a feeling that something tragic was going to happen. People kept coming in and leaving the café, laughing and chatting among themselves, but I sat in numb silence. I gazed out the window at the peaceful Cornish countryside and wondered about his wife and one-month-old baby left behind in the Soviet Union. I wondered about the crew. I wondered about Alexei. What had compelled him to take his life? What was he thinking as he sat alone on deck staring at the water rushing past the hull? What was he thinking as he sat alone on the branch seconds before taking his life?

No one ever found out why he did it. There was a note with some vague reasoning, but his words hardly came close to explaining his actions. They never do. The crew rallied and decided to press on with the race, but it was a different team that sailed for Australia. They were tempered by tragedy. If any good came out of Alexei's death it was a single-minded desire among the remaining crew to finish what they had set out to accomplish years earlier, when the idea of racing around the world seemed an impossible dream.

    I was there five months later when a slightly battered boat with a seasoned crew on board came charging up the Solent. They would have been the first Soviet boat to finish the race had the Soviet Union not disintegrated while they were away. Vladislav will tell you, with a twinkle in his eye, that the *Fazisi* project was the beginning of the end for the Soviet Union. Their foray onto the world stage was more than just the nose of the camel under the tent. It was nose, hump, and hind leg; and Eastern Europe was changed forever.

CHAPTER 8
TEA WITH CONDORS

"All other creatures look down towards the earth, but man was given a face so that he might turn his eyes towards the stars and gaze upon the skies."
—*Ovid*

    A cold wind blew from the west, whipping up white caps and spraying spindrift high into the rigging. Occasionally a williwaw would plummet down from the surrounding peaks and flatten the surface of the water, lacing the channel with white, foamy streaks. I was cold. My fingers were numb from holding the wheel, and the side of my body that faced the wind ached from a constant pelting. It would be a relief to be below, out of the wet where a warm stove and hot coffee laced with rum awaited. "Not much longer," I thought. I could see the island up ahead, and knew we would be anchoring within an hour. The leeward side was a secure place to spend the night, and the island offered good shelter and good hunting. There was an abandoned sheep station near the anchorage, and a lot of rabbits.
    Forty minutes later we dropped anchor and let out 200 feet of chain. Skip and one of the crew ran bow and stern lines

ashore and tied them off to trees, while the rest of us stowed the sails and put the kettle on to boil. I ducked below gratefully and warmed myself in front of the stove. The cabin was strewn with gear hung out to dry, but it was cozy and warm and smelled of damp socks and dinner. There were a few colorful decorations adorning the main salon and a calendar counting down the days until Christmas. Home sweet home—at least it had been for the better part of a month. We were living "off the land" in Tierra del Fuego, hunting and fishing for our food and enjoying the remoteness of the Chilean archipelago.

A full decade had passed since we capsized at Cape Horn and despite my fervent promise to return to pay my respects, the opportunity had not presented itself—at least not in the way I had imagined. I did return to Cape Horn four years later, sailing aboard *Drum* and our rounding was far less spectacular. In fact, it was perfectly pleasant. Despite a rough Southern Ocean passage we arrived at the Horn with a light easterly wind blowing, and with full sail set we short-tacked around the legendary landfall. The Horn was shrouded in low fog, and because the weather was pleasant and predictable, we were able to sail close in to land. We sailed right past the place where *Alaska Eagle* had taken her first knockdown, but this time the ocean was calm, with gentle, undulating swells giving no sign of the storms that for centuries have wracked the area. The boom of water hitting land was still there, but it was subdued and sounded more like a pleasant greeting than an ominous roar as before. Ice cold vodka and smoked salmon was served on the after-deck and we saluted the corner in grand style before heading north for England once again.

Now I was back, this time on an expedition to hunt and climb, and of course, to pay my respects. Skip had since built a 54-foot steel cruising boat, designed and engineered for high-latitude sailing. He based the boat in Ushuaia, the southernmost town in the world. Ushuaia is located in the Beagle Channel, a narrow strip of water that parallels the Straits of Magellan, three hundred miles to the south of it. It lies a mere seventy miles due north of Cape Horn, and while the feeling of a frontier town still exists, Ushuaia has started to take on a more modern feel with trendy boutiques springing up on Main Street, and a fledgling tourist business promising prosperity. We provisioned in Ushuaia and then left for a month of sailing in some of the most remote cruising grounds in the world. Our boat, *Pelagic*, was a perfect base camp.

The forepeak onboard served as a temporary larder, and amongst the cans and carafes of wine, a half dozen Upland geese were plucked and hung to cure. They were the spoils of the past week's hunting. Along with the geese was a slab of reindeer meat that we had traded with the crew of a French yacht, and the remains of a beaver that we shot the first day out. Its pelt lay nailed to a board, salted and curing. The yacht's steel hull was immersed in frigid Beagle Channel water, and without insulation it was cold and damp up front so with the forepeak closed, it was a perfect place to hang the catch.

"Who's up for a little rabbit hunting?" Skip asked. I was tempted to stay below and sit by the heater, but everyone else was going ashore, so I roused myself and pulled on my thermal gear. The fleece was warm and dry from the heater, and felt good. I grabbed my rifle and a hip flask of red wine, and followed the others into the dinghy. There was less wind in the anchorage, and the yacht bobbed in the leftover slop. We beached the dinghy, tied the painter to a tree, and scrambled up through the low scrub.

There were signs of rabbits everywhere, but not one to be seen. In a cove near the anchorage a flock of geese hung near the water's edge, but we were not interested in them. We had eaten our fill of geese and had more than enough in the larder. A couple of steamer ducks churned past, but we left them alone. They were tough and stringy, and too gamey for eating. We were out looking for rabbit, but it was more the fresh air and exercise we were after.

The island was less than a mile across, and its vegetation grew at a 50-degree angle, blown that way by the persistent wind that buffeted the trees and scrub. The prevailing wind is from the west, so all the vegetation leans towards the east. We walked partway around the perimeter, and after seeing nothing to shoot, made our way to the south side to pay a visit to the sheep station.

At the turn of the century there had been numerous stations scattered throughout Tierra del Fuego, but foot-rot wiped out much of the profit, and the idea was eventually scrapped. For a while many station owners left someone to watch over the place in an effort to lay claim to the land that was locked in an ongoing territorial dispute between Chile and Argentina, but eventually they left and the buildings fell to ruin. As we approached the old shearing shed, we were surprised to see smoke drifting from one of the outer buildings. On the opposite ridge a horse and rider appeared. He galloped towards us brandishing a rifle, and in rapid-fire Spanish explained that he was looking after the station and we should follow him to his hut. He said his name was Miguel, and he pointed towards a rough-looking corrugated iron shack alongside the shearing shed, motioning for us to follow. We climbed over the low stone wall and made our way towards the building.

His place was crude, but comfortable. The front area was strewn with rough hand-hewn furniture, and there was a tattered curtain hanging in the doorway, separating the front area from the back. Beaver pelts stitched together warmed the floor. We made ourselves comfortable while Miguel tidied up and rolled himself a cigarette. After his initial enthusiastic greeting, he had not said much. Instead he beamed mysteriously, clearly pleased to have company. His cabin had a few colorful streamers hanging from the rafters, a simple acknowledgment of the Christmas season. Miguel broke some twigs and threw them in the fireplace. He poked at the coals, coaxing life back into them, and before long, the fire was cranking and warming the cabin. The warmth dispelled the otherwise damp, mildewy smell that permeated the place when we first walked in.

Miguel's face was weathered and worn, and shone like an old boot. Cigarettes had discolored his teeth, and the nicotine added a yellow hue to his skin. He told Skip, who translated for us, that he was watching the station for the owner, and would be on the island for a nine-month stint before his relief came in the spring. Once a month a Chilean supply ship would stop by with provisions; otherwise, he was all alone, isolated from the rest of the world. He would supplement his diet by hunting and fishing, occasionally gathering mussels from the rocks.

Miguel continued with his mysterious manner; he was clearly planning something. He produced a half-dozen goose eggs and told us how he had robbed a nest and stolen the eggs. He then cracked the eggs into a bowl and scrambled them with a fork, beaming at us, but not saying a word. I wondered if we were getting an early dinner. He clearly had something up his sleeve. After ten minutes of vigorous beating, he headed into the back room and reappeared with a bag of sugar. He placed the sugar on the table, spooned ten heaping tablespoons into the goose-egg mixture and stirred the contents. I wondered about the mixture, but Miguel was not saying a thing.

He returned to the back room and reappeared a moment later with a small bottle of vanilla essence. It was obvious that the essence was part of a precious supply, and he carefully measured a few drops into the cap, and then dumped the vanilla into the bowl. He scrambled the mixture, and then left the bowl and tended the fire. Skip asked him what he was doing, but Miguel just pointed to the Christmas decorations and didn't add any information. He was clearly enjoying himself and the secrecy only added to his fun. "Too long alone," I thought.

It was starting to get dark outside and the wind in the channel had subsided. The front room of Miguel's cabin had a clear view of the water. It was no longer being whipped into white caps. Instead the water was a cold blue-gray, marked with an occasional streak of white foam. Miguel lit a lantern, and the soft light cast a content glow on the faces in the room. He was enjoying his one-man show, and I was looking forward to whatever it was he was making. He disappeared to the back room again, and reappeared with a six-pack of Old Milwaukee beer and a grin stretched across his face. Our surprise at this strange appearance of American beer in a shack in Tierra del Fuego was only heightened when Miguel ceremoniously cracked the top of one of the cans and poured it into the goose-egg and sugar mixture. It immediately foamed up, and then quickly subsided.

He added a second beer, and then a third. The bowl was overflowing with froth, so he set it aside and returned with a larger one. Skip held the new bowl while Miguel tipped in the slimy mixture, and then added a fourth beer. He was clearly having fun—we were clearly becoming alarmed. It had occurred to us that this might be something we would have to drink, and because we were well-mannered visitors, we would not be able to decline.

By the time the sixth beer was added and the mixture stirred, the slimy froth was overflowing onto the table and dripping on the floor. Miguel grinned at us and then disappeared once again. We could hear him digging around for something. I glanced at the others who were staring at the bowl of froth, not saying a word. A moment later Miguel returned with four cups. He blew into them and banged them on the table to dislodge the dust. He then produced a ladle, and meticulously spooned the goose egg–beer mixture into each of the mugs. There were four of us, plus Miguel, and I wondered who would not be getting the treat. I hoped it would be me.

It wasn't. He placed the first mug in front of me and handed the others theirs. I peered into the cup. The froth from the beer had subsided, and the drink looked just as you might imagine it would—like slimy yellow egg yolk floating in cheap American beer. Miguel stepped back and admired his work. He pointed to the decorations hanging from the rafters, smiled at us and said, "Chreestmas." We were not smiling.

"Chreestmas," he said again, and gestured for us to drink up. The sugar had dissolved and the vanilla essence added a sweet smell to the mixture. I took a sip and fought a gag reflex, but the mixture slid down my throat and I was surprised to find that it tasted quite good. I recognized the flavor, sort of. The concoction tasted like eggnog—with a twist. The others drained their mugs and started to laugh. Miguel poured another round. This time we all drank without hesitating, but the mixture was rich and one mug was enough—the second cup tasted more like beer and eggs. Miguel beamed and then headed into the back room once again. He returned with a cold Chilean beer, popped the cap and sat by the fire. He leaned back and drank the beer. He looked at us and laughed, drank more beer, and then told us what had happened.

Some French sailors had palmed a case of cheap American beer off on him. He had hoped that they would return so he could play a trick on them, but they never came back. When he saw us sailing up the channel, he decided we were to be his victims instead, and we were. Miguel laughed, then brought out a case of cold Chilean beer. "Much better," he said.

"Much better," we agreed.

It was late in the evening when we left the hut and made our way back to the dinghy. We had finished the beer and enjoyed Miguel's cooking—stewed beaver with rice. The night air was clear and cold, the Southern Cross visible directly overhead. We rowed out to the boat and climbed aboard. I looked towards the now calm Beagle Channel where a full moon was reflected on the still water. Another day in Tierra del Fuego was coming to an end. I slid into my sleeping bag and thought of Miguel alone in his hut. It would be weeks before he saw another face, and four long months before he saw his family. "We all carve a life for ourselves," I thought. Some, like Miguel, and others, like the gas station keepers of the Nullabor, clearly enjoyed their own company. I could relate. While I enjoy the companionship of others, especially when on land, I was becoming increasingly interested in sailing alone, and it was that night while laying in my bunk that I began to plan a solo voyage around the world. It would be a long while before

I would get the chance, but the seed had been planted. For me, that's always the first step. First, though, I had to fulfill the reason I had come to Tierra del Fuego: to climb a high mountain to pay my respects to the wind gods of Cape Horn.

The next morning we sailed west towards the small village of Puerto Williams. Snow was falling and the wind came in gusts as we made our way slowly along the coast. It was rugged country, thick bush making the shoreline almost impenetrable. Above the tree line the sides of the mountains were laid bare from incessant gales, and they were steep sided and covered in a dusting of new snow. Our plan was to climb a 6,000-foot peak on the south side of the Beagle, a jagged peak with a daunting name: Dientes de Navarin, the Devil's Teeth. The peak is the highest point on Navarin Island and we hoped that the view from the top would reach as far as Cape Horn. We anchored early so that we could get to bed early, the plan being to start the climb before daybreak.

It was still dark when Julia, my guide, and I left the boat. We rowed ashore, grateful that the snow had stopped. It was cold and there was ice on water where we tied the dinghy. We followed a dirt track into a shallow valley watching steam rise with each breath. Three miles up the track we turned right, forded a shallow stream, and then sloshed through sphagnum bog until we reached the incline. That was where the difficult part began. The thick undergrowth made it hard to find any kind of a path and in places we had to carve one of our own. I watched Julia hack at the undergrowth swinging her machete in a wide arc, chopping branches and then clearing the debris with her free hand. Her back was soaked with perspiration.

"Let me take over, Julia," I said. "Take a break." She moved aside to let me pass, and I took the machete from her. We had edged up a narrow valley, gradually gaining elevation. I swung at the brush and pulled the loose branches aside. It was hard work and before long I was sweating and panting from the effort. Finally we could see a break ahead. We were almost at the tree line.

"I'll finish up," Julia said. "Pass me the machete." I handed her the blade and stood back. She hacked at the final bushes and moments later we spilled out onto the level area above the tree line. The view was spectacular, even though we had not gained much elevation. The sun was just rising, casting a pale pink light on the fresh snow, and below us, thick Tierra del Fuego scrub stretched as far as we could see. In the spring the scrub is a canopy of firebush with a blaze of red flowers scattered amongst the dull green leaves of the beech trees. Late in the season they give way to the piercing yellow bloom of the calafate, and if one is lucky enough to be there when the calafate bears fruit, one can feast upon its delicious berries.

We rested for a few minutes taking in the view, and then continued on towards the top. The summit was a further four thousand feet above us, and at times the peak was shrouded in fog. There was an ice field on the south side, but the sheer cliffs below the peak were black rock. It was going to be a difficult climb.

"We need to keep moving," Julia said. "It's a long way to the top and we need to traverse the ice field before the sun gets on it." She was worried about the snow becoming soft and unstable. The air was much colder now that we were out of the trees, but at least the going was easier. There was a low butte ahead; beyond we would be into the real meat of the climb. From our vantage it looked very steep, almost vertical in places. We kept a steady pace to conserve energy, gradually making our way higher. The view was more spectacular with each step, and after a while we could see a thin sliver of blue below. We were high above the Beagle Channel and saw sunlight dance on the water. Beyond, the snow-covered mountains in Chile reflected the morning sunshine. It was a magnificent setting in a remote part of the world. My kind of place.

Tierra del Fuego is a land of high, rugged mountains and flat, grassy plains, that stretches from the fifty-second parallel south to Cape Horn. It is flanked on its northern border by the Straits of Magellan, the west by the Pacific Ocean, and the east by the Atlantic. The area was named Tierra del Fuego by Ferdinand Magellan, who saw columns of smoke rising from the shoreline. "It looked as if the land was on fire," he was reported to have said, and so it became Tierra del Fuego, Land of Fire. The smoke was, in fact, from the cooking fires of the Fuegan Indians who lived along the shore. They hunted and gathered for food, cooked over open fires and huddled for warmth around smoldering embers. They are gone now, wiped out by disease brought to the area by the missionaries that followed Magellan. Mark Twain had it right when he wrote, "Soap and education. It's as lethal as guns. It just takes a little longer."

As we trudged higher I thought about the Indians, and their melodic names rolled around my tongue. The tall Ona Indians hunted guanaco with carefully made bows and arrows. They used the skins for clothing and shelter, and feasted on meat. The Ona were the most powerful of the tribes and would occasionally attack the others, but mostly they lived in peace, keeping to themselves.

I wondered about the Yahgans, who wore little or no clothing and scrounged a living along the shore. They used spears and harpoons to hunt otter, fish, and seals, and carried fire with them in their dugout canoes. I smiled at the thought of wooden canoes nosing their way through kelp beds with a blazing fire to keep the occupants warm. The Yahgan men never learned how to swim, and would leave it up to their wives to anchor their canoes out in the channel. The wives would then have to swim ashore.

The Huash were the oldest of the Indian tribes, and were pushed to the eastern tip of Tierra del Fuego by the more numerous Ona and Yahgan. They also hunted and gathered for their food, and lived in huts made of sticks and branches.

But it was the Alacaluf with whom I identified. They roamed the northern plains dressed warmly in guanaco skins, rigging sails in their canoes and navigating the deep waters of the Straits of Magellan. Their resourcefulness should have helped them survive, but all the Indians are gone now, along with their colorful history.

Tierra del Fuego is also Darwin country. It was here a century and a half earlier that Charles Darwin and Robert Fitzroy passed through aboard the HMS *Beagle*. It was the first trip for Darwin; Fitzroy was returning to repatriate three Indians he had seized on a previous trip. Fitzroy had traded a shiny button from his tunic for the youngest Indian, and named him Jimmy Button. When they returned to England, Jimmy Button became an immediate celebrity. They clothed him (for the first time in his life), paraded him in front of British aristocracy, and generally assimilated him into British society. He was even granted an audience with the King. Jimmy Button adapted well to his new celebrity and cultured lifestyle, and soon learned the language.

Fitzroy's motives, however, were not all charitable. He had plans for Jimmy Button. He and Darwin would use Jimmy as a conduit to the rest of the Indians. Jimmy would translate, and it would only be a matter of time before the godless Indians became god-fearing Christians. As they sailed up the Beagle Channel, Jimmy Button set eyes on his homeland for the first time in three years. He was wearing a British naval tunic adorned with bright shiny buttons, looking every bit the part of cultural ambassador. Darwin was fascinated with the Indians and wrote, "It was without exception the most curious and interesting spectacle I ever beheld. I could not have believed how wide was the difference between savage and civilized man: it is greater than between a wild and domesticated animal, inasmuch as in man there is a greater power of improvement." Using Jimmy Button to understand the Indians would be key, but Jimmy had other plans. The moment the H.M.S *Beagle* made contact with the Yahgans, Jimmy stripped naked and bolted. He disappeared into the thick Tierra del Fuego bush and was never seen again.

Darwin's efforts were not totally in vain. The Indians were as curious about the rest of the world as the rest of the world was about them, and Darwin set about studying their language. He was surprised to find among their vast vocabulary of more than 30,000 words no words to describe a higher power. "They were the original Godless nation," he wrote. In their primitive ways he found no signs of civilization of any kind. It has been said that excess production is a basis upon which a society becomes civilized. There must be at least a little surplus food to support a chief, a priest, an artist, or an artisan, but the Indians had none of even the simplest requisites. They had existed without any contact with the outside world, and as such were "unspoiled." They were perfect for Darwin's purposes.

Climbing in Tierra del Fuego I felt a deep connection with Darwin and the Indians. There is something immensely primitive about the landscape, something about the massive peaks whose sheer presence is timeless. It's a rugged wilderness that has escaped man's overwhelming need for more room on an already overcrowded planet. I felt privileged to be there, secure in the knowledge that I was there for the right reasons.

By mid-afternoon we approached the ice field. Beyond was the vertical rise to the summit. At first we trudged through shallow slush that soaked our boots, but after a while the slush got deeper and it took more effort to make progress. A damp chill seeped into my bones, and I battled to walk without falling. We were roped together, Julia leading. Occasionally I would glance at the scenery, but mostly I was lost in my thoughts, thinking back to our capsize at Cape Horn. I knew that we had been spared when really we deserved to pay a higher price for our foolishness.

Cape Horn had not come by its legendary reputation easily. Many had perished on its rocky shore. We had been lucky to get by with blown sails and shattered egos. I remember feeling the presence of the sailors who had been there before us, the seamen who had plied those waters bringing wealth to the west. It was a dangerous time, a time when men with dreams of a Cape Horn rounding never lived to see their families again; a time when massive clipper ships were tossed about and snapped in two by the force of the waves. We were lucky not to be counted among them. Cape Horn had taken many lives, but we had been spared.

As Julia and I edged up the steep face below the summit, I felt as if I was paying my dues. The gods would be watching. I had vowed to return and was keeping my word. My body ached from the climb, and a cold wind cut through my jacket. There was less than sixty feet to the summit. We shuffled slowly towards the top and then suddenly there was nowhere left to go but down.

We sat atop the "Dientes" and rested. The view was breathtaking. To the north the Andes were bathed in bright sunlight, stretching up the west coast of Chile as far as I could see. Below, the Beagle Channel snaked its way between Navarin Island and the southern reach of Argentina. Far to the west I could see Ushuaia nestled along the coast, and below us Puerto Williams snuggled in the lee of the mountain. There was a brisk wind blowing in the channel and I could see white caps marking the surface of the water. They caught the sun and reflected like diamonds, and I swear I could see Fitzroy and Darwin on a close reach just fetching the Murray Narrows. To the south, heavy clouds obscured the view, but I knew somewhere down there Cape Horn was shrouded in fog.

It was time for a celebration. I looked at Julia sitting with her back against a rock. She had collected branches on the way up and gathered them into a small fire. A clump of snow was already melting in the billy can.

"We're good for something, us Brits," she said, and produced two tea bags. "I never leave home without them." She was a good guide and a great sport. Before long the tea was hot and ready for pouring. I leaned back against the rock, Earl Grey in hand, and contemplated the climb. It had been more exhausting than I had anticipated and we still had to head back down, but so far it was all worth it. The area held a strong fascination for me. The ocean, the Indians, the wildlife, and Darwin. I wondered where Jimmy Button spent his last days.

Clouds still shrouded the area south of us, occasionally lifting to allow a fleeting glimpse of the islands, before quickly closing in again. I threw a few dry twigs onto the fire and shoved another handful of snow into the billy. The branches spluttered and crackled as thick smoke rose from the embers. Far above me a small speck wheeled among the clouds and I wondered if there was a smudge on my sunglasses.

And then I saw them. Andean condors. The most magnificent of all South American birds of prey cruised the thermals high above us. They soared among the clouds and then disappeared from sight. I rubbed my eyes, and when I opened them again the condors were right above us, so close I could almost reach out and pluck a feather from their magnificent plumage. Their primary feathers arched with exquisite perfection, gaining maximum effect from each minimal movement. Their beady, inquisitive eyes reflected the majesty of Tierra del Fuego, and I knew in that moment that the gods had acknowledged my effort. To the south, the clouds slowly parted, and far away in the murky distance Cape Horn stood like a silent sentinel guarding the gateway between the Pacific and Atlantic oceans. I could almost make out huge rollers thundering into the steep sides, flinging spindrift skyward—and beyond the Horn itself a bunch of baby-faced sailors trying to round the Cape in a full gale, spinnaker flying and dreams of adventure fixed on their faces.

CHAPTER 9
A LONG DAY

"I travel not to go anywhere, but to go."
—Robert Louis Stevenson

    The truck was packed and ready to go. I had changed the oil the night before and stowed most of our gear in the back, covering it loosely with a tarp. Erin was inside fixing a thermos of coffee and making sandwiches for breakfast. Her footsteps were soft on the tiled floor, and the pale early dawn light cast gentle shadows on her face, softening her features and giving her skin a warm glow. She looked beautiful with her thick auburn hair pulled back and fastened with a childish hair clip. She was not a morning person, and I knew that I would be better off outside until she was good and ready to go. I started the truck to let it warm up and checked one more time to see that our gear was secure. The ride to the "wild coast" was long, most of it on bumpy dirt roads, and our gear was sure to be jolted loose if not properly secured. The tarp would help keep out the dust.

    I wandered around the side of the house to the back, and sat on the edge of the lawn looking over my father's small avocado orchard. The ground sloped away from the house, and the orchard ended up against the woods that abutted our land. In the trees vervet monkeys swung with wild abandon, poaching onto our property and swiping an occasional avocado before scurrying back to the relative safety of the trees. If they weren't such pests it would have been amusing to watch their antics. Instead I picked up a stone and flung it in their direction. The stone crashed through the branches and the monkeys chattered among themselves, scurrying up the trunks and out onto the uppermost limbs. They stared down at me with their large, inquisitive eyes, muttering to themselves. I aimed another stone and flung it, instantly renewing the chattering. Behind me I heard a low whistle. Erin stood at the edge of the porch, thermos in one hand, and a bag of sandwiches in the other. She smiled. It was time to go.

Erin was one of the first people I met when I arrived in the United States in the early 1980s. I was immediately attracted to her light skin and dark brown eyes, and before long we were living together. She had never been to Africa and this trip was to introduce her to the land that I loved so much. I wanted her experience to be pure Africa—the people, the countryside, and the downside, and there was no better place to find these things than the "wild coast." There are few places left on the planet that remain completely untouched by man's indiscriminate need for space. The "wild coast" is one such place. It runs two hundred miles from the Natal border, south towards the Cape Province, and forms the coastline of the Transkei, one of South Africa's so-called "independent homelands." It remains unspoiled for one simple reason: it is largely inaccessible. All the roads that run to the coast run perpendicular to it, and it is a long, dry, dusty slog to get there.

Only true believers make the effort, and we were planning a week-long trip.

We drove through town, past the glitzy department stores, past the old railroad station, and beyond, towards the outskirts of the city. The streets were still deserted with only a few early risers to be seen. This was my town, Pietermaritzburg. This was where I had grown up, and the streets and buildings felt as familiar to me as old friends. Before long the buildings thinned out, and we were into the country, rolling hills gently undulating as far as the eye could see. It was winter, and an occasional pocket of frost stood stark against the brown landscape. The early light was filtered by low cloud, and in some places a gentle mist hung in the valleys. It dampened my windshield and made the road slick, but the sun would soon be up to burn off the remaining wisps of mist and pockets of frost. A hot day lay ahead. The truck was running well, and I felt a warm contentment in anticipation of another adventure.

Africa is ingrained in my spirit. I can feel the rhythm of the land resonate through my blood the moment I return. Each continent has its own beat, and you can feel it as soon as you arrive at the airport, but it is only the land of your birth that has that special effect on your being. All those formative years seep slowly into your system and are instantly triggered as soon as you breathe the air that you were born into. I felt the rhythm intensify with each mile.

The sun broke the horizon behind us, and before long it had climbed high enough to beat down on the car, warming the inside. I rolled my window down, and the cool, sweet-smelling air drifted in as we made our way through the rural villages of western Natal. The mud huts were painted in bright colors, giving them a gaiety that belied the surrounding poverty. Barefoot kids scrambled down to the roadside to watch us pass. They stood and waved, some of them cupping their hands in hope of a handout, but we blew by, intent upon getting to the Transkei border before lunch. I could see the look of dismay on Erin's face as we passed without stopping, but after a few more miles and hundreds more kids she knew, as did I, that helping out a single family would hardly dent the overwhelming poverty. We swallowed our guilt and kept on going.

The road was a narrow, single-lane highway, and occasionally a truck carrying livestock would pass us heading towards town. The trucks were piled high with their precious cargo balanced precariously. The vehicles swayed dangerously. I pulled over onto the dirt shoulder to let them go by, and felt the wind buffet our car as they passed. The smell of scared animals hung in the air long after they were out of sight. Occasionally we would encounter a piccanin, a young farm boy, herding a flock of sheep down the road, and we would slow to let them pass. Mostly, though, it was just a rolling road heading west.

By late morning we made the border of the Transkei and pulled up to the disheveled Customs buildings. A uniformed guard strolled up to the car, picking his nose and sweating profusely. Customs were a mere formality and passage was automatically granted to all South African citizens. We did not expect any problems. Erin was traveling on an American passport and I had been using a British passport for the past few years, thanks to my father having been born in England. Neither one would present a problem.

"E' passiport, please." The guard extended a sweaty hand. I reached into my bag for the passports and a travel permit, and handed them over. We sat in silence while he studied the documents. I noticed his pistol bulging in its holster. The guard squinted at each stamp, fingering the paper and flipping the pages until he came to the photographs.

"Where you going, Sah?" he asked. I explained that we were headed to the wild coast for a few days.

"And whose bakkie is dis?" he asked, using the Afrikaans word for pickup truck. I told him that it belonged to my brother, and watched while he wandered around the car, inspecting the gear in the back.

"You want to sell it?" he asked. "I give you three thousand Rand today."

"No, thanks," I replied, "I can't do that. It's not my car." He stopped at Erin's window and peered inside.

"You sell dis bakkie to me today," he insisted, wiping his hand across his nose.

"I can't," I said. "It's not mine to sell. Besides, we need it to get to the coast." He sniffed and spat on the ground.

"Very well, then. You sell dis bakkie to me now otherwise I will not let you pass," he continued, his voice rising with an edge that made me uneasy.

"I can't sell it," I insisted. "It's not my car. I don't have the papers." Arguing was pointless, judging by the guard's demeanor. I sat in silence and watched him. He wandered around to the rear of the truck lifting the tarp once more to inspect our gear, and then returned to the Customs building. "What now?" I thought. The heat was making it uncomfortable in the car, and I was getting anxious and agitated just sitting and waiting. "Christ, this is ridiculous," I muttered under my breath. I was keen to keep moving. After twenty minutes he reappeared.

"You, Missus." He gestured to Erin. "You get out of the

car." She looked at me and I nodded. "You stand against the car and wait, and you Mister, you stay in the car." I sat quietly behind the wheel feeling the level of agitation rising.

"Where you from, lady?"

"America," she replied.

"You like men?" he asked. Erin did not reply. "You like American blek men?" he continued. Erin said nothing. "You tell your boyfriend to sell me this car." What was it about the car, I wondered? Why was he being so insistent? Three thousand Rand was about half its value, but that was likely not the reason. He was just out to harass us and exercise his newly granted powers. The "independent homelands" were a lousy idea anyway, I thought. Give a guy a gun and a uniform, and he loses all sense of reason.

"You like blek men?" he asked again moving closer. Erin stepped back.

"Yes," she said softly. "I like men." The guard beamed.

"Now we're getting somewhere," he said. I glanced in the rear-view mirror and noticed another car approaching. The guard saw it, too, and spat on the ground.

"Shit," he said. "You get back in the car, lady." He handed her the passports. Without further comment he raised the gate and waved us on. A lime-green VW beetle pulled to a stop at the gate, and I looked back in time to see the guard spit one more time, adjust his nuts, and stroll up to the driver's side window.

We pulled away, and a few miles later the tar abruptly ended, and the road turned to dirt. The pickup drifted sideways as it hit the new surface, and dust billowed out behind us. It was a while before either of us spoke.

"What was that all about?" Erin asked. I shrugged and stared intently at the road. The guard had been acting strange, but strange guards were nothing new in Africa. Who was it that said, "Power corrupts, and absolute power corrupts absolutely," I wondered? The independent homelands were a bad idea, bound for certain disaster. The guard was just a small example of what might happen. I was looking forward to the day when there would be an equal vote in the country. It had to happen, and the sooner it did, the better it would be for everyone.

"I don't know," I said. "Too much power and not enough brains." I watched the dry land pass by and wondered about the future. I wondered what would become of South Africa? What would happen to this beautiful land? What would happen to my country? I had once been told that rape was the national sport of the idle African, but didn't subscribe to that kind of thinking. Still, the guard had unnerved me. I was pessimistic about the future.

"What do you think would have happened if the other car hadn't arrived?" Erin asked. I stared at the road and didn't answer. I had no idea. The incident made me feel uncomfortable, but I was not going to let it ruin my day.

We stopped in Umtata for lunch. Umtata is the capital of the Transkei and housed the puppet government during the days of apartheid. We picked up a six-pack of Lion Lager and some biltong to go with the sandwiches. South Africa is famous for its dried meat, and a slab of ostrich biltong would be a great addition to the lunch that Erin had packed. We were eager to make Magwa Falls by dark and piled back into the truck, which by now was a dull red, thickly coated with Transkei dust. I could feel it caking the back of my throat. Erin cracked the top of a Lion Lager and passed it to me. I drank gratefully, and the beer washed away the film of dust that coated my tongue and the bad taste left by the guard. I steered the car with one hand, clutching a thick sandwich and the beer with the other, while the truck drifted around the corners in a billowing of dust. "Bakkie surfing," it's called, and to an African kid it's about as close to heaven as it gets.

The afternoon drifted lazily by. The dirt road gradually narrowed as we got further from town, until it was a track barely wide enough for a single car. There was no other traffic on the road, so it didn't matter. The countryside was flat and featureless and dotted with small clusters of huts. There was no organized grouping to the villages. They had sprung up in a haphazard way, cluttered around what water they could find. Scrawny farm animals scrounged whatever nutrition they could from tufts of dry grass. I was amazed that they survived in such a harsh place, but Africa is all about survival.

We finished the six-pack and stopped for another at a roadside stand. The shelves were mostly bare, and everything was covered with a fine film of dust. In the rear of the store a refrigerator chugged desperately, struggling to keep its contents cool against the heat of the day. It reminded me of the one in Australia that housed the kangaroo in the crazy old man's house. A radio played, and the attendant sat bored by the door. I asked if there was a place to buy petrol. She waved her hand in the general direction of the coast and shrugged.

"Somewhere down there, Baas, you can buy petrol." She didn't seem too certain. I wished I had brought along a spare jerry can, but it was too late now. I paid for the beer and headed back to the car. The air had turned still and hung heavy. Towards the west I noticed a bank of cumulus clouds rolling in, their anvil shaped tops reaching up beyond the cirrus.

"I think we might be in for some rain," I said to Erin. I could feel the moisture wrap itself around everything, and the air was thick with dust and humidity. Erin dozed off from the heat and beer, and the clouds closed in as we pulled into Magwa Falls.

The sign at the gate might once have greeted all visitors gaily, but it now hung lopsided on a wooden post with the paint peeling. We passed over the cattle grid, down a tree-lined avenue, and up to the main reception area. The sign on the door was faded, but it too beckoned a welcome, and while Erin stayed in the truck to watch our gear, I went inside to register.

The reception area was cool and dimly lit. As my eyes adjusted to the low light, they focused on a rundown counter with a few faded promotional posters from a bygone era hanging on the wall. There was no one around. I rang the bell and waited, but no one came. I rang again, and then noticed a door off to the side. I knocked tentatively, and when there was no answer, I quietly pushed it open. The room was dark with all the curtains drawn. A faint wheezing and puffing emanated from the far corner, and I could just make out the slouched form of someone in a chair. The receptionist was fast asleep, oblivious to my presence. Her huge breasts rose with each wheeze, and fell gently with each puff.

"Hello," I called, "hello, hello." The breasts rose and fell. "Excuse me, ma'am. Hello, hello." No movement. The wheezing continued while her ample mounds of flesh rolled in rhythm. I looked around the room, and then went back to the reception area and banged the bell. Through the window I could see Erin waiting patiently. I decided that I had better wake the receptionist, and tentatively approached the wheezing body, gently nudging her shoulder and calling out a soft "hello," but the body only wobbled to my touch. There was no response. I prodded again, and my finger sunk into the fleshy folds. All of a sudden her eyes flashed open and she jumped to her feet.

"Sheeeeet, Baas, wad you doin'?" She stared at me with wide eyes and then slumped back into the chair. "Sheet, Baas, you dam' scared me. What you want here?"

"I'm here to check into a room," I stammered. "I have a reservation."

"Sheet, Baas," she said again, using a servant's term for an employer. "You don' need a reservation around here. No one comes here any more. If you want a room, jus' take a room." She rose slowly from the chair, a lot slower than the first time. "You wan' a room, you can have any room. Twenty Rand for the night." I followed her out to the reception area and pulled a R20 bill from my jeans pocket. She shuffled over to the counter and reached for a bunch of keys.

"What do you mean no one comes here any more?" I asked. I was looking for a quiet place, and it seemed as if I had found one. Thunder rumbled in the distance and the windows rattled.

"Dis place is under new management," she said. "Since the Transkei became independent, dis place been under Government management. "You take any room," she said, "any place you fancy. The key fits them all." I thanked her and took the key. The air outside was cool and fresh after the stale smell of the reception.

Erin smiled as I approached the car. "Where have you been?" she asked, "I was worried about you." I looked at her happy face and thought I noticed a look of anxiety cross her eyes. Perhaps it was just my imagination. "Is everything okay?" she asked.

"Oh, fine, yeah," I replied. "We have a room for the night." For the first time I noticed an eerie, still feeling in the air. Not like the calm that precedes a storm, but an ominous, languid feeling. I shivered despite the warm temperature. Something did not feel right. The air was too still. There were no birds. No sounds at all. Nothing was moving. In the distance I could hear the surf crashing onto the beach, but it was only a muffled roar. We drove down the dirt road towards the huts where guests stayed. There was no one around. The road reached the edge of the beach and the surf thundered louder. The sand was a brilliant white, and the warm blue ocean crashed onto the shore in a frothy wave washing up to the high-water mark. Beyond the breakers I saw white caps on the ocean and felt another unease as I realized that not 50 yards offshore a strong wind was blowing, but where we stood it was calm. Dead calm. Erin stared at the whitecaps, and then looked at me.

"Weird," she said.

"Very strange," I agreed. We pulled up to the first hut, a rondavel, as it's called in Africa. It was round with white-washed walls and a thatched roof, and was close to the beach. The wonderful sound of the ocean would lull us to sleep. I immediately felt better as that small part of being African connected with the remote setting and the rondavel. It had been a long day and I was looking forward to a swim. It felt good to be back home with the wild coastline bursting with energy. Maybe a good swim and a decent meal was all we needed.

Thunder rolled overhead and rumbled a low bellow that echoed across the dry land.

"We'd better be quick if we want to swim before the rain comes," Erin said. We piled out of the truck, and I opened the door to the rondavel. It was cool inside, but smelt damp and stale. The light didn't work, and Erin pulled the curtain aside to let the outside light stream in. The place was a mess, with the bed unmade and clothing scattered on the floor.

"It looks like someone is staying here," Erin said. "I thought you said that we were the only guests."

"That's what she told me at the reception," I replied. "Let's try another hut." We walked over to the next hut and went in. It was bright inside, but smelt worse than the first one.

"Maybe it just needs a little air," Erin offered hopefully. I went into the kitchen looking for the source of the smell and found a pot bubbling on the stove. The stink in the tiny room was overwhelming.

"This is really strange," she said. "It looks as if there is someone staying here as well, and whatever they're cooking smells disgusting." Her American nose was sending strong signals to her brain. There was no way she would stay in this hut. The pot bubbled away, and as I lifted the lid to peek inside, a cloud of foul smelling steam escaped. The steam dissipated and I looked into the pot. Staring back at me was the half-boiled head of something. The front teeth were exposed. They were extra large and white and incongruous against the darkened eye sockets. I slammed the lid down as the hairs on the back of my neck stood straight out.

"Shit, let's get out of here!" I bolted for the door. From where Erin was standing, she had not been able to see into the pot, but she knew that it wasn't good. We ran back to the car.

"Let's get the hell out of here," I said. "This place gives me the creeps. There may still be time to find somewhere else before it gets dark." Erin didn't need encouraging. We raced back up the dirt road not bothering to stop at the reception to pick up my twenty Rand, crossed over the cattle grid, and drove back to the main road. My heart was pounding, the hairs on my neck were still standing on end. There was no way we were going to stay one moment longer; however, our problem was going to be finding another place to stay before nightfall. Accommodation was scarce, and the sun was already waning towards the western horizon with rain imminent.

I pulled the truck to the side of the road and grabbed the map. Umzimvubu was down the coast a little, not far as the crow flies, but there were no roads running along the coast. We would have to drive the better part of an hour inland before finding a crossroad to link up with the road running to Umzimvubu. It was our only choice. Erin opened a couple of beers, and we headed back the way we had just come.

"That place was downright spooky," she said. I agreed and gunned the engine. We would have to hurry.

Sunsets in Africa are like no other on earth. The air is filled with dust and moisture, and the sun's rays reflect off the minute particles. The landscape is brown and dry and absorbs the late afternoon sun with warmth and beauty. We were being treated to one of the best, enhanced by an approaching thunderstorm. The clouds were black, laden with rain. We drove in silence watching the fingers of light paint the sky. It would be dark by the time we arrived in Umzimvubu, but I was more concerned about beating the fading light to the crossroad. There are few signposts in the Transkei, and finding the road would be difficult even in daylight. We pressed on steadily as darkness approached.

I glanced at the gas gauge and cursed under my breath. The needle hovered just above red. We should make Umzimvubu without any problem, and I hoped that someone there would have a few gallons to sell us. I didn't mention anything to Erin. She had been a good sport all day, but I could sense her unease. I was feeling a little uneasy myself, and I was in a familiar environment.

"Beautiful sky," I muttered. Just then, large splats of rain fell heavily onto the hood of the car. They dissipated the dust on the windshield, immediately forming small rivers of mud. The warm drops drummed the roof, and in a few moments the din inside was too loud for talking. The wipers ran at full speed. It was hardly possible to see more than a few feet in front of us, and I prayed silently that there would not be any hail. A late afternoon hail storm can be a spectacular sight, but devastating to anything in its path. Thunder rolled across the heavens, and the dry earth drank up the moisture. We plodded on, looking for the crossroad.

As suddenly as it had started, the rain quit. Storm clouds lined the horizon and I knew that the worst was yet to come. Up ahead I saw a small road running perpendicular to ours. It had to be the crossroad. I stopped the car, checked the map, and then pulled onto the intersecting road.

Road was probably a misnomer. In Africa the roads sometimes become paths, and other times they are just ruts that your tires fit into. This one started as a road, but after a few minutes began to fade. The dirt turned to a path, and soon the path turned into two ruts. Two narrow, mud-filled ruts. I thought about turning back, but the level of the gas gauge convinced me to press on. If we turned back we would not make Umzimvubu that night. Fortunately the ruts gave way to a wider track, and after a while it resembled a road again. And then the rain resumed. It came down with less urgency than the first foray, but it was still a heavy downpour. At times we were driving off the path when I would notice tracks running alongside of us, and pull back onto them. Night had fallen, and the headlights reflected brightly on the drops of rain. Every now and then a rabbit would stand frozen in the beams, and at the last moment it would regain its senses and bolt off into the black. Erin clutched the door handle, holding on as the car skidded in the mud. My hands were glued to the wheel, palms sweating. I felt a slight chill despite the tropical air.

Our situation was deteriorating rapidly, and our options were limited. The gas needle hovered just above empty, at times dipping below. The crossroad was a little over ten miles long, or at least that was how it appeared on the map. I was starting to feel that we were on the wrong road. We had been driving for almost an hour, and there was still no sign of the road leading to Umzimvubu. We slipped and slid and sloshed and bumped in the pitch black, finding no trace of civilization, and no other road. The wind picked up and buffeted the car while the rain pelted loudly on the hood. I was clearly worried, and Erin, to her everlasting credit, was biting her tongue. I knew that she was scared and I felt scared myself. We were well beyond the point of turning back. The level of gas in the tank would barely get us off the crossroad, and definitely not all the way back to Magwa Falls. We pressed on.

The rain continued to fall heavily. Without a moon, it was the darkest night I could remember, and the Transkei is so flat and featureless that there were no landmarks by which we could gauge our progress. Suddenly I noticed a break ahead, and with a bump and a skid we landed squarely on a larger crossroad. It ran perpendicular to ours—in the direction of Umzimvubu. I stopped and checked the map. This time I was sure that we were on the right road and swung the truck, pointing it south once more. South in the direction of the coast. Umzimvubu looked to be about twenty-five miles away, and with a little luck we would be there by 10 p.m. It had been a long day and we were ready to get out of the truck and into a warm bed.

The new road was a lot better than the cross-track, and we made good progress. The truck was sliding in the mud, and I was having a hard time keeping it on the road. At each bend the rear-end would slide out; one time it swung all the way around until we faced back the way we had come. It might have been a problem had there been other traffic, but we had not seen another vehicle since leaving Magwa Falls. We passed small clusters of huts and could smell the wood smoke from their cooking fires. I envied them, and thought of families gathered out of the rain, cooking big pots of food over open fires. I was hungry and longed for someplace warm and dry.

"You okay?" I asked Erin. She nodded slightly.

"Better now than I was on the other road," she replied. "I was scared back there. I didn't think we were going to make it." Her face was pale and drawn. "Were you scared?" she asked. I nodded. It was obvious that we had been in trouble.

"It's okay, sweetheart," I said, "we will soon be in a warm place, and out of the rain."

"I don't care if Umzimvubu is like the other place," she said flatly. "We're not leaving."

"Okay, then." I had no intention of doing any more driving. If we made it, it would be on fumes only. The rain continued to pelt down, and the drops reflected brightly in the headlights. The visibility was almost zero when the road suddenly took a sharp turn to the right. Out of the corner of my eye I saw the track heading up a hill and reflexively swung the wheel, slamming the brakes. The car skidded sideways, and then spun a full 360 degrees. I shut my eyes and hung onto the wheel as we took a violent bump, and then became airborne before making a soft landing in a ditch alongside the road. The engine screamed and the wheels spun violently, kicking up mud. My foot was jammed on the accelerator. I pulled it off and the car stalled. It was suddenly very quiet. I looked over at Erin. Her face was white and she looked vulnerable and scared hanging onto the door handle. All of a sudden tears popped from both eyes. They ran down her cheeks and dropped onto her lap. She sat there looking at me and I hung my head. We were now in real trouble.

"Shit," I muttered. "Damn, how bloody stupid." I cursed at the rain and at the mud. "What the hell are we going to do now?" I sat with my head resting on the wheel and stared into the dark night. The headlights were pointing up at the sky fading out into the inky black. Beside me I could hear Erin crying softly.

"What a bloody idiot I am," I said. "What a stupid fool." It had already been a tough night and we were now in a real jam. I turned off the headlights and we were pitched into complete darkness.

"Turn the lights back on," Erin said. "I'm scared, it's too dark." I flicked them on again and the beams pointed skyward. The rain had stopped momentarily and I rolled the window down. I could smell wood smoke in the air and guessed that there must be a settlement nearby. Perhaps I could walk and get help, but I knew that Erin would not stay alone in the car and I wasn't too sure how safe we were, anyway. We were most likely the only white people for fifty miles, and strange things have happened to lost travelers.

"We'd better save the battery," I said, and turned the lights off again. This time we were ready for the darkness and it did not take us by surprise. I took Erin's hand in mine; it felt cool in my clammy hand. She squeezed it gently and in the darkness I could see a trace of a smile cross her face.

"This ain't no America," she said. "Where is AAA when you need them?" I smiled back at her and wondered what to do next.

"There's not much we can do until morning. We're stuck in this ditch, and we'll need a tow to haul us out. I am sure we are safe here, though." I stated the obvious, and added the bit about being safe more for Erin's benefit than mine. I had no idea if we were safe, but saying it out loud seemed to reassure us both.

"Feel like a beer and something to eat?" Erin asked. "They are not that cold anymore, but it's better than nothing." She passed me a lukewarm Lion Lager, and cut a few slices of biltong. We sat quietly sharing the can and chewing on the salty meat. The night was quiet and the clouds seemed to be breaking up. Occasionally a weak half moon would appear through a break in the clouds, and shed its watery light onto the landscape. The mud glistened and reflected the silver beams. On any other occasion it would have been beautiful to sit and watch the huge storm clouds roll by a waning moon, but this was not a night for cloud watching. We finished the beer and decided to save the last one for breakfast.

"Why don't we try and get some sleep?" I said. "We'll see what tomorrow brings." At least it was warm and dry in the car. We tilted the seat back as far as it could go, and I shut my eyes trying to block out our predicament. I must have dozed for a moment because Erin was suddenly shaking me.

"Quick," she said. "There is a car coming." I looked where she pointed and could just make out headlights winding their way towards us. I kicked my shoes off and hopped out of the truck. My foot sunk into a few inches of soft mud and squelched with each step as I made my way up to the road. As the car approached the driver flicked his beams on high and caught me directly in the glare. I waved and it pulled up alongside me. I felt a sudden pang of anxiety. What if these people were not friendly? The car stopped and the driver wound down his window. A lone black man sat behind the wheel.

"Hey, Baas, wad you doing out here?" His white teeth glistened, and I could see that he was suppressing a laugh. "You're in trouble, man. Wad you doing with your bakkie in the ditch? That's no place to park." He laughed at his own joke and opened the door. He was a big man and more laughter rumbled deep inside of him. He shook my hand still laughing to himself, and led me to the back of his car. The trunk opened, and he reached in and grabbed a short length of rope.

"You the second person I pull from a ditch tonight. Five miles back there," he said, pointing back the way he had just come, "I pull another bakkie from the ditch." He laughed again and patted me on the back. "Don't worry, Baas, I have you out in a few minutes." From the car I heard Erin in a small voice.

"Are you all right, Hancock?" she said. "Is everything okay?"

"We're going to get pulled out," I shouted back.

I plodded back to the car with one end of the rope, while my new friend tied the other end to his tow hitch.

"Sit tight, Erin, he's going to pull us out."

"Should I get out of the truck?"

"No," I said, "just hold on and we will be out of here in a

moment." I tied the rope around the tow hitch and sloshed my way back up to the road. The rope went tight and the engine roared, but our truck didn't budge. He gunned the engine again—still nothing.

The black man pointed towards the truck.

"You better get down there and push," he instructed. I skidded down the bank, made my way to the front of the truck, and leaned my shoulder up against the bumper.

"Okay," I yelled, and heard the engine roar. There was a soft sucking sound as the truck moved, and then suddenly it was free. I shoved harder, and with a pop the car was pulled backward out of the ditch, leaving me flat on my face in the mud. I looked up at the road and the man was standing there laughing.

"Come on, Baas. Wad you doing down there?" I could see white teeth glinting in the moonlight.

"Shit," I said. "I have had enough." I heard more laughter as I slipped my way back up to the road. He had untied the rope from both cars and extended a hand to help me up the last few feet.

"Hey, Baas, where you goin' tonight?" I told him that we were headed for Umzimvubu for a few days and he laughed even louder.

"There's nothing at Umzimvubu any more," he said. "There's no place to stay there. Everything is closed." I stared at him.

"There's nothing in Umzimvubu? No rondavels?"

"No, Baas, it's all closed. Since the new government took over, it has been closed."

"Oh, man," I cursed softly "What now?" Our predicament had hardly improved since being pulled from the ditch. No gas for the truck and nowhere to stay. Erin had not heard the conversation and was sitting patiently waiting for me to come back to the car.

"Do you know any place to buy petrol? We need petrol for the truck." The man laughed again and pointed to the north.

"About 15 miles up the road there is a pump. There is also a small hotel there. Not very fancy, but cheap. I must go now." He shook my muddy hand, jumped back into his car and sped off. I could hear laughter as he pulled away. In a moment his tail lights had faded and it was dark again. I climbed in alongside Erin and she grinned at me.

"What's so funny?" The mud was starting to cake, and dry bits flaked off in the car. Erin laughed and took my hand.

"So what did he say about Umzimvubu?" I told her about the hotel and we headed back the way we had just driven. The town would be north of the crossroad, and if our luck held we might just have enough gas to get us there. I drove slowly. Without the rain it was easier to see where we were going.

Half an hour later we pulled into a small village with no name and drove slowly down the main street. The town was deserted and very run down. A few ramshackle houses lined the only street, and halfway down a sign read OTEL. The H was gone, but that was the least of its problems. The roof was sagging and all the paint had peeled off. I stopped out front and jumped out of the car.

"I'll go and get us a room," I said, and looked for the reception area. There did not appear to be one so I peered through one of the open windows. In the corner of the room a narrow cot was covered with a filthy spread. The room was tiny, and on a wooden bed stand there were a few candles and a box of matches. An unwashed smell permeated the place. We were both tired, but I could not see Erin agreeing to stay in that room. I hoped the good rooms were in the back.

I told Erin what I had seen and she still insisted that we should stop for the night.

"How bad can it be?" she said. Maybe she was right. We found the reception area and let ourselves in. There was no one around. I banged on the window and called out, but no one came.

"This place is not so bad," Erin said. "I'm so tired that I would not even notice if the bed was hard."

"Hello," I called out. "Hello. Anyone here?" In the corner I heard a small rustling sound and glanced down. Two rats were chewing on an old newspaper, and then one of them scurried across the floor and ran across Erin's foot. She screamed and fled back to the car. I found her sitting with her door locked and her legs pulled up under her.

"Wewwe . . . are not staying there," she stammered. "Let's get out of this place. I want to go home," she wailed. I agreed. It was time to bag the vacation and get back to civilization. If we were lucky we might even make it home before dawn.

"Let's go," I said, and then remembered the gas. We had been running on fumes for a long while. We were not going anywhere until we found a pump.

We drove up and down the main street looking for something that might resemble a petrol station, but without luck. On the edge of town I saw some kids hanging out and stopped to ask them if there was a place to buy petrol. They directed me behind a rundown warehouse where an old-fashioned gas pump stood looking like it had not been used in years. The kids told me that old Mr. Mbeki was in charge of the pump, and he lived a short walk down the dirt track that ran adjacent to the warehouse. I looked where they pointed and the track faded into the dark night. The storm clouds still hung low, the sliver of moon barely shedding light. I told Erin to wait in the car and lock the doors.

We had to get gas and if old Mr. Mbeki had the keys, then I would have to find him. I fumbled through our bags, found a flashlight and set off down the path. It was slippery from the rain, and narrow. Some branches grew across the path and I had to duck to get under them. I was glad for the flashlight, but even its faint beam did little to calm my nerves. The night was so black that the feeble beam faded out a few feet in front of me, swallowed up by the darkness. I began to wonder if the kids were sending me on a wild goose chase when my ears caught the sound of muffled laughter. It had to be Mbeki's place.

Back in the car Erin sat quietly with her feet tucked up under her, all doors locked. She left the engine running and every few seconds glanced nervously down the path hoping that I would reappear. It had been a long day and her imagination was working on overdrive. The skewed American view of Africa being a wild and savage place was haunting her, but so far without reason. With the exception of the guard at the border crossing, all the people we had encountered in the Transkei had been good to us. Still, the shadows bothered her, just as they were bothering me.

The muffled laughter grew louder as I stumbled my way towards the sound. In a clearing ahead I discovered a small cluster of huts grouped together against a low cliff. There was a pungent smell of wood smoke in the air. I guessed that dinner would be well over and the fires were being kept going to keep out the dampness. It had started to drizzle again and the drips ran down my face. My wet hair hung in my eyes. I wasn't sure what to do. I was nervous about knocking on the door and asking Mr. Mbeki to crank up his pump, but there was no way that we were going to return to the hotel, and sleeping in the car for the night was not a great option. I wanted to go home.

The loudest voices seemed to be coming from the main hut and I cautiously approached the front door. I listened for a moment and then called out.

"Hello? Hello? Mr. Mbeki?" Immediately the voices inside hushed. "Is Mr. Mbeki in there, please?" The door swung open and a teenage boy stood in the entrance, naked to the waist. He stared at me. Behind him the room was filled with smoke, and I could make out a number of people sitting on a bed.

"Is Mr. Mbeki in?" I stammered. The boy moved aside to let me in. An old man was sitting in the middle of the bed with a number of small children snuggled around him. He was wizened with a scraggly gray beard. Most of his front teeth were either yellowed or missing.

"Yebo, Baas," he said, "I am Mbeki." The children sat silently staring at me with big brown eyes and snotty noses, and cuddled closer to the old man when he spoke. It was very hot and very smoky in the hut, and my eyes smarted. I explained that I needed to get some petrol and Mr. Mbeki nodded and asked me to sit down. I looked around for a chair, but he patted the mattress motioning for me to join him on the bed. There was a long pause while I sat uncomfortably waiting for his answer. I was worried about Erin alone in the car and wanted to get moving, but Mr. Mbeki had the key to the pump and I was not about to hurry him. In broken English he asked why I was there and why I needed to get petrol now and not in the morning. I lied and told him that my wife was feeling sick and I wanted to get to Umtata. He nodded thoughtfully and said something to the teenage boy who disappeared into the adjacent hut. Mr. Mbeki rubbed his chin, deep in thought, and then rose slowly from the bed. His small frame was stooped and he walked with an awkward shuffle. The teenager returned with a bunch of keys and Mbeki nodded to me.

"Follow me," he said, and we set off back up the hill. I followed his frail frame, attempting to light the path in front of him with my flashlight, but Mbeki knew his way. We inched our way along as he chose his footsteps carefully, and after a while the smell of the huts disappeared and we approached the top of the hill. I could see the pump and hear the truck running.

Erin jumped as I approached the car and smiled with relief when I told her that we would be able to get gas and keep moving. Pietermaritzburg was still a long way away, but now we had a chance of making it back home. I swung the truck around and shone the headlights at the pump while Mbeki fumbled with the lock. And then the engine spluttered and died. It was suddenly very quiet—we were out of gas.

Mbeki fired up a small generator. The noise broke the stillness of the night and the pump spluttered. He smiled thoughtfully while pumping, and beamed gratefully when I paid him three times the going rate. It was 11:30 p.m., and still drizzling.

I studied the map and found a road that would take us back to Umtata. The road was slippery and driving was difficult with poor visibility. Thunder rumbled in the distance and the smacking of the wipers lulled us as we drove on through the African night. Erin soon fell asleep while I fought desperately to keep my eyes open. I was tempted to pull over and rest, but opted instead to press on.

A little after midnight it started to rain again, while sheet lightning lit the sky. The road had turned into a narrow, wet gully. I checked the map. We seemed to be on the right track. I thought I could make out a light in front of us and rubbed my eyes, sure they were playing tricks on me. We had not seen another car since being pulled from the ditch, but as we got closer I could make out the faint taillights of another vehicle. I was happy to have someone to follow because the visibility was all but gone, and the road had started to drop off down a steep hill. I was worried about skidding off the track. I slowed to a crawl and followed the two red lights as we pressed on in the dark. I was glad that Erin was asleep. At times I lost sight of the car ahead only to find it again around the next bend.

Suddenly the road leveled out and the car ahead stopped. I stomped on the brakes and skidded to a stop inches from the car in front. The headlights reflected on rapids directly in front of us. The river had broken its banks and was flowing strongly. The driver hopped out and walked to the water's edge to inspect the flow. He waved at me, and then, without hesitating, jumped back in his car, gunned the engine, and sped into the water. Waves splashed and the car drifted sideways. In a moment he was on the other side. He leaned out of the window and beckoned to me to follow. I glanced over at Erin, who was still asleep, gulped, and gunned the engine. The truck hit the rapids on the upstream side of the bridge, and Erin woke just as the first wave crashed over the car. The wheels lost all traction and suddenly we were afloat.

"Hancock, what the hell are you doing?" she yelled.

"Hold on," I said. I clutched the steering wheel and prayed. The truck bobbed in the rapids, but there was enough momentum to carry us to the other bank. The tires spun until they caught, and we skidded up the other side and pulled to a stop alongside the other car. My feet were in a few inches of water so I opened the door to let the flood pour out. Erin glared at me. The rain kept pounding down.

In the car beside us were five well-dressed black men returning from a party somewhere. They were all smashed, the three in the back fast asleep. The smell of cheap whiskey hung over their supine bodies. The driver was dressed in his Sunday best with mud caked to his knees. His once-smart shoes were now blobs of clay, and his jacket was wet and covered with mud. He was grinning heartily, flashing a perfect set of teeth, and enjoying every minute of this great adventure.

"That was the easy part, Baas," he told me. "The river is no problem except once my brother was washed away." He waved in the general direction of downstream. "The hard part is dis' hill." He was right. On the way down to the river the car had been sliding all over the place, and it looked as if the hill ahead was even steeper. I shook my head and wondered again what else could possibly go wrong.

"Don't worry Baas, you jus' need speed. Lots of speed. And a good driver." He grinned and then yelled at the three sleepers in the back. "And no passengers." The three dazed passengers tumbled from the car and staggered around in the rain trying to gain their bearings. It was obvious that they had been through this routine before, because they set off up the hill, leaving only the driver at the bottom with the car.

"You, Baas," he said, pointing at me. "You follow them, and you, Missus," he said, pointing at Erin. "You stay in the car."

He seemed sure of himself and I took off up the hill. It was very steep and the rain had washed away a portion of the road. We rounded a bend and lost sight of the two cars. My companions looked miserable as their wet suits hung loosely and mud caked their legs up to just below their knees. We stood in the rain waiting patiently and I wondered what the plan was. In the distance I heard an engine revving.

A moment later headlights appeared at the corner, and then the car hurtled into view at full speed. It slid sideways at the bend and almost ditched itself, but the driver was obviously practiced and deftly steered it back on track. The engine raced and the wheels spun wildly, flinging mud everywhere. The car pulled abreast of us just as its momentum was waning, and the four drunks and myself jumped in behind and started pushing. Mud squirted out from each tire as we pushed and shoved the car to the top of the hill. With a roar, it crested and took off on the flat. The driver pulled over to the side and then walked back to join us.

"Good job," he said. "Now your car, Baas. Jus' be sure you have lots of speed." I walked down the hill to the river and found Erin sipping on the last Lion Lager. She shook her head at me.

"You're a mess, Hancock."

I looked down at myself. Mud was plastered everywhere. I tried to rinse some of it off in the river, but the flow was running swiftly and I was worried about being washed away. Now it was my turn for some deft driving. I climbed in beside Erin and revved the engine. We took off up the hill with as much speed as I could coax in the slippery conditions, and approached the first bend with a good head of steam. The car drifted sideways as we took the corner, and I gunned the engine. With the car still drifting the added power thrust us into a spin. In a second we were pointing back down the hill. Erin yelled, and I hung on as we skidded towards the edge of the road. The car stopped in time, but we had lost our momentum. We slid back down the hill to the bottom.

The second time I took off a little slower, and we hit the corner just right. The car drifted slightly and then straightened out as I accelerated for the stretch to the top, but we had lost our momentum. The wheels skidded and slipped and we ground to a halt. I could vaguely make out five shadowy figures huddled against the rain about a hundred yards up the hill.

"Shit," I cursed, "we're never going to make it up this damn hill." I looked at Erin in the dark and could see lines of fatigue around her eyes. She started to giggle and then laughed out loud. What a night. What a dumb, stinking, strange day it had been, and the end was still not in sight. In a few hours the sun would be up and perhaps then it would be dry enough to make it up the hill. Erin's laughter was infectious and soon we were both laughing out loud. Tears ran down my face, but they were tears of frustration more than joy. I glanced over Erin's shoulder to see a black face peering in. When he caught my eye his face broadened into a huge grin and he shook his head at us.

"I drive, Baas," he declared and opened my door to get in. Without much thought I hopped out while he took off down the hill with Erin still in the passenger's seat. The lights turned the corner and we were plunged back into darkness. I shivered from the cold and waited for the lights to reappear. I heard the engine roar and then saw the truck hit the bend with a full head of steam. They drifted sideways and then straightened out. The truck passed me at full speed and to this day I have a clear picture of the driver hunched over the wheel with a maniacal look in his eyes, and Erin alongside him, sitting bolt upright, staring straight ahead. Her pale, gentle face contrasted with the determined look of the driver. In a few seconds they were gone and the noise of the engine died away. They made it all the way to the top without a push. I ran after them, and by the time I got to the crest the other car was gone. I opened the door and jumped in. Erin glared at me.

"Hancock," she said. "You now owe me one, and it is going to take you the rest of your life to pay it off. You're a bloody mess," she declared. "Just take a look at you." She had not been out of the car since Magwa Falls and was sitting clean and pretty alongside me. I had mud caked everywhere, from the blobs that were once my shoes, to the crusted bits stuck in my hair. I covered my face with my hands and shook my head.

"What the heck," I muttered. "What the hell else can go wrong?" I pushed the car into gear and let the clutch slide. "Home," was all I said.

The road was flat and in reasonable condition and before long we passed through Umtata for the second time. The rain had tapered to a fine mist by the time the dirt road turned back to tar. The small store where we had bought the beer and biltong was dark, and the streets were deserted. Erin dozed while I struggled to stay awake until just before dawn when the border post came into view. The buildings were dark and I was tempted to drive right on through without stopping, but there was a single light burning in the guard post. Erin volunteered to take our passports in to have them checked. I was hardly recognizable and thought it wise to stay in the car. She took both passports and disappeared into the building. I tilted my seat back a little, and dozed off. I dreamed of mud and boiling heads and swift flowing rivers, and jumped suddenly when Erin shook me.

"You need to come in," she said. "There seems to be some problem with your passport and they won't let us pass until they talk to you." I staggered out of the car littering the path with flakes of mud as I made my way into the building. The walls were cold and intimidating. We passed an open cell and walked to the office at the end. Behind a small desk sat a huge Afrikaner, his expansive gut hanging limply over his belt, his shaved head reflecting the bare light bulb.

"Meneer Hancock," he addressed me sternly in Afrikaans. "It seems to me that there is an issue here with unpaid taxes." He spat out the word taxes, and eyed me over the rims of his glasses. I said nothing, too tired and numb to respond.

"Meneer Hancock," he continued. "Were you not born in the Republic of South Africa?" I nodded. "And, Meneer Hancock, it seems to me that you have been traveling for quite a few years, have you not?" I nodded again.

"So, Meneer Hancock, I must ask you this very important question. Where do you pay your taxes?" I stared at him blankly. What on earth was he getting at? "It seems to me," he stated matter-of-factly, "that you have been traveling for a number of years, obviously earning money, and probably not paying taxes." He spat the word out again, as if it was a bad taste in his mouth, and waited for my reply. My head was spinning and I could not think of a good answer. I stared dumbly at him and noticed a fine sweat breaking out on his brow. He licked his lips.

"I need an explanation, Meneer Hancock," he said. Erin said nothing. I said nothing. The room swayed and the fatigue seeped up my legs. "I am waiting, Meneer." I glared back at him and then in a clear voice, answered.

"I do not have to pay tax on the income I receive. The money I get comes from my family. You see," I said, "my father sends me money to stay away from home because I am an embarrassment to the family." Erin shot a quick glance my way and the Customs man burst out laughing. His body shook and his gut wobbled.

"Meneer Hancock," he said. "My job is very boring as you can imagine. But you have made my evening." He laughed again and I could see Erin visibly relax. "That was funny," he said. "Very funny. But, Meneer, I am going to have to lock you up for the night anyway." He paused, waiting to see what effect his words would have on us, but we were too tired to care.

"Why?" I asked.

"Meneer, look at you." He lowered his voice to a softer tone. "You're a bloody mess. You can hardly stand up because you are so tired. If I let you go now you will crash your bakkie before the next bend. I'll put you both in a cell and you can rest until the new guard comes in at seven o'clock." There was no point in arguing with him. He was right. He rose from behind the desk and pulled a bunch of keys out of the drawer. "Follow me, please." He led us back to the open cell and stood aside as we filed in.

"You are the only ones here tonight so you have the place to yourself." He pointed to the two small cots. "They're too small for two people to sleep in," he said with a chuckle. "I know because I have tried." We both collapsed fully clothed onto the cots and in a second we were fast asleep.

It seemed to be only moments later when I heard the cell

door rattle and forced an eye open. The Customs man was standing there with two steaming cups of sweet tea, and announced that it was morning. He pointed us towards the showers and said that we would have to leave in 15 minutes before the other guard came on duty.

"He's a sonofabitch," he declared. "He'd leave you locked up for a week, just for the hell of it." I was tempted to ask if it was the same black guard that we encountered the day before, but thought better of it. We showered, and feeling better, stepped out into bright sunshine. All trace of the storm was gone and everything was washed clean. Someone had washed and waxed our truck and it shone brightly in the sunlight.

"What do you think?" I said to Erin. "Should we head back to the coast?" She glared at me without answering.

It was almost noon when we rolled into Pietermaritzburg and the city sweltered in the midday heat. We passed through town and then drove on north, up through the more affluent suburbs that surround the city. The air was cooler, and I could feel the temperature change as we arrived back home. The hydrangea bushes that lined our driveway were still in full bloom, and their sweet fragrance greeted us as I stopped the truck in front of the house. The long day was over.

CHAPTER 10
PETE

"Please do what you can to take care of the beautiful places. Hear the deep song of the land and sea. For if we lose this place, this sense of place, then we shall truly have nothing at all."
—*Rachel Carson*

The bushmen have a time-honored saying that we would have done well to heed: "When you see a black rhino," they say, "you first look for a tree to climb, and then you look at the rhino." It was good advice, but we were already halfway across the clearing before it sank in. This was not a good idea. Behind us was open veldt, with the nearest tall tree at least a half mile away. Ahead lay the rhino and short scrub. We were on foot with nowhere to run, and worse still, nowhere to hide.

The pair of black rhinos that we had spotted earlier had wandered into the thicket ahead and were now out of sight. Pete was the first to see them. They had been browsing along the edge of the scrub, blending perfectly with the bush. It was only the sudden movement of the tick birds that caught his eye. A quick flash of white.

"Shh. I think I can see them," Pete said. He kicked at the dry ground with his good foot and watched the dust drift lazily towards us. He kicked again to be sure and then nodded. We were still downwind. "We need to be quiet from now on," he said.

It had been a long, dry winter on the northern plains of South Africa. The sun had sucked the moisture out of every living thing, leaving behind a parched and harsh earth. It had been easy to spot game. Just find water and wait, and soon you would see all there was to see as the heat of the day forced all living creatures from their cover out into the open to drink. We had seen just about everything we wanted to see, except for one of Africa's most dangerous animals, the black rhino. They have short necks and are usually found browsing on the inch-long thorns of acacia trees, a diet akin to eating nails. They are also the ones with bad attitudes, probably caused by a belly full of undigested thorns. Their gnarly nature and impressive stature combine to make them dangerous and unpredictable. A black rhino is likely to pulverize you rather than run off into the woods to avoid a conflict. What they lack in eyesight they make up for with their keen sense of smell and robust personality. We were psyched to see one. A game guard told us of a pair that could usually be seen browsing near the old airstrip.

"Get up early," he advised. "You're most likely to see them at first light." I was traveling in South Africa with a few of my crewmates from *Drum*. It was during the Whitbread stopover in Cape Town and we were attempting to get as far away from the water as possible to recharge our batteries. Erin was with me and Bill had his girlfriend, Alice, with him. Rounding out our party was Roger, our eccentric Swedish navigator. We were staying with my brother, Pete, who lived and worked in a game park in the northern Transvaal. We camped out under a blanket of stars and rose before dawn. The air was soft and smelled of dust and dew. It was quiet, the time of day when there is a truce between the hunters and the hunted. The terror of night slowly gives way to the cruel reality of day, but for a while in the predawn, all is still. It's a power vacuum.

As dawn broke in the east, we watched the sun rise over the scorched bush. It rose quickly like a giant orb breathing fire. The drops of dew that had settled on the grass overnight quickly evaporated into instant humidity. The soft landscape became hard and harsh as the lushness of the early morning disappeared with the first fingers of warmth. Another hot African day had begun, and as we hiked across the clearing I felt the first drops of sweat run the length of my spine.

"Let's stop a moment," Pete whispered. "Let's see if we can see them." We stood motionless for a few minutes, and then suddenly, another flash of white. The tick birds were having a feast. "There," Pete said, "just behind that clump of bushes." I squinted into the nearby bush looking for a sign of life, but saw nothing. Pete kicked at the ground again and watched the dust rise and drift lazily on the gentle breeze. We were still downwind.

"Let's get out of here," I whispered. "Those guys will fucking maul us if they see us." I had spent many years in the bush and knew better, but the others were intent upon seeing the rhino and said nothing. Pete tilted his head to the left and nodded in the direction of the tree line.

"There," he said. "There's the other one browsing in the scrub." I followed his gaze and could just make out the bulk of the other rhino. It was less than a hundred yards away, standing motionless. I wondered if they knew we were nearby. I glanced over my shoulder at the open veldt with cropped, sun-scorched grass, and remembered again the bushmen's warning. "First you look for a tree to climb . . ." In the distance the shrill cry of a fish eagle broke the silence. It was the only sound other than my heart pounding and the gentle clanging of Pete's crutches.

"Pete," I said. "Let's get out of here." He smiled and said nothing. This was his environment and I knew that he would not take any chances, but still I had an uneasy feeling.

"Okay, be very quiet now," he said. "Let's see if we can get a bit closer." Pete rose slowly and started to make his way forward. His crutches clanged quietly as he placed them carefully to avoid cracking dry twigs. I felt sweat leak from every pore and followed a few steps behind. The others fell in beside me. Both rhinos had blended back into the bush and were nowhere to be seen. We crept forward, a small party of rag-tag tourists and one man of the bush. The heat was becoming more intense. I watched beads of sweat run the ridge of my nose, coast slowly towards the ground, and splatter on the dry dust at my feet. The moisture was instantly swallowed up by the parched dirt. We moved carefully towards the edge of the clearing, closer to the rhino.

Pete stopped and knelt down. He picked up a handful of sand and let the dirt filter slowly between his fingers. I watched the dust drift towards the rhino. He glanced at me and then picked up another handful. The dust drifted in the same direction.

"Shit," was all he said. The wind had changed direction and we were now upwind. The rhino would soon pick up our scent.

"Now what?" I asked.

Pete smiled at me and said, "This should be interesting." I heard the fish eagle call again from its faraway perch. It was hunting for breakfast. My shirt clung to my back in a wet, soggy mess.

As I followed Pete, I thought about man's ability to adapt to his environment. Pete did not seem to notice the heat like the rest of us; in fact, he was hardly breaking a sweat, but then a decade in the African bush conditions you for hot weather. Since graduating from university with a degree in wildlife management, Pete had been living in the wild as part of the conservation crew at Pilansberg Nature Reserve, a wildlife sanctuary a hundred miles west of Johannesburg. The elements had tempered him, and with time he gradually became part of the African landscape, equally at home with its harsh climate as most of the four-legged creatures that roamed the plains around him. His skin color blended perfectly with the hard earth, and his hair waved like the bleached thatching grass found abundant across the South African low veldt.

We were always close. I think it was the streak of individuality seared into each of our personalities that drew us together. Perhaps it was our mutual love for the outdoors and adventure. Maybe not, though. Maybe it was just that as his younger brother he could use me as a fall guy for his many schemes, and so he tolerated my presence. Whatever it was, we spent a lot of time together—and we got into a lot of trouble. In the mid 1970s, while climbing in the mountains, we crossed the line from innocent fun to dangerous stupidity, and our lives were forever changed.

As children we spent our family holidays in the Drakensberg mountains, hiking, swimming, and soaking up fresh air. The mountains were only an hour's drive from Pietermaritzburg and it was an environment that tested us and allowed us to play outside of our comfort zones. While the mountains are wild and rugged and unspoiled, they were still a relatively safe place for kids to roam. If you hiked up towards the escarpment and lost your way, you simply hiked back down again and chances are you would end up back where you began. Our parents let us roam freely and I would follow Pete on many treks into the bush. Sometimes he tolerated my presence; other times he would stride on ahead, purposely trying to lose me. I would always hang on grimly, trying to match his stride, always a few steps behind, never giving up.

I remember one particular walk. We hiked higher and higher into the hills while the fog rolled down to meet us, and before long we were engulfed in its wet embrace. Pete has an uncanny sense of direction and strode ahead while I staggered along a few paces behind, trying to keep up. The damp fog mingled with my tears. My legs were bloody from branches and thorn bushes that had scratched them, and my entire body was tired and sore. Occasionally we would startle a secretary bird and it would take flight, rising like a ghostly apparition as it disappeared into the mist.

We kept going up and up until late in the day when Pete finally turned around, and I gratefully followed him back to camp. It was dark when we arrived back at the hut, and I discovered the first adrenaline high of my life. The exhilaration of a tough day, combined with the relief of making it home safely, made for a heady feeling. Like most addictions, however, getting the high soon became harder, and after a while it required more daring and trying feats to achieve the same effect. For two barefoot African kids, the mountains were a veritable feast where we could test our courage and our blossoming climbing skills. It was all fine fun until the day we tried to go straight up.

It was not a high cliff, or at least it did not appear to be that high from the bottom looking up, but then it always seems higher from the top looking down. The day before we had climbed a much higher cliff in an effort to get above an eagle's nest. Pete wanted to check for chicks without disturbing the nest, so we climbed an adjacent cliff hoping to look down into the nest. The first 30 feet were an easy scramble up the side of the rock, and then a more difficult climb to a narrow ledge that would take us to a vantage point above the nest. We clambered onto the ledge, and with the enthusiasm of two kids on a mission, quickly made our way out onto the sheer part of the cliff. Initially the ledge was quite wide, but it narrowed rapidly, and suddenly we were standing on the verge of a 300-foot drop. I looked down and was instantly paralyzed with fear. Pete felt it, too. We pressed up against the side of the cliff and stood frozen. My mouth was dry and I could hear my breath rasping in my throat. We were in big trouble. Up was out of the question. Down was not an option, and the way back looked like the north face of Everest. Worst still, Pete had been leading on the way out, and to return, I would have to lead. My gut tightened and I could taste the bile rising from my stomach.

I stood frozen until Pete ordered me to head back. There was no way. I couldn't move. My feet were glued in place. Pete kept urging, realizing that if I didn't move, he, too, was stuck. The urging soon changed to commanding, and then with gentle coaxing interspersed with loud threats, I slowly started to make my way back towards easier terrain. My shallow, quick breathing combined with a shot of adrenaline to make me light-headed, and it soon felt as if I was floating, until the ledge widened and the ground rose up to meet us. We were safe again, and the heady feeling of an overdose of adrenaline took over. We flew back to camp, our feet a few inches off the ground. We had conquered our nerves, or so we thought, and the rush was incredible. We were kids; Pete had just graduated and I was about to enter my first year of high school. We were kids with more energy and enthusiasm than brains. These days they have a name for it: Young Male Immortality Syndrome.

By the previous day's standards, this cliff we were about to climb did not look that high. Eighty feet at the most and no chance of a sudden, sheer drop. It was late in the day and the shadows were lengthening, but we figured we would be to the top and down again before it got dark. We lingered at the base trying to decide the easiest way up, and then without much of a plan, started climbing. My bare feet made easy going of the initial climb. I wrapped my toes around small branches and quickly inched higher. Pete was leading, using his longer reach to drag himself up the rock. His mind was focused on the top and his concentration complete. He seemed to have forgotten the near miss of the day before. I hadn't, and kept looking down.

It soon became obvious that I wasn't going to make it. The panicked and paralyzing feeling of the last climb was foremost in my mind and I knew I was going to quit. My legs were weak and my heart was racing. I turned around and carefully made my way back down. At the bottom I sat with my back against a rock and watched Pete continue his climb towards the top. He stopped just below the summit and perched on a narrow ledge resting and contemplating the last few feet. Standing up and reaching as far as he could, the ledge above was a few inches beyond the tips of his fingers. I saw him feel to one side and then the other, but there was no easier way. He looked down at me and signaled with a thumbs up. He looked much more confident than I felt.

"Come on down Pete, let's go home," I yelled up at him. "It's getting late." Pete just grinned and stretched for the handhold again. He was still a few inches short.

"I'm going to make it to the top or bust," he yelled, and I could see that there was no talking him out of it. The challenge was taking over, the adrenaline had kicked in.

"Come on Pete, let's go back, it's getting late," I persisted, but he ignored me and continued to search for a handhold. I thought for a moment of leaving him and heading back to camp in the hope that he would follow, but instead decided that I might be able to help him.

A short distance back along the path was another trail that I was sure led to the top of the cliff. Perhaps I could get above him and see if there was another handhold for him to reach for.

"I'm going to try and get above you," I shouted, and Pete gave me a thumbs up.

I made my way along the path and soon found the other track. It was nothing more than a faint trail used by the hundreds of rock rabbits that made those cliffs their home. I scrambled up through the underbrush, eased along the contour line, and in a few moments found myself on the flat area above the cliff. I tentatively climbed down to a point where I thought he would be, and peered over the edge.

"Hey, Pete, can you hear me?" I yelled. "Can you see me?"

"Don't shout, you'll scare the animals. I'm just below you," a quiet voice a few feet below replied. I couldn't see him. I gingerly lowered myself until I could make out the handhold which Pete had been reaching for, and then peered over the edge into his grinning face.

"If you can get a grip on this ledge you'll be able to pull yourself up." My voice had an edge to it. I was worried. I looked down at my brother and he didn't seem the least bit concerned.

"How far above my fingers is it?" he asked.

"About eight inches."

"What if I just jump up and grab it? Is it big enough to hold onto?" I looked at the small ledge below my feet. It was amply big enough for him to grip onto.

"Sure," I replied, "it's bigger than the one you're standing on."

"Okay," Pete whispered, "I'm going to jump for it," and without hesitating, he jumped. His fingers found their target and gripped the bare rock.

"Just pull yourself up, Pete," I yelled, my voice tense with excitement. I could feel my throat tighten. Something didn't seem right. "Just pull yourself up," I urged.

"I can't. I can't." His words hung suspended in the air for a few seconds before sinking in.

"What do you mean you can't?"

"I can't pull myself up. My arms are not strong enough. I'm plastered against the rock and there is no way to swing my legs under me." Pete was right, he was going to have to pull himself straight up using just the tips of his fingers.

"What about going back down again?" I asked, but as I said it I knew that it would be impossible. He'd jumped from a ledge that was smaller than the one he was grimly hanging onto. There was no way he would be able to land back where he had been. Beads of perspiration were popping out on his forehead and I felt my limbs slowly turning to jelly. The paralyzing feeling was returning.

"Shit, I'm in trouble," Pete yelled. "Take off your shirt and lower it to me." I looked at him in terror. "Take off your goddam shirt," Pete yelled, and I could hear the fear rising in his voice. I looked at his fingers and the tips were white and bloodless.

"Lower your shirt down to me and you can pull me up," he yelled. His arms were starting to shake from exhaustion. My whole body was frozen with fear. There was nothing I could do. I reached for my shirt and pulled it over my head, but when I looked back down, Pete was gone. I stared at the ledge where he had just been hanging, and there was no trace. A second later I heard a dull thud from below the cliff. A thud, and then nothing.

"Pete," I croaked. There was no sound from below.

"Pete!" I yelled, "Are you all right?" No reply. I screamed, and the sound of my voice jolted my body from its paralysis. I scrambled up the bank and along the contour line letting the bushes tear at my clothes and skin. I did not feel a thing—my mind and body were numb. I slid down the trail in a flurry of dust and broken branches until I found the main path, and when I got to Pete he was lying listless at the base of the cliff. I ran to his side and for a moment I thought he was okay. He was just laying there not moving. His eyes followed me as I knelt beside him.

"Shit," he said. "We really fucked it up this time, didn't we?" I nodded trying to fight back tears. "My back is broken," he stated matter-of-factly. "Go and get Dad."

The rest of that day remains a blur. It was dusk by the time I made it back to camp. My father was sitting in his easy chair sipping his first whiskey of the evening. We summoned the camp warden and some helpers, and in the fading light made our way back along the path to where Pete lay. He had not moved. I thought he was dead. There was a thin line of blood running from his mouth and pooling on the grass, but other than that nothing had changed. Pete blinked his eyes open and looked at my father.

"Dad, my back is broken," he stated matter-of-factly. "Be careful how you move me." I was still sure he would be fine until he was rolled onto the stretcher. Pete's screams still ring in my head, as does the memory of the slow trek back to camp, feeling our way along the path by the dim light of a single flashlight. Pete was loaded into the back of a van and transported down a rocky mountain road to the nearest hospital. Each bump and turn in the road sent waves of pain through his body until he slipped into the merciful abyss of unconsciousness.

A year later, with calipers fastened on both legs and crutches for support, Pete was able to inch his way out of his wheelchair and onto the parallel supporting bars. With his physiotherapist encouraging every move, he slowly crept along the bars to the end, and then painfully inched his was back to the chair. It was a slow, tedious process. Healing a broken body takes time. Healing the mind takes even longer, but that process was already well underway. There is something magical about the human spirit that kicks in when it is needed most. As soon as you accept the inevitable, the practical kicks in. Pete quickly accepted his fate and got on with making the best of a compromised situation.

Another year passed before the calipers were ditched and Pete was able to get by on crutches alone. His back had broken at the same spot where he'd earlier cracked a vertebrae on his spine. It was a weak link, and when his spine snapped, it severed the nerves to both legs. A lot of surgery, and a lot of bed rest eventually healed most of the nerves to his right leg, but his left leg was ruined and hung withered and limp.

Being confined to a wheelchair brought its own blessing. Instead of heading straight into the bush out of high school, as Pete had planned to do, his wheelchair restricted him to a less hostile environment, and university seemed a good alternative. He graduated seven years later with a degree in wildlife management. As soon as he was released from the constraints of academic life, he headed straight for the hills to put it to good use. Throughout it all he maintained his sense of humor.

We sat crouched less than thirty yards from the rhino. They had still not picked up our scent, even though the wind was blowing directly towards them. Instead they ambled along the edge of the scrub, stopping occasionally to sniff the air. At times they would lift their heads and stare straight at us, but see nothing. I was not worried about their eyesight; it was their noses that concerned me.

"Let's back up and get the hell out of here," I offered, but the others sat motionless, intently watching the rhino. There was something fascinating about our predicament. "Maybe they will move off and not bother us," I thought. They were slowly heading away and I hoped they would disappear into the bush and be gone. A troop of baboons sauntered out from the scrub and came our way, but as soon as they saw us they bolted off, muttering as they went. The rhino meantime had stopped moving away and were heading back in our direction. Pete grabbed another handful of dirt and watched the wind blow the dust directly in their direction. We were still upwind. They would soon catch our scent, and when they did it would only be a matter of time before they came to investigate.

Our options were limited; none of them promising. The nearest trees were either towards the rhino, or back across the plain. If we moved slowly we still had time to beat a retreat, but instead, we remained glued to the spot. The fish eagle called again from its high perch, and my heart continued pounding in my chest. I glanced behind at the open veldt and watched a family of warthogs scurrying towards us. They are a clear indication that god has a sense of humor, and I smiled to myself, remembering the story Pete had told us the night before. We were sitting around the fire, camped under a clear sky—a perfect place for storytelling.

"I know many animals more brave than the warthog," he started, "but none more courageous, and definitely none quite so dumb. He is a peasant of the plains, a drab and dowdy digger of dirt, but despite his funny looks, the warthog is not an animal to be taken lightly." Pete's face sparkled as the coals reflected in his eyes and the flames threw patterns on his weathered features. "The average warthog stands just higher than a domestic pig, but that is the only thing average about them. Their skin color is the shade of mud, and their eyes are small, dark, and have only one expression—suspicion. What they see, they suspect, and what they suspect, they fight. So," he continued, "let me tell you about my encounter with a warthog."

His story took place at Manyaleti Game Reserve, a small private reserve annexed to the larger Kruger National Park in South Africa. Pete had worked there for a few years before moving to Pilansberg. A game guard had spotted an injured warthog, and they decided to track it with the intention of darting the hog to take a closer look at its injuries. Pete set off with two game guards, and by late afternoon they were firmly on its trail. They followed the spoor through thick bush, and knew that they had the right hog by occasional drops of blood smeared on the grass. The tracks led to a burrow with obvious signs of an occupant in residence. Warthogs often commandeer the burrows of other animals, easing themselves in rear end first to lie there facing out observing the passing scene. They use their long snouts to pile a heap of fine dust in the hole and wait until their enemies come within range. The dust serves as a smoke screen as the hog launches itself out of the hole in a frenzy of dust and tusks, ready to do battle.

The injured hog had backed itself deep into the hole, and Pete and the game guards carefully approached the den. They were well aware that there is no animal more dangerous and more inclined to fight than an injured warthog. There were streaks of dried blood on the dirt around the hole, and it was obvious that the hog had been using the den for some time. Pete peered into the dim interior and could just make out a long sloping snout, two piercing eyes, and the glint of two razor-sharp tusks. He balanced on one crutch, and poked into the hole with the other. The warthog shrunk deeper into the den, secure in its burrow, clearly resenting the intrusion. Pete had read somewhere that the only way to get a warthog out of its den was to shake a piece of paper in front of the entrance. It appears that there is nothing more insulting to a warthog that this flagrant disregard for its privacy, and the shaking paper is more than it can stand.

He sent one of the guards back to the car to fetch an old newspaper, and while they were waiting scouted around for a place to hide where they could get off a clean shot. They would have to hit the warthog square-on with enough force to embed the dart so that the tranquilizer could take effect. Occasionally, from deep within the burrow, the hog would snort its displeasure, but most of the time it just lay still.

The guard arrived with the newspaper, and they stood together in front of the den trying to figure out a plan. Pete poked into the hole one last time, but the hog just snorted in disgust and refused to budge. He stepped back from the entrance and motioned to the guard to bring the newspaper. Suddenly, with a loud snort and a billowing of dust, the warthog emerged from its cover, head lowered, tusks extended. It barreled straight at them. Pete turned, and with a reflex action balanced on both crutches, raising his legs up into the air. The warthog ran between his crutches directly into the game guards behind him.

It slammed into the closest guard, knocking him off his feet, flattened the second, and without losing momentum bolted off into the bush leaving Pete still perched on his crutches, and the two guards battered and bruised on the ground. Pete came through without a scratch, the guards were less lucky, and the hog was found dead a week later. It had backed itself into another hole, and died from loss of blood. When they found the body, vultures had picked its head clean, but the rest of the hog was preserved, jammed tightly into the hole, facing out.

I smiled to myself while I recalled the story, and watched the family of hogs approach. As soon as they saw us they scuttled off with tails in the air and tusks at the ready. Their sudden movement had frightened the rhino and they stopped browsing and lifted their heads, testing the air. The closest rhino moved its head from side to side, sniffing the breeze. It was looking in our direction and took a few steps towards us.

"Just sit still and don't move," Pete warned. We sat motionless and watched the rhino watching us.

"Damn," I muttered, "this doesn't look good."

"Shhh." Pete said. He kicked the sand and looked at me. "Still upwind. okay here's the plan. If this guy charges we're stuffed. Our best bet is to get out of here and up a tree." He looked at Alice and nodded towards a thorny acacia on the edge of the scrub. She looked back at him in disbelief.

"You want me to climb that tree?" she asked. "It's full of thorns." Even from where we were sitting, I could see the inch-long thorns. They were bleached white and razor sharp.

"Alice, you have two choices at this point. Either you can get up the tree and hope for the best, or you can get trampled by a pissed-off rhino." Alice did not need additional coaxing. She stood up and started for the tree. "Move slowly, and if the rhino charges, make a run for it." She crept forward, one eye on the tree, the other on the rhino. Within a minute she was at the base of the tree and looked back at Pete, hoping he had changed his mind. He nodded to her to start climbing. "Erin," he said, "you're next." She crept towards the tree, but stopped when the rhino started to move in her direction.

"Don't worry," Pete said. "He can't see you. He thinks there's a problem and is coming to investigate. Just keep moving." Erin made the tree and started climbing. "Okay," he said, "the rest of us might be in the shit, but let's sit still and see what they do." Bill, Roger, and I held our collective breaths, and didn't move.

A cloud passed in front of the sun throwing a shadow across the bush. Pete grabbed a handful of soft sand and let it slip through his fingers. I saw the dust drift towards the rhino and wished I was somewhere else.

"When he charges, don't move," Pete said. "He doesn't know we're here. He just thinks there might be trouble and is taking no chances, but he will not see us until he is a few feet away."

"Great suggestion," I thought. Five tons of pissed-off rhino pummeling right at us, and all I had to do was remain still. Then I remembered. I could make a run for it; Pete had no choice. His only defense was to stand still and hope for the best. The rhinos were less than sixty feet away. I no longer noticed the heat.

"Bill," Pete said. "You try and get up the tree, but move slowly, and Roger," he added, "you follow him. Just move slowly. This guy knows something is up and will trample you if he sees you." They both looked at me, and Bill muttered something about it being safer at sea. He crept slowly towards the tree, Roger just behind, and had covered half the distance when the rhino fixed its radar on them. It swiveled its ears until it homed in, and ambled over to investigate. It did not look pleased. Pete flung a crutch in the opposite direction, and the rhino stopped. Roger stood up and bolted for the tree, and then it all happened in an instant.

The rhino charged, Bill followed Roger, and Pete yelled at the rhino. It stopped, turned, and looked directly at us. Pete flung his other crutch, and as the rhino ambled over to investigate, I took the opportunity to get out of there. I spun around and fled across the plain. The rhino heard me leave, stopped where it was, and fixed Pete in its radar. It took two steps in his direction and then charged again. Pete stood motionless as it approached, gambling against the odds that it was only a fake charge. The rhino kept coming, its massive bulk picking up speed, and then ten feet from him, it abruptly stopped. It raised its head, sniffed the wind, and then pawed at the ground.

I kept running. Pete stood perfectly still.

In the acacia tree, Roger had trampled over Erin and Alice in his eagerness to escape the rhino, and was hanging out on a high limb, scratched and bloodied. He yelled at the rhino and it swiveled and looked in their direction, and then lumbered over to investigate. The rhino walked towards the tree, stopped at the base, sniffed the wind, and then without further investigation took off into the bush. The other one followed, and from my vantage halfway across the plain, I could hear them crashing into trees, knocking down bushes as they ran into the thick scrub.

It took over an hour for the tree climbers to make their way down—it had taken only a few seconds to shimmy up, thorns be damned. They were covered with scratches, and their blood dripped onto the dry earth. I made it back to where Pete was stranded, and gathered his crutches.

"What is it about you and me?" he said. "Every time we are out together we end up in trouble." I looked at him and laughed.

"Another close call. Next time we might not be so lucky." I heard the fish eagle call from its faraway perch and saw a speck of white on a high branch overlooking the river. It was still fishing for breakfast. "Didn't you say there was a pride of lions near the south gate that you thought we could get close to?" Pete picked up a handful of dirt and flung it at me.

"Maybe next time," was all he said.

"Maybe not," I replied.

CHAPTER 11
A SLEIGHT OF HAND

"We have to change our pattern of reacting to experience. For our problems do not lie in what we experience, but in the attitude we have towards it."
—*Akong Rimpoche*

We could see the "smoke" from Victoria Falls from a long way off. Flying over the area, it's nothing but a vast expanse of dry African scrub until an oasis of green and plumes of "smoke" appear near one of the world's most spectacular waterfalls. The "smoke" is a fine mist that rises up from the foot of the falls, and saturates the surrounding savanna. The scrub turns green and lush from a constant watering, and contrasts starkly with the dry bush.

Our pilot banked over the waterfall, allowing us a clear view of the spray and the thin ribbon of blue that snaked its way towards the edge. The Zambezi River winds through barren veldt, and then plummets 350 feet into a deep crevasse. The earth has split apart and swallows the river, sending spray high into the air. The falls thunder to an ancient rhythm and we felt its roar resonate through the thin panels of the plane. The pilot circled one more time, and then headed for a small landing strip on the edge of town. I was in Zimbabwe fulfilling a promise that I had made to my daughter years before. She was named Victoria, although everyone calls her Tory, and when she was small I told her stories of a big waterfall deep in the African bush. It was a place where magic could happen; I promised to take her there and now that she was seven-years old, we were making the trip.

Tory was the only child from my marriage to Erin, who, despite that never-ending trip to the wild coast and the incident with the rhino, still agreed to marry me. It was a marriage based on travel and adventure, but when Tory was born the traveling ended, and the marriage started to fall apart. Tory was not quite three when we divorced.

Our six-seater plane touched down on the runway and taxied to the terminal. I could see the heat rise in waves off the tarmac, and felt the humidity buffet us as soon as the door was flung open. I grabbed Tory by the hand and we climbed down onto the apron. The air was warm and smelled of jet fuel and cooking fires. It smelled of Africa—the old and the new. I was glad to be home.

We shared a taxi for the trip downtown, and headed for the village of Victoria Falls, or Vic Falls as it's known to the locals. The small town has prospered from the tourist trade, and from the downtown area you can see the spray and hear the muffled thunder of the falls. The striking beauty of the waterfall, cheap accommodation, and abundant wildlife attracts visitors from around the world. They come to admire the crack in the earth where millions of gallons of water plummet each day. Occasionally, a helicopter flies close to the face of the waterfall on a scenic excursion, allowing high-paying passengers a closer view. Mostly though, it is a town of young transient tourists, arriving in beat-up pickup trucks and combi-vans, wearing braids in their hair and sandals on their feet. They come for the bungee jumping and whitewater rafting, and they come because it is cheap, exciting, and spectacular. We would fit in just fine.

Tory and I had been in Africa for three weeks. We had hiked the Drakensburg Mountains in South Africa, camped out in Botswana, and felt the beat of the land slowly creep under our skin. For me it was a time to reconnect; for Tory it was a time to discover a world beyond television. A few nights before we had camped alongside a shallow lake, and watched while elephants bathed and drank in the moonlight a few feet from our fire. In the night we heard lions roaring, and the next day saw fresh tracks where a pride had wandered through our camp. Vic Falls would be a bit more civilized. We had a hotel for the night and planned dinner on the town. First, though, a trip to the Falls was in order. We changed our clothes and headed out onto the streets.

With the exception of the main road that runs through downtown, the streets are dirt. A fine coating of dust settles on everything. Goats and chickens scratch an existence off the land, and we passed a donkey tied to a post. The dirt was worn in a circle around the post, and the donkey stared at us with indifference. Some of the locals nodded as we passed, and then I heard a voice calling out.

"Hey, Mister, you need to change some money? Twelve for US, sixteen for UK." A young man slid in alongside of us and said again, "I give you twelve dollars for US, or sixteen for UK."

"No, thanks," I replied. "I don't need to change money." I felt for the familiar lump of my wallet and kept on walking.

"My name is Jacob, like in the Bible," he said. "When you need to change money you come and see me, okay?" I nodded.

"Sure, man," I said. "Maybe tomorrow." The boy winked at us, and slid back into the shadows. I did a quick mental calculation. I had heard that you could get a better rate changing money on the street in Zimbabwe, and twelve for US was better than I had expected. The exchange rate at the airport had been eight Zim dollars for each one of my US dollars. It translated into Cokes for a dime, and cold Tusker beers for seventy-five cents apiece. I still needed to buy our air tickets out of Zimbabwe, and would have to change a pile of cash before we could leave.

"Hey, Mister." A different voice called out. "You want to see some carvings?" Another kid slid into step alongside us and lifted his filthy jacket to reveal a magnificent stone carving of an elephant. I looked for a moment, resisting the temptation to touch it.

"Oh no, thank you," I replied. "I am not interested." I had seen similar looking carvings in the curio shop at the airport, and thought that I might charge one on my credit card.

"One hundred and fifty Zim dollars only," he replied, "but of course, price is negotiable." I did not want to start up a bargaining session with him, and recalled that the elephant in the curio shop was around two hundred dollars.

"No, thanks," I said. He dropped back and offered a final pitch.

"One hundred, Mister, and if you are interested my name is Michael." I wasn't interested.

We walked towards the noise and spray and soon found a sign that read, "Welcome to Victoria Falls." Beyond was a path. The roar of water increased as we slipped our way down the wet trail, and it was only when we were right opposite the waterfall that the full effect hit us. It was obvious why the locals had named the place Mosi-Oa-Tunya, "the smoke that thunders." The water plunged towards a deep pool at the base of the Falls, and thundered as it hit the surface. A heavy spray rose up and saturated the surrounding area. Our clothes quickly became wet, and the trees and bushes dripped constantly. We stood alone at the edge of the gorge, and I let the spray wash over me. It washed away weeks of dirt and years of grime and slime from living in a fast-paced world.

I could smell the earth and feel the water's thunder deep in my gut. The ancient rhythm was anchoring my spirit. Africa was calling me home. Soon I would be on a plane heading for New York, but for now I was enjoying the moment. I closed my eyes and purged the thought. The bustle of life in America held no appeal.

Tory shivered from the cold. She grabbed my arm.

"Can we go now, Daddy?" She was cold and wet and ready to leave. I took her hand in mine and we walked back along the footpath towards the gate. In a few moments we were out of the spray and back into the hot African sun. The heat quickly evaporated the moisture from our clothes. At the gate I took a photograph of her standing under the sign.

"Victoria at Victoria Falls," she said. "Can I have another Coke when we get back to the hotel?" The ten-cent Cokes had become a hit.

"Sure, sweetheart," I said. "I'm dying of thirst, too." I was looking forward to a cold beer.

We stopped in town to buy some sandals, and as soon as we left the store Jacob slid in beside us.

"Hey, Mister, if you need to change money I give you good rate," he said. "What you have? US or UK?"

"US," I answered. "But I don't need to change any money."

"I give you twelve for US and there is no commission." I stopped and looked at Jacob. He looked to be in his late teens, perhaps twenty. The earnest look on his face made him appear younger than his years. His clothes were tattered and he was barefoot.

"Let me think about it, Jacob," I said. "Maybe tomorrow."

"Yeah, Mister," he said. "Tomorrow I see you." He slipped back into the crowd and was gone.

Back at the hotel I sat by the pool writing in my diary, while Tory charmed the barman with stories of America.

"It's true," I heard her say, "we have over fifty television channels. There's Nickelodeon and Cartoon Network and . . . and lots of others." The barman looked at her in amusement and total disbelief, and plied her with more Coke. I ordered another Tusker and my mind drifted back to the street hawkers. "Twelve Zim dollars for one US dollar," I thought. That would be fifty percent better than the bank. I needed to change a fair amount of money before we left Zimbabwe, and my mental calculator soon figured a savings of over fifty dollars. I pondered the amount for a moment, and then went back to my diary.

It was winter and the days were short. By late afternoon the long shadows of the mopani trees shaded the pool, and the air turned cool. Tory extracted herself from the water, and waved to the barman who was still smiling in disbelief at the thought of fifty television channels. A fiery red sky washed the western horizon as the sun dipped below the tree line. We changed for dinner, and went back into town to find a place to eat.

The village had come to life after the heat of the day, and exhibited all the sights and smells of a small, third-world town. Dust hung suspended in the flickering street lights, and the street hawkers were bothering the tourists with their persistent sales pitches. They all had some great bargain, negotiable of course. In the distance I could hear the Falls thundering. There were other sounds of Africa as the wildlife slipped from the slumber of daylight into the harsh reality of night.

We ate steaks in a street café, and I drank a bottle of South African wine while Tory continued to take advantage of the ten-cent Cokes. It was our last night in Africa. The next day we would fly to Johannesburg in time to make a connection to New York, and then on home to Boston. I could hardly imagine being back in the US, to crowded sterile streets, and the cut and thrust of day-to-day commerce. African dust had seeped into my system and slowed my pace to a crawl. It was going to take a lot to jump start me again. I paid the bill and we headed back to the hotel.

"Pssst. Hey, Mister, it's me, Jacob." A familiar shadow fell in beside us and continued the sales pitch. "I have the best rates in Vic Falls and no service charge. I see you tomorrow. My name is Jacob like in the Bible." The inflection on the word "Bible" added to his sales pitch. He was surely someone I could trust.

"Maybe," I replied, quickly adding, "but don't count on it."

We fell asleep to the chorus of wild creatures staking their territory and hunting in the dark. Sometime before dawn I heard the far-off roar of a lion. It came from across the Zambezi River, somewhere in Zambia, and I savored the sound, knowing that it would soon be traded for the more domestic sounds of my American life. I heard the mad giggle of hyena, and the persistent call of the African nightjar, but the sounds faded as light brightened the eastern sky. We were out of bed early and ate breakfast by the pool. Our flight was mid-afternoon and I needed to change money and buy the tickets. I thought about trusting the street hawkers, then thought better of it and opted instead for a bank. It would be a safer bet.

On the way into town a silent figure fell into step beside us. A tattered boy no older than thirteen with solemn eyes and a snotty nose tugged at Tory's sleeve and lifted his jacket to reveal another carved elephant. It was beautifully crafted and I couldn't resist touching it. The elephant was cold and smooth and very heavy, and the boy told me that it was carved from a local stone. The tusks were carved from real ivory and he had removed them and stuffed them into his pocket so that they didn't break. He carefully unwrapped them and they fit neatly into two small sockets either side of the trunk.

"You want to buy elephant?" he asked. "One hundred and fifty Zim dollars only. Very good deal." I hefted the elephant and liked the feel of it. It was a better carving than the one I had seen the day before, and better than the one at the airport.

"No, thanks." I said. "I am not interested," and returned it to the boy.

"One hundred only," he said, and he knew I was weakening. I could almost picture the elephant on my mantle at home, and felt a twinge of pity for the boy.

"Seventy-five." I countered, and he knew that he had me.

"Eighty, Mister, and we got a deal." The boy took my money and left. Moments later we were surrounded by half a dozen kids all producing a carved animal, all willing to negotiate, all knowing that I was a buying customer. I felt smug at the deal that I had struck and knew I had paid around ten US dollars for a carving that would reach close to a hundred back home. A skinny kid touting a hippo caught my attention, and after some negotiation I owned the hippo for a little under sixty Zim dollars. I packed both carvings neatly in my backpack.

We sat for a while watching the passing trade. I bought Tory an ice cream, which dripped in the sultry heat and before long Jacob appeared and sat down beside us.

"What's your name, little girl?" he asked.

"Victoria," she replied. "Like the queen."

"No, Mon," Jacob responded. "Like the Falls, and you are much more beautiful." I knew that he was softening us up, but his manner was gentle and Tory was enjoying the attention.

"Can I get you some sweets?" he asked. Tory looked at me and I shook my head slightly. I saw a momentary flash of sulkiness in her eyes, but she knew better than to accept candy from a stranger. Jacob told me that life in Zimbabwe was difficult since the revolution that changed it from the British colony of Rhodesia to an independent country. He told me that he worked for one of the store keepers who needed foreign currency to buy goods for his store, and that was the reason why he was able to make such a good exchange rate. His story seemed reasonable, and feeling flush from my recent bargaining sessions, I asked him for his best rate.

"Twelve for US," he said. "It's the best rate in Vic Falls and no commission." I thought for a moment and then countered.

"I need at least fifteen."

"No, Mon. I can't do fifteen. If you change over a hundred US, I can do thirteen." Now we were getting somewhere. The greed was starting to stir. I had to change close to two hundred dollars and my savings would be significant.

"I'll change two hundred US if you'll give me fourteen." I was willing to hold out for the best rate. There were plenty of other traders on the street.

"No, Mon," he laughed. "I can't do fourteen. It's too much." I decided I would stir him up a bit by walking away from the deal.

"Sorry, Jacob," I said, "I have to go." I took Tory by the hand and walked away. I felt smug. I knew that I had him. He would go for fourteen and I would save a bundle. I was glad that I had not changed money at the bank. We wandered in the direction of the banks, and before long Jacob fell in beside us.

"Hey, Mon," he said. "I can do fourteen if I give you half of my commission." I had him now.

"Okay, then, we have a deal." I was anxious to make the transaction before he changed his mind. Jacob smiled at me and I felt good about being able to help him make a little money. The banks always make a ton of profit; this was more direct. This would really be helping the locals, and he seemed to be a nice kid.

Jacob pulled me aside, and in a low, secretive voice told me to meet him back at the place where we had been having ice cream.

"Just keep on walking past there," he said. "I have to stop at the store to get the money." I worried that the store keeper might try and talk him out of the deal, but knew that he had to go there to get the money.

"Okay, Jacob, but don't be long. I have a plane to catch."

"Don't change with anyone else," he said. "I will see you in five minutes. My name is Jacob, like in the Bible." With that he was gone. Tory looked at me with a quizzical stare, and asked if she could have another ice cream. We stopped and bought one each, and then wandered back towards the hotel. The taxi to take us to the airport would be there to pick us up in less than an hour, and we would soon be on a plane heading home. It was very humid and I could feel small rivulets of sweat running down my back. I was nervous about changing the money, but fourteen Zim dollars for one US was a great deal. I could feel the solid weight of the elephant and the hippo in my back pack, and it gave me confidence. Jacob fell into step beside me.

"I've got the money," he said. "Two thousand, eight hundred Zim dollars." I had already slipped two one-hundred dollar bills into my front pocket. "Just keep on walking," he said. I thought he looked a bit nervous and worried he might back out of the deal.

"Are you sure you want to change money at that rate?" I asked. I felt a twinge of guilt at the lopsided exchange rate.

"Sure, Mon," he said. "No problem. Just up ahead there is a small alleyway. I don't want the other people to see us making a deal because they always hassle me. We can change there." We kept on walking, and at the alley I stopped. For a fleeting moment I wondered if I was doing the right thing. Perhaps I should change at the bank, but their rate of eight Zim dollars was not much. Jacob pulled a wad of notes out of his jacket. They were bound by a few rubber bands.

"Quick," he said. "We change money." I pulled the bills out of my pocket and handed them to him. He counted the money, and then handed me the wad of Zimbabwe currency.

"Wait a moment," I said. "I need to count this." It appeared to be in small bills.

"Count it at your hotel," he said. "Don't worry, you can

trust me. You know where to find me if it's not all there." I had seen him on the streets since we arrived in Vic Falls, and I knew that I could find him again if we were a few dollars short.

"Okay, Jacob," I said, "but I will come looking for you if it's not all there." I suspected that he might have skimmed a few dollars for himself, but was not concerned. Fourteen Zim dollars was a good exchange rate.

"Thanks, Mon," he said. "And you Victoria, you are the most beautiful girl in the world."

With his final compliment he was gone. I could feel my wet shirt sticking to my body. We needed to hurry back to the hotel. There was just enough time to pay the bill and get to the airport. I slid the wad of cash into my pocket and wandered out into the sunshine. Jacob was gone. Tory ran ahead and I ambled behind feeling the heat and dust, wishing there was time for one last Tusker. The cash was burning a hole in my pocket. I walked on, a small knot starting to form in my stomach. I knew that I should have counted the money.

"Tory, wait a moment," I said. I stopped under a big acacia tree and looked around to see if anyone was watching. The knot in my stomach was getting tighter. There was something about the deal that did not feel right. Jacob had left too quickly. I pulled the cash out of my pocket and looked at it. The note on the outside was a clean blue hundred-dollar bill. I flipped the rest and they were all blue. For a moment I felt better, but when I pulled the bands off, the bills fell open and the knot got tighter. The top bill was also a blue note, but it was for one Zim dollar. I flipped to the next one, and then the one after it. Jacob would be smiling to himself by now. He had just made one hundred and ninety American dollars profit for a few hours work. I had been caught by one of the oldest scams in the book and that was the least of my problems. We were going to miss our plane. I felt rivers of sweat running down my spine.

I still had the problem of buying the plane tickets, and Jacob had stolen the last of my money. I already had the flights from Johannesburg to New York paid for, but getting back to South Africa was going to be a challenge. It was eleven-thirty in the morning. Our flight was due to leave Vic Falls at one-fifteen to arrive in Johannesburg in time to make our connection back to the United States. If we missed the plane we would have to wait three days until the next flight, by which time our nonrefundable return tickets would not be worth the paper they were printed on.

I grabbed Tory by the hand and ran back into town. The banks closed at noon, and I had to try and get there in time to get a credit card advance. I had already checked and knew that the airline would not take a credit card.

Tory was surprised by the sudden rush, but kept up with me as we ran through the center of town. We arrived at the bank just as a stern-looking doorman was shutting the front door. I managed to get one foot inside and pushed it open. The teller looked bored and disinterested when I explained my plight. I would need my passport, she said, hoping that her revelation would suddenly discourage me from pursuing the matter further. It was a few minutes before lunch and she was mentally out of there. Luckily I had both passports on me. She took mine and my MasterCard, and disappeared behind a closed door.

I waited impatiently looking at the clock on the wall, wondering if we would make the plane. It was scheduled to leave in a little over an hour. The teller reappeared with the bank manager. I was told that they had to call the US to get authorization on the card, and I would have to fill out some forms. I mentally calculated the time difference, and knew that the US banks would not be open for another few hours. I prayed that there was some direct link to a computer that would give us the okay. The manager escorted Tory and me to a small, airless room and produced a long questionnaire. It demanded all sorts of irrelevant information. I scribbled as quickly as I could, and handed the forms back. It was almost twelve-thirty. We sat waiting; the doorman shuffled his feet noisily; the teller looked bored and hungry; and the clock ticked loudly, taunting us.

After a while the manager reappeared, beaming. He had my money. He shook my hand and told me that it was the first credit card advance he had done. We took the cash and bolted outside in time to grab a cab. First a stop at the hotel to get our bags, and then full speed to the airport. There is nothing more frightening than a Zimbabwean cab driver with an incentive for haste. His car was more than twice the age of my daughter, and badly in need of repair. Bits of it were breaking off as we sped towards the airport, dodging donkeys and goats, and finally with its last gasp, we pulled into the passenger departures. The place was deserted.

A couple of flies buzzed noisily, but that was all. The airport is small, and out of the window I could see a South African Airways jet taxiing on the runway. I banged on a door that said

"Customs Only," startling the on-duty Customs man who was about to nod off to sleep. I explained that I needed to catch the plane. He jumped to his feet, yelled into his walkie-talkie, and before I knew it, out the same window, I saw the plane stop, turn around, and return to the gate to pick us up. We paid for our tickets, cleared Customs, and boarded. It was the first time a jet had come back for me. As we took off I looked down and saw the "smoke" rising from Victoria Falls, and the thin blue line snaking its way through dry African veldt.

CHAPTER 12
JAMAICA FAREWELL

"The cure for everything is salt water—sweat, tears and the sea."

—Isak Dineson

The highest peaks of the Blue Mountains in Jamaica are usually shrouded in mist, which coats the coffee crop with a fine dew, especially in the early morning before the sun breaks through. The plants drip constantly, the moisture seeping slowly into the groundwater, flowing in small rivulets until they meet up with other tributaries to form a lacework of small streams. By the time the sweet water has tumbled towards the ocean, it has become a churning river, cascading over boulders and tumbling between narrow, steep-sided cliffs. The undergrowth is thick and lush, a tangle of vines and tropical vegetation. We found it easier to wade and rock-hop our way upstream than to struggle with the dense foliage, and after an hour of dank coolness we suddenly found ourselves out in the bright sunshine at the edge of a deep pool. The sight was spectacular, just as we had been promised. The edges of the pool were a pale turquoise, becoming darker towards the middle. The very center of the pool was black, an indication that it was very deep. I looked over at my Jamaican friend and asked, "How deep?"

"I guess about fifty, sixty feet, Cap," he replied. "Maybe more. Don't worry, you will not touch the bottom." I couldn't detect anything in his voice, but I guessed he was probably right. The far side of the pool was dominated by a waterfall, wider than it was high, with a steady cascade of water crashing into the pool below. A fine mist rose, saturating the surrounding trees. We had come to jump over the waterfall and for a brief few seconds I thought to myself, "You crazy bastard, this time you've gone too far."

The idea had sprung from too many beers the night before. At the time it seemed like a good suggestion, like many of them do. However, in the cold light of day standing at the base of the falls looking up, I realized that the idea bordered on lunacy. Still, a small part of me knew that I could not back out. Men are strange that way.

"What do you think?" Sigrun asked. I ignored her question, knowing that she knew exactly what I was thinking. Women have a way of seeing straight into our hearts and Sigrun was no exception. "I'm going to have to jump," I mumbled, adding quickly, "but I am not going to go first. Hulk's going first so that I can be sure I'm not the only idiot." I looked around for Hulk, but he was already making his way towards the base of the falls.

John Brown is one of the kindest, most gentle men I have ever met. His friends call him Hulk and it's not hard to see why. A lifetime spent working hard and living close to the earth had toned his body and given his skin a deep, dark glow. He's missing a front tooth and his eyes are perpetually bloodshot from smoking too much marijuana, but other than that he's large, perfectly built, and very strong. A few days earlier when I sailed into Jamaica, Hulk had come out on a fishing boat to guide us through the narrow cut that separates Port Antonio from Navy Island, once the secret hideaway of Errol Flynn. He pointed us to an anchorage and then hopped on board, introduced himself, and asked if I had any work for him. His casual, forthright manner was engaging and I liked him from the very moment I met him. At that point I had no idea how much trouble he and I were going to get ourselves into.

A few hours after we arrived in Jamaica, Hulk introduced me to the owner of a small waterfront bar in Port Antonio, and she agreed to let me tie up alongside. From the foredeck of my boat, *Great Circle*, to the nearest bar stool was a distance of twenty feet, and I knew that my stay in Jamaica was going to be a good, albeit brief, one. I was planning on leaving the boat for a few weeks and returning home to the US, so after a few Red Stripe beers I contracted Hulk to caretake the boat, and grabbed a taxi to the airport.

On New Year's Day, 1997, I sat down with a pen and blank piece of paper, and made a resolution that would change the course of my sailing career, and in some ways, change the course of my life. The resolution was based on a seed first planted years before during my visit to Tierra del Fuego when I lay awake thinking about a solo voyage around the world. Shortly before going to Tierra del Fuego, Erin and I had divorced. In fact, that trip was as much about an escape from the stress of a broken marriage as it was about paying my respects to the gods of Cape Horn. Being single and making every effort to be a good father had clipped my wings and I was spending as much time on dry land as I could. To buy a boat and sail it around the world was as far removed from reality as a visit to the moon, but time is a great healer of wounds. A seed once planted eventually starts to bear fruit, and on that first day of a new year I decided it was time to get things going. I was not getting any younger, and a solo circumnavigation would be physically demanding, no matter my age.

I decided to enter the Around Alone, a tough event similar to the Whitbread, only the 27,000-mile course would be sailed single-handed. The only thing that stood between me and certain victory was a boat and a half-million dollars to campaign it. I had neither. I did, however, have a good campaign slogan and once the idea was committed to paper, I kept the slogan in mind. It read, "Goals are dreams with a deadline." My deadline was the start of the race twenty months away.

We need to be careful what we wish for, since some wishes do come true. Living in a land of prosperity does help, but in general if there is something we really want, we can have it. I wished for a boat; not just any boat, but one designed and built for solo sailing. During my land-bound years I had been working as a sailmaker, and made sails for a client who had built a boat for the 1994 Around Alone. It was beautifully designed and engineered, and the client, who soon became my friend, named the boat after his wife. Unfortunately, they got divorced and he ended up not doing the race. Three years later, shortly after that New Year's Day when I had committed my dream to paper, my friend called. He had a boat for sale. Without going into the details, a few short weeks later I was the proud owner of the perfect boat for a solo circumnavigation. My friend, with a boat named after an ex-wife, was what salesmen call a "motivated seller." My trip to Jamaica was the maiden voyage aboard the yacht, newly renamed *Great Circle*.

Jamaica was to be my training base for the Around Alone race and I returned several times to take the boat out to get used to its size and power. Each visit to Jamaica strengthened my friendship with Hulk and through him I was introduced to Pressley. Soft spoken with a rakish angle to his cap, Pressley Mackenzie was another warm Jamaican longing for a life in America. Both he and Hulk had dreams of visiting Miami and making it big, and almost from the outset they besieged me to take them back to the US. I politely declined, not wanting to hurt their feelings, but also knowing that doing so would be asking for trouble. If I took them to the US they would be my responsibility, and I already had too much on my plate.

On my final trip to Port Antonio, Sigrun and her friend Cricket joined me. Sigrun was my neighbor in Marblehead, Massachusetts, and there was more than mutual interest. I was hoping that the tropical heat and sultry air would coax her into a relationship. It was still winter up north and with snow on the ground, both Sigrun and Cricket jumped at the opportunity to help me sail the boat back to the US. We would leave after a few days in Jamaica and sail through the Windward Passage between Cuba and Haiti before passing the Bahamas and stopping in Fort Lauderdale.

We provisioned the boat at the nearby supermarket and left on a clear, warm afternoon. As I looked back at the island I saw the low clouds resting on the higher mountain peaks, and marveled at what a beautiful, diverse country Jamaica was. That night the wind picked up from the north and we crashed and banged our way towards Cuba with all on board feeling less than a hundred percent. Sigrun kept glaring at me, wondering what I had coaxed her into, and my chances at love were looking less favorable with each mile. The following morning the weather had not improved, and by the time we got closer to the Windward Passage and encountered the stronger winds that funnel between Cuba and Haiti, we were ready to turn back. I was reluctant to give up, but when a jerry can of diesel burst, filling the boat with a slippery, rank mess, it took only moments to decide. I turned the helm, pointing the bow towards Jamaica once more. Almost immediately, life improved dramatically. A fresh trade wind from behind, a tropical destination ahead, and once again life was good. It was the night we arrived back in Port Antonio that the idea of jumping over the waterfall came up.

I am sure that I would be a better person if I could only learn to swallow my pride. Age and experience have not helped, and have perhaps even made it worse. Hulk and Pressley were pleased to see us again, but I felt like a failure for having turned back from my trip north and I felt that I needed to earn their respect again. These were two simple, barely educated men—at least by our standards—but there was something in the way they carried themselves that I envied. Sometime in the evening Hulk mentioned the waterfall and commented that only a brave few had jumped from the top, and I rose to the bait. I also thought that the jump would impress Sigrun, and the way things were going I needed to do something to revive the interest. I knew it was the Red Stripes talking, but how high could the falls be?

As the three of us made our way around the pool I envied Sigrun. Not one to be suckered into anything, she had politely declined to be drawn into the jump. Cricket, on the other hand, was up for it and she and I followed Hulk to the base of the falls. The easiest way to get to the top was to climb in behind the falls and drag ourselves through gaps in the rock until we were above the lip of the waterfall. As I climbed higher I thought again how crazy the idea was, but there was no backing out. That would only have added insult. It's not that I am afraid of heights; it's falling that I'm afraid of, and whether it's a jump or a slip, to me it's still a fall. Within moments we were at the top. Both Cricket and Hulk looked confident and relaxed. My stomach was in a knot. Not only would we have to jump over the waterfall, we would also have to jump far enough out so that we did not hit the side on the way down. I peered over the edge and saw Sigrun sitting on a rock sunning herself like a lizard. Born in Iceland, she was making up for lost time and enjoying every ray of warm sunshine.

"So, Cap, what do you think?" Hulk asked. I pretended not to hear. All I could feel was my heart racing. "You want me to go first?" His teeth were white, except where the gap was, and his eyes smiled along with his mouth. He knew I was scared despite my cool pretense. Surprisingly Cricket was looking forward to the jump, but then she's a talented skier and used to the pull of gravity. I was almost tempted to ask Hulk if he had brought any marijuana, but decided against it. Now was not the time to start any new habits. It actually looked higher from the top than it did from the bottom, the same way climbing a mast does.

I edged closer to the lip and then heard a scuffle behind me. In a moment Hulk passed me, striding towards the edge and then throwing himself into the air before disappearing from view as he jumped towards the pool. From below I heard the splash and moments later saw him surface away from the falling water. I could mostly see his white teeth, his black face lost against the dark water. I did not feel good about it, but I was going to have to jump. Any final thoughts of backing out simply disappeared. I had not paid attention on the way up and I was sure that I did not know the way back down. Cricket smiled at me and said, "Should we jump together?" I wondered if being stuffed in a barrel and sent over Niagara Falls would be any easier. "Sure, Crick," I said. "Tell me when you're ready."

We backed away from the edge and then on the count of three started our jump. I remember the takeoff and the landing, but like my fall so many years before, the bit in-between is gone. The body's natural defenses take over, I guess. Sigrun says it took the longest time for us to fall and we made a huge splash; I only remember being in very cold water and seeing shafts of light reaching down to me as I swam for the surface. I also remember thinking that I would never do anything stupid in my life again, but little did I know I would break that rule within weeks. As it turned out, Sigrun also thought that it was a dumb thing to do, and my chances of a relationship were still looking slim.

We returned to the US, leaving the boat once again tied to the waterfront bar. It had become a fixture in Jamaica and when I walked through the crowded streets of Port Antonio people recognized me and waved. "Hey, Cap," they would say. "You need help on that boat? I'm a good sailor. I crew for you." They were all looking for a way out of the country and a free ride to the land of opportunity. Despite their abject poverty they were happy people and not all of their happiness came from smoking marijuana. I learned from the Jamaican people how little we need to be happy, not how much. I rented a car and drove all over the island on narrow, pothole-filled roads, constantly amazed by the skill and devil-may-care attitude of the drivers. Many times I wished that I did smoke grass just so that I could handle the traffic. There were times when I was passed at full speed on a blind corner with chickens in the road and oncoming traffic, only to get back to Port Antonio to see the maniac driver fast asleep in the shade of a tree. Only in Jamaica do the drivers put their lives in danger to get someplace as quickly as possible to spend the rest of the day lazing about in the sunshine. My only advantage was that I grew up driving on the left-hand side of the road; otherwise it would have been a total nightmare.

The day after the jump, Hulk asked me if he and Pressley could sail back to the States with me. "Cap," he said, "we really need to go to Miami to earn some money for our families." I knew Hulk had no family; in fact, he had made up his last name of Brown because he did not know who his parents were. Pressley, on the other hand, had three small children and a wife, but he was willing to leave them for a few months so that he could send money home. He had just built himself a new house and needed money to finish the interior. His house was modest by most standards—a corrugated iron shack on a cement slab with indoor plumbing was all there was, but it was a mansion to Pressley. I looked at Hulk and weighed my options. I was either going to have to negotiate the Windward Passage alone, or take along some crew.

"Sure, Hulk," I said. "I will be back in two weeks. You and Pressley get your papers in order and you can come with me."

"No problem," he replied. I should have known better.

I flew into Kingston where Hulk and Pressley met me at the airport. As soon as we exited the building the heat and humanity hit me like a wave. Reggae music blared from every car radio and window sill. The place throbbed with energy while Bob Marley urged the population to "get up and stand up for their rights." On previous visits I had flown in and out of Montego Bay, and by Kingston standards it was a quiet, organized city. Hulk grabbed my bags and tossed them into a waiting taxi.

"Cap," he said, "we have a small problem." The heat was my only problem so I was sure that whatever Hulk had on his mind would not be an issue. "We still need to get visas," he said. I stared blankly at him. "Hulk, you've had two weeks to get visas," I said. "We can't leave without them."

"It's not a problem, Cap," he said. "We just go to the American embassy and apply. With you here it should not be a problem." I was less sure, but waved to the cab driver who sped off at top speed dodging dogs and cutting in and out of traffic. I rolled the windows down and gasped for breath while watching the scene in downtown Kingston pass by. A few minutes later we pulled up in front of the American embassy. The line stretched hundreds of yards out the door. I looked at Hulk who smiled sheepishly. "It's not a problem, Cap, we just have to wait."

We stood in the sun inching our way closer to the front door. People produced radios and turned the volume to max.

Others had obviously anticipated the wait and had brought food to eat. My stomach craved a Red Stripe, but I thought better of showing up at the application window with beer on my breath. Late in the afternoon we made it in the door and just before closing got up to the window. A well-dressed, surprisingly cool-looking man handed us forms to fill out and said it would not be a problem. My letter of introduction and the fact that I had a boat for the trip made things a lot easier, he said. We filled out the forms and returned to the window. The well-dressed man studied the forms, asked for an application fee and told us to come back in six weeks to pick up the visas. I looked over at Hulk, who was concentrating on something near his feet.

The air was noticeably cooler for the ride to Port Antonio. Heavy storm clouds had built up and they hung low over the Blue Mountains. Jamaica is a place where you can really smell the air. It has a thick scent of frangipani and cooking fires, but on this particular evening I could smell rain. Despite my casual assurance that there was no rush, the cab driver sped along the narrow roads, winding his way higher and higher until we crossed over the ridge of the mountains and headed down the other side to Port Antonio. As we pulled into town I could make out the top of my mast sticking above the buildings. We really had become a fixture in the town, and while I was reluctant to leave I knew that it was time to head back to the US. If I was to keep my campaign to sail around the world alone on track, I needed to be back in New England by mid-May. Thunder rumbled as we drove through town. Both Hulk and Pressley had been uncharacteristically quiet for the trip back, both feeling a bit embarrassed by the visa situation. I had still not decided what to do. I was reluctant to do the trip alone, getting Sigrun and Cricket back down again was not an option, and sailing to Florida with two Jamaicans without visas did not seem like a smart idea. "Hulk," I said. "Let me get the boat sorted and have dinner and then we can talk about what to do."

"Sure, Cap," he said. "No problem."

Being on the boat was beginning to feel like home. I could hear the tug of the dock lines and the slap of water as it lapped against the flat aft sections of the boat. I poured myself a Red Stripe and relaxed at the navigation table listening to the sounds of Reggae mix with the sounds of an approaching storm. I ordered a cheeseburger at the bar and took it back to the boat, wondering what I should do. I always think best in the shower so I grabbed my shaving kit and headed for the small bathroom behind the restaurant. It was quintessentially Jamaican. A family of kittens lived in the corner and the Trade Winds blew in under the door. A bare light bulb hung from the roof with exposed wires half-taped together. It looked as if the electrician had decided to stop for a smoke break and had forgotten to come back. It had been like that since I first arrived.

I turned the water on and felt the wind buffet the shower stall. Suddenly there was a loud crack of thunder and the light went out. I fumbled for my towel, which was hanging over the door, but accidentally touched the wire. Somehow there was still power flowing, ingenious Jamaican wiring I guess, but it was the last thing I needed. I felt the first shock of electricity hit my hand like a dull pain and then because I was standing in a pool of water, it traveled through me. Luckily it was only a quick jolt, but it was enough to scare me and I fled from the shower dragging my pants on as I went. The rain started to fall in heavy sheets and the small harbor was whipped up with white caps. Back on the boat I poured myself a huge glass of rum and fell asleep to the sound of water banging against the hull and the dock lines tugging at their cleats.

The next morning I had made up my mind. I was not ready for my first solo sail and because I had to get going the only option I had was to take Hulk and Pressley, visas be damned. I would deal with it on the other end. The storm of the night before was still lingering and it, more than anything, had me feeling uneasy. *Great Circle* is a handful when the wind is up and I was worried about the sail up the Old Bahama Channel on the north side of Cuba. It was a busy shipping area. Right on cue, Pressley showed up for his day job; sweeping out the bar and deck and straightening the chairs. Even though it was a small place, Pressley usually stretched the job out to two or three hours. His monotonous sweeping mingled with bird calls, and the soft sound of rain falling on the water. The sounds of paradise, I thought.

"Where's Hulk?" I asked. Pressley looked a bit sheepish and pointed to a room behind the restaurant where Hulk sometimes stayed.

"We drank a lot last night," he said. "Rum mostly. Hulk is still sleeping." I walked to the room and knocked on the door, but there was no reply. "Hulk," I said. "It's time to get going." When there was no reply I pushed the door ajar. It was dark in the room with the shades pulled, but I could just make out the shape of two naked bodies. The girl had a sheet draped over her breast, but that was all. Just then Hulk sat up. I felt guilty about entering their room, but Hulk just smiled, his white teeth with a small gap obvious in the dark room, and said, "Are you ready to leave, Cap?"

I bought some provisions at the small supermarket and we left shortly after lunch. I was still unnerved by the weather, maybe the electrical shock had something to do with it, but as we short-tacked out through the narrow harbor entrance I had an uneasy feeling about the trip ahead. It was not a sparkling Caribbean day like I had become used to. Instead, the clouds over the Blue Mountains reached right down to the village, shrouding some of the homes on the edge of town. "The river would be flowing strong today," I thought, thinking back to the waterfall jump. We cleared the harbor, flicked on the autopilot, and set a course for Cuba.

Other than a slightly bumpy seaway, the first night's sailing was pleasant. I had Hulk and Pressley stand watches, while I monitored my radar from below and listened to the sound of Jamaica on the radio until the reception faded to static. Because of the wind direction we could not steer a direct course for the Windward Passage, and shortly after dawn I saw the low coastline of Cuba on the horizon ahead. The vegetation was in marked contrast to the lush richness of Jamaica. Low scrub and a few trees were all that grew on an otherwise barren landscape. I did not want to get too close so we tacked over and spent the day short-tacking up the coast just in sight of land.

Sure enough as we approached the Windward Passage the wind picked up as it funneled between Cuba and Haiti, and the seaway began to get choppy. Pressley's usually dark skin took on an interesting tone and I noticed him swallowing hard. His mouth was dry—the first sign of sea sickness. I asked him how he was doing, but he only swallowed harder and told me that he missed his family. Moments later he was hanging over the rail, moving from side to side as Hulk and I tacked the boat. By nightfall we were halfway through the Passage, the sun dipping slowly behind Castro's Cuba. I could not help but think of what life was like on the island and wished we could stop for a few days. Unfortunately, the American flag snapping briskly in the breeze behind the boat made us unwelcome.

Once we rounded the corner into the smooth waters of the Old Bahama Channel we set a spinnaker. The moon was up (and so, finally, was Pressley) and we sailed under autopilot with none of us saying a word. Off to port the lights on Cuba twinkled in the distance while we made good progress with a fair current and following breeze. For an African white boy, the irony of sailing past Cuba with two black crew members was not lost on me. It reminded me how sailing is a great equalizer and how important travel is for the human race. It's the only way we will ever get to understand each other. Growing up in lily-white South Africa I would never have imagined that I would find peace and happiness, say nothing of trust and friendship, from the company of two black men. "Try telling that to Castro," I thought. Trust and friendship is what builds nations.

We finally made Florida after three days of sailing. It had taken longer than I planned, but a "complimentary boarding" by the US Coast Guard while still in Cuban waters lost us a few vital hours and we ended up losing the wind at the end. Fortunately I hooked onto the edge of the Gulf Stream and we drifted north, first picking up Miami, then Fort Lauderdale radio stations. Sigrun and Cricket were flying down to meet us and I was looking forward seeing them again. I hoped that the warm Florida nights would loosen Sigrun's resistance to a relationship. The trip up from Jamaica had been good and I had barely given any thought to the problem of my two visa-less crewmembers. That was until I called Immigration moments after dropping anchor in one of Florida's numerous waterways. It was a Saturday afternoon and the person on duty was clearly not happy about having to work weekends.

"Get up here with your crew and paperwork right away," he growled, "and everything had better be in order." I stared at the pay phone with my heart thumping and wished that all I had to do was jump over a waterfall. Facing Immigration was not going to be easy. How was I going to explain Hulk and Pressley? I had already told the man that I had two crew on board. I walked slowly towards the beach where the girls and the two Jamaicans had gone, my stomach feeling heavier than lead. I crossed A1A and found them lying in the sun, a cooler of cold beer hidden under an umbrella.

Then an idea dawned on me. I had not told the man at immigration who my crew were. For all he knew they could just have easily been two girls, especially two girls with recent Jamaican stamps in their passports. I knew they had stamps in their passports because we had gone together to clear Customs when we first left Jamaica. I smiled when I remembered the trip to the Immigration office in Port Antonio. We had been given directions by the barmaid at the waterfront bar, but somehow we missed a turn. Farther up the road I ran into a man I knew from town and asked him the way. "Sure, Cap," he said. "You just follow the road back until you see the Rasta man under the tree, and then you take a left." Both Cricket and Sigrun had given me a quizzical look, but sure enough back up the road and under a tree was an old Rasta man, fast asleep in the shade. He had probably been there for years. I longed to be back there where life was simple, eating jerk chicken and sipping local rum. Instead I had to convince the girls to go along with my plan. They were skeptical.

"What if someone saw us sail in?" Sigrun asked. "What if they don't believe you?" They were good questions and ordinarily I would not have asked, but desperate times call for desperate measures and this situation, by my standards at least, was desperate. I had still not officially purchased the boat. It was under charter to me until I could get a survey done. Until then the boat was the property of its previous owner. With loudly touted zero-tolerance laws in Florida, I was sure that the boat would be seized if it was found out that I had brought two illegal Jamaicans into the country. Earlier that week the Coast Guard had intercepted a raftload of Haitians heading for the US. The problem of illegal immigration was very real and very much in the news in South Florida. I looked at Sigrun and Cricket and they must have seen the desperation in my eyes. "Sure," they said, "what can possibly go wrong?"

We grabbed the ship's papers and a cab, and drove to the Immigration building. It was a typical featureless government building, cold and daunting. Immigration was on the third floor and as we knocked on the door I felt my heart pounding in my chest. My palms were sweaty and I was sure that guilt was written all over my face. I opened the door and rang the bell on the desk. No one came. As we sat waiting, I had the same sinking feeling I'd had thirty years earlier, waiting for the headmaster to open the door to his office before he caned us. After a few minutes we heard some loud voices and then an angry man appeared at the counter.

"You off the boat, then?" he demanded. "Are you the one who called?" I nodded. "Yes," I said, trying to look sure of myself, knowing very well that I was not doing a good job. "These are my crew," I said pointing to Cricket and Sigrun. They looked equally nervous. He barely glanced at them and for a few moments I thought we might be all right. "Your papers had better be in order," he grunted, snatching the documents out of my hand and handing me some forms to fill out. I was thankful that I had not brought Hulk and Pressley. There was no way this guy was going to find that story amusing.

I filled out the paperwork while he disappeared into the other room with the papers and passports. Fortunately, both Sigrun and Cricket still had their passports on them. I could smell sweat and by now knew that it was my own. Sweat from being scared has a very different smell than sweat from hard work. It was the former that I could smell and it was dripping down the inside of my shirt, despite the air conditioning.

"So these are you crew," he said coming back into the room. He gestured towards them as if to indicate that they did not look much like sailors. "Yes," I said. "Very good crew." I smiled hoping that he would respond, but he just scowled. He leafed through the passports pausing for a moment on the Jamaican stamps and then satisfied, passed one of them back to me. I saw that it was Cricket's.

"You are from South Africa?" he said looking at me. I nodded. "What is your status in this country?"

"I am a resident alien," I replied, wondering who had come up with the word alien to describe people from other countries.

"Where is your green card, then?" he asked. I reached for my wallet and saw Sigrun stiffen slightly. Tucked behind my credit cards and drivers license was my green card and I handed it over. The immigration man studied it sternly and then turned to Sigrun. "You are from Iceland?" he said. I saw Sigrun stiffen again. "Yes," she said.

"And what is your status in this country?" he asked. I looked at Sigrun who replied in a small voice. "I am also a resident alien." I was not sure why she looked so frightened.

"Your green card, then," the man said. "I need to see your green card." Sigrun patted her pockets, but she knew it was in vain. She had left the card at home, never once thinking she would need it for a simple two-day trip to Florida. I saw her turn pale and then she said, "I left it at home." For a few seconds the Immigration man did not respond and I thought he was not concerned, but then his face darkened and he stared straight at me.

"You, Captain," he said, "have committed a very serious offence. You have arrived in the United States with crew whose paperwork is not in order." I could hardly keep from laughing at the thought of Hulk and Pressley back on the boat, but I kept a straight face. We were in enough trouble as it was and I was now certain that a relationship with Sigrun would never happen. She stood alongside me, swaying a bit on her feet while we waited to see what would happen next. "Come with me," the man said gesturing to me, and I followed him into the next room. I sat at a small table trying to think what to say while he shuffled papers, a permanent scowl etched on his face.

"Captain, you have committed a very serious offence," he repeated. "I am going to have to deport your crew and seize your boat. This is Florida. We take immigration very seriously."

I had no idea what to say. The man was probably right. I sat staring at the floor while he rose to leave. "That's all there is to it," he said as he walked out of the room. "Deport the girl and lock up the boat until you pay the fine." I swear I saw him lick his lips in anticipation, but maybe I was just being paranoid. He left me sitting at the small table feeling very desperate. The heady sailing of the last three days and the months of carefree living in Jamaica were suddenly a distant memory. I was back in the US, facing, as he put it, a very serious charge.

I heard voices in the other room and wondered what was going on. Sigrun told me later that she was taken to a separate room and told that she was being deported to Iceland. Cricket sat alone. She was told that she could leave, but she remained, waiting to see what was going to happen. After a while I heard a knock on the door. A new face appeared and asked who I was and why I was in the room. I explained that there was a problem with my immigration paperwork and that one of my crew was being deported for not having a green card. The person left and I heard some loud voices coming from another back room. Then it fell silent. I wondered what Hulk and Pressley were doing. Suddenly the door flew open and the new face smiled at me.

"Don't worry," he said, "my colleague can sometimes over-react. There is not a problem. We will just take Sigrun's passport and she has ten days to reclaim it in Boston. All she will need to do is show her green card." I felt a huge weight lift from my shoulders. Visions of the boat being impounded had been at the forefront of my mind, to say nothing of figuring out how to get Sigrun back into the country. We left the Immigration building floating a few feet off the ground.

Many years earlier, when I first visited Florida, I had gone to a place called the Southport Raw Bar, a somewhat divey place that served cheap beer and oysters on the half shell. Now I told the cab driver to take us there; we had some celebrating to do. The beer is served in chilled pitchers with the oysters on a bed of ice. After the stress of the afternoon nothing had ever tasted better. We reluctantly left after the first pitcher. The Jamaicans were on the boat and probably in need of a shower. The plan was to return to the raw bar for dinner. The cab dropped us off at the hotel that Sigrun and Cricket had booked for the night and we walked from there back to the boat.

The evening air was warm and all the weird and wonderful people that call South Florida home were out cruising the streets. Some were on roller blades, others riding bikes, most of them dressed in colorful clothing, all of them sporting deep suntans. We passed an elderly couple whose skin looked as if it had be treated in a leather tannery. Fake bleached hair and elaborate earrings made them true Florida residents. As we crossed the bridge to get to where the boat was anchored, we looked down at the traffic cruising the inland waterway. Off to the side in a small cove I could see *Great Circle*, but there was something strange about it. There was a boat tied up alongside. A large boat. In fact, even from a distance I could see that it was an official boat.

I broke into a run, hoping that my eyes were deceiving me, but the closer I got the more obvious it looked. The official government seal on the side of the boat was evident even in the fading light. I could just make out Hulk and Pressley sitting on the aft deck looking very subdued. Hulk looked up and saw me on the bridge. He looked right at me, but did not wave or gesture. Instead he turned his back towards me. I knew that he had seen me and I took his body language to mean that things were not good. I could see a few uniformed people standing in the companionway talking to others below. I thought I recognized one of them as the first Immigration officer, but I could not be sure. They were still quite a distance away.

We hid behind part of the bridge watching the scene below. Our worst nightmare was about to come true. Not only had I brought two illegal immigrants into the country, I had dragged two others into the mess. We were all in deep trouble. I watched the officials going over the boat and then suddenly they climbed back on board their boat and with a roar of engines, they left. Hulk and Pressley did not look our way until the boat was well out of sight. We rowed out to *Great Circle* and tied up alongside. Hulk looked more serious than I had ever seen him.

"What's up, Hulk?" I asked, and then something I had never thought of dawned on me. What if the Jamaicans had brought a small stash of marijuana with them? They told me that they were clean and I believed them, but they might have thought one small joint was hardly worth mentioning. "What did those guys want?" I asked.

"Cap, those guys were from Customs," he said. "They were just checking out the boat. They said they had never seen such a boat."

"What did they want?" I asked again.

"Nothing," Hulk said. "They asked if we had drugs, but we told them we were clean. I told them that you had gone to clear Immigration and they said that they would be by in the morning to check your papers."

I could not believe our luck. It seems that Customs and Immigration work from two different offices and unless they were planning on comparing notes on a Saturday evening, they would not know until the following morning that the names of the two Jamaican men were not Sigrun and Cricket. I had just been handed my second reprieve of the day and I was not about to wait for a third. It was time to get the heck out of South Florida. I gave Hulk and Pressley some spending money, their air tickets back to Jamaica and told them to forget they had ever heard of me. If anyone asked, they had no idea how they got to Florida.

Those clean sheets and warm bed in the hotel would have to wait. So, too, an attempt at romance; I was heading north. Without further delay, I upped anchor and motored slowly out down the inland waterway and out through the harbor cut. A slight swell greeted me as I found the open ocean and raised my mainsail. For most of the first night I kept looking over my shoulder expecting to see chasing lights, but they never appeared. As dawn broke on my first night ever sailing alone, I was far out to sea riding a fair wind north.

CHAPTER 13
ALMOST SIDESWIPED

"Twenty years from now, you will be more disappointed by the things you didn't do than by the ones you did do. So throw off the bowlines. Sail away from the safe harbor. Catch the Trade Winds in your sails. Explore. Dream. Discover."

—*Mark Twain*

Three days after leaving Fort Lauderdale I was running before a strong southerly wind approaching Cape Hatteras off the Carolina coast. The seas were large and even, the Gulf Stream adding a good three knots to my ground speed. *Great Circle* was performing better than my best expectations and for my own part I was starting to settle into the routine of sailing alone. The adrenaline was keeping me focused, coffee keeping me awake. Sailing alone was still new to me.

Late in the afternoon I poured myself a large rum drink and sat on the windward side watching the spray rise from the bow and drift across the foredeck. At times the speedo was registering over twenty knots, but it didn't feel like it. The boat sailed effortlessly through the water and the autopilot kept us on a straight course. I knew that I was in for a long night and that I should get some rest while it was still light, but the excitement of sailing alone with a spinnaker up had me wired and sleep would not be easy. Instead I relaxed by feeling the rhythm of the waves and listening to the whine of the wind in the rigging.

As we closed on Cape Hatteras the traffic increased as ships moving north and south converged at the corner. I kept on the outside of the northbound lane and watched freighters pass in single file. Before dark I doused the spinnaker and took a reef in the main, figuring that it would be wise to run the night under reduced sail. It would prove to be a smart move.

Night fell with the last of a waning moon heading for the western horizon. As it dipped into the water it suddenly got very dark and all I could see were whitecaps lit by florescence. I turned off all the interior lights and put a shade over the radar so that it would not blind me. *Great Circle* hissed through the water, still making twelve knots. Occasionally a light spray would splash me and I could feel the warm Gulf Stream water on my face. I was thankful that the night was clear. Even though we had passed Hatteras there were still several ships in the area and I was glad that the squalls of the previous night were gone. The night before had been one of the most terrifying nights I had spent at sea and I was not in any rush to repeat it.

It had started benignly enough, a light wind and quartering sea pushing us north, but around midnight small, powerful squalls developed on the edge of the Gulf Stream. I reduced sail, wallowing a bit in the lulls and feeling over canvassed in the squalls. It was a bit of a balancing act, but since I was new to solo sailing I erred on the side of caution. At around three in the morning I saw a large cloud line approaching from behind. It was clear on my radar as a distinct wall. I took a second reef and set the storm staysail. It was not the wind and waves that had me worried, it was the lightning that accompanied the front. The first bolt streaked from the sky and seemed to collide with the water right behind us. A thunder clap followed a second later.

As soon as the rain started, so did the lightning show and I was the center attraction. Within minutes there were bolts all around the boat with a deafening noise of thunder rolling across the sky above. I could not help but think about my mast being the highest point for hundreds of miles, and knew that I was a helpless sitting duck until the squall passed. It did, but only after an hour, by which time my legs were quite literally knocking together. Wind, waves, and water are one thing to have to deal with; bolts of electricity striking randomly were quite another. So with the sky clear, I hoped that this night would be uneventful.

Sometime after midnight I saw a ship on the horizon behind me, its leading lights clearly visible. I could also see a green running light indicating its starboard side. I watched the lights for a few minutes and then ducked below to see if I could pick it up on my radar. The problem with monitoring both a visual and a radar is that the bright light of the radar often kills your night vision. For now anyway it made sense to check both places and sure enough a solid blimp showed on my screen eight miles behind and slightly off to port. Back on deck, after my eyes had adjusted to the darkness, I could still clearly see the ship. It is a habit of mine to place a call to any ship whose course looks like it might converge with my own, and this ship appeared to be heading for the same point. I grabbed the VHF radio and switched it to channel 16, an emergency frequency that all mariners monitor.

"This is the sailing boat *Great Circle*, *Great Circle*, *Great Circle*," I said repeating the boat's name clearly. "This is *Great Circle*, whiskey, oscar, mike, 2242," I continued, giving the boat's radio call sign. "This is the sailboat *Great Circle* calling the ship off my aft, port quarter heading northbound in the vicinity of 35 degrees 12 minutes north, 74 degrees 56 minutes west." This is a typical procedure and usually after a few tries you make contact with the bridge of the ship. VHF radios have a range of thirty to forty miles, sometimes more depending on how high your mast is and how much power you have for transmitting. I called again and waited for a reply. Moments later I heard a ship reply asking me to switch channels to another working channel in order to keep channel 16 free for emergencies. I flicked the switch and called again on channel 9.

"Yes, *Great Circle*, I read you loud and clear," a foreign and somewhat sleepy voice replied. It's a part of sailing that I love. When you are at sea you are part of a big floating community made up of dozens of different nationalities, and more often than not you find yourself talking with Chinese or Russian radio operators. Fortunately most of them speak a little English. "Yes, captain, what can I help you with?" he asked.

"I was just checking to see if you could see me on your radar," I said.

"Yes, captain, I see you clearly ahead of us," came the reply. I asked where they were bound and while he told me where they had started their trip, where they were heading, and what cargo they were carrying, I thought back to an encounter with a ship that had occured almost two decades earlier.

It happened during the Parmelia Race, a race from England to Australia. Our crew was young and looking more for adventure than victory. Back in the late seventies almost everyone smoked and a long ocean passage was considered a good way to quit. If there were no cigarettes on board you would just have to do without, and by the time you arrived back on land six weeks later, hopefully the cravings had passed. A week into the trip we were sailing off the Portuguese coast and for those who were trying to quit, the nicotine withdrawals were painful. Then we saw a ship approaching on a similar course. It was daylight and we made contact with the captain explaining that we had a dire need for cigarettes and asked if he could help. In the spirit of sailors everywhere they agreed to dump a package overboard, which we would scoop up as we sailed by. It worked perfectly and for a while the cravings were sated. The following afternoon, buoyed by our cigarette experience, we asked another passing ship if they had any beer on board. We were a dry boat—we were racing after all—and with the tropical heat beating down a cold beer had been on everyone's mind for days.

"Sure," came the reply from the bridge, "how many do you need?" We could not believe our luck and half an hour later we plucked a case of cold Brazilian beer from the ocean. There was a note taped to the box. "Good luck to the crew of *Independent Endeavour* from the captain and crew of *World Navigator*." The following day we asked for rum raisin ice cream, but only got the sound of static as a response. I guess goodwill on the high seas has its limits.

After talking to the ship I went back on deck to get a visual. Sure enough, I could see the leading light right where they had been earlier, only now they were closer. I was glad that they had come back on the radio and rested easier knowing they had seen me on their radar. Even under reduced sails I was still sailing at ten knots. I was contemplating rolling away some of the headsail, but decided to wait until the ship had passed. I went below and called again. The radio operator came right back on the air.

"Can you please confirm your position?" I asked. "I have been having some trouble with my GPS [global satellite navigation system] and I am not sure if it's accurate." Earlier in the day as we passed Cape Hatteras it seemed as if my GPS was off by a few miles. Moments later the radio operator came back with their coordinates. I thanked him and checked them against my position. Something did not seem right. Their position was twenty-nine miles away from mine. Either my GPS was really off, or I had copied the numbers incorrectly. I called again, and very sheepishly asked for a confirmation of their latitude and longitude. It was the same as I had already written down, taking into account that we were both moving. I was very confused. How could my GPS be so far off? It had been many years since I had navigated by sextant, and although I had one on board I was not sure if my sight reduction tables were current. It concerned me. The area around Nantucket Island has numerous shoals and I had to be sure that I knew exactly where I was if I was to pass that area safely. I called the ship back and thanked the radio operator for his time and wished them a safe passage. At least the radio was working properly.

I was getting tired and wished that I had forced myself to sleep earlier in the day. I put the kettle on for coffee. Then I heard a strange noise. It sounded like a low rumble and I wondered if we were going to get some rain. The rumbling continued. It started to become more persistent, interspersed with a dull thud, thud, thud. "Strange," I thought to myself. I should have checked my radar, but I had been so perplexed by the GPS situation that I had not taken a moment to look. The ship had seen me and they were changing course to pass a good distance away, or so they said.

Suddenly I realized what the noise was. I ran on deck where the night was pitch black. It was more than night blindness. Earlier I had been able to at least make out the horizon, but now it was just solid blackness. The thud, thud was louder and then I looked up.

I was staring at the side of a ship that completely blocked out the horizon. Almost directly above me I could see lights. I heard voices yelling and a searchlight beam shone down onto my deck. The ship was no more than fifty feet away and I was on a collision course. I don't recall exactly what I did. I just acted reflexively. I must have disengaged the autopilot and swung the helm because in seconds *Great Circle* was laying on its side. The boom came crashing across, slamming into the rigging, momentarily pinning the boat. I skidded out of the cockpit and felt my feet hit the water as I landed up against one of the stanchions. The force with which I had swung the boat threw me out of the cockpit and almost overboard. Fortunately, I straddled the stanchion and although the pain was more than I care to describe, it was a lucky break. I was wearing a harness, but in the rush to avoid the ship, I had not clipped on. Had I not hit the stanchion, a sore crotch would have been the least of my problems.

The sails flogged violently and the boat was shaking as we rounded up into the wind, but through it all I was able to look up and see the stern light of the ship. It was so close that I could see the name clearly, despite the spray and darkness. *"World Navigator"* it read, and under the name in smaller letters, the hailing port of Monrovia. The crew were still training their searchlights on me, but soon they stopped and the thud, thud noise faded, replaced by the sound of waves banging into the side of the boat, and the flapping sails. I scrambled back into the cockpit and gybed the boat back onto course. Immediately the noise stopped. We were sailing with the wind from behind again while the stern light of *World Navigator* faded into the night.

Once the autopilot was back in charge I went below and called the ship. The radio operator came back on the air as soon as I called. "Yes, captain" he said, "we can see you just fine. We are now passing you about a mile away." I stared at the hand piece. A mile away! I called back about to blast them for their ineptitude, but instead asked a question. "Can you tell me the name of your ship?" There was short pause and then, "Yes, captain, our ship is *Ocean Heritage*." I could not believe my ears. Moments later another ship called. "This is *World Navigator*, *World Navigator*, *World Navigator* calling the sailboat. Did we hit you?" they asked. I slumped into my navigation seat feeling very much older. I had been talking to the wrong ship all this time. *Ocean Heritage* had another boat in view. *World Navigator* had not seen me and I had not believed my GPS. A combination of coincidences had a near fatal outcome.

I picked up the hand piece and called back. "No, *World Navigator*," I said. "You did not hit me. I'm fine." I repeated, "I am fine." I thought I might thank them for the beer given all those years back, but it was a long time ago and they would likely not have remembered. I was older now, but obviously not wiser.

I sat the rest of the night on deck keeping a close eye out for ships, but there weren't any. I sailed out of the shipping lanes and once again I had the ocean to myself. Sailing alone has its hazards, but I had also discovered its rewards. Flying through the night with all sails set, the boat vibrating from the speed and spray and me alone on deck feeling the thrill of being far out to sea, had heightened my senses to a place where they had rarely been before. For the first time in many years I felt alive, really alive. My dream was coming true. Now if only I could figure out how to get Sigrun to see things my way.

CHAPTER 14
REMEMBERING ERIC

"Have you gazed out on the ocean and seen the breaching of a whale? Have you watched a dolphin frolic in the foam? Have you heard the sound a humpback hears five hundred miles away, telling tales of ancient history, of passages and home?"
—*John Denver*

It had been a week since we left Marblehead and the sun had just dropped into the ocean behind us, spluttering and sizzling as it set, leaving a starlit night and a lumpy sea ahead. We were four hundred miles west of the Azores Islands. I pulled the fishing line in and we settled on canned spaghetti for dinner. Other than the gale that blew through a few days ago, it had been an easy passage, marked by a series of strong low-pressure systems that fed us a steady westerly flow. *Great Circle* was sailing well, riding the wind like a cork full of jet fuel. She was designed for that kind of sailing and flew along oblivious to the conditions, both good and bad. As I headed below to write up the log, I glanced at the instruments mounted above the companionway. Boat speed was ten knots. I felt a fine spray from the bow wave and ducked as solid water splashed the coach roof. The red night lights illuminated the interior. I settled into my nav seat, flicked the single-sideband radio on, and tuned in to the BBC world service.

"This is London," the rehearsed voice announced, and the theme music transported me back thirty years. For a few moments I was a small child at dinner, eating in silence while my parents listened to the world news on the BBC. It was a mealtime ritual in our house, and stories of war-torn villages and drought-ridden areas went hand-in-hand with lamb chops, peas, and mashed potatoes. Five sharp beeps, one long tone, and a voice announced, "The search for a well-known yachtsman presumed missing off the coast of Wales has been called off until morning. Authorities announced this evening that they had suspended their search until daybreak tomorrow for the sailor who apparently fell overboard from his yacht. In other news . . ."

"In other news?" I said to myself. "What other news?" Someone I knew, or knew of, was missing and I needed to know who they were talking about. I would have to wait until later in the broadcast to find out who it was. While I waited, I tipped back my chair and gazed out the window. My nav seat was comfortable and the view from inside the cabin was outrageous. I had a clear panorama of the world to leeward, and watched swells drift lazily by. A sliver of moon reflected on the water, casting dancing shadows on the waves. For a moment my thoughts were back on the news, and then I saw dolphins. Actually, I heard them before I saw them. There was a sharp squeak and a rattle, followed by a quick exhale and a blur as two Bottlenose dolphins flew by my window. They slid into the water without a splash and were gone.

My crew was in the cockpit. They were deep in conversation and saw nothing.

"Dolphins," I said as I clambered over them and headed for the bow.

"Come on guys, let's see you jump." The ocean below me was still and I watched the bow rise and fall with each swell. It knifed through the water and cut a clean path across the surface. I hung onto the bowsprit and watched the waves for movement. "Come on guys," I pled. This passage had been devoid of wildlife and I was aching to see a sign that other life existed. I hung over the bow until I could just see the keel, and they came at me like children playing with a water hose. I heard their squeaks and watched a dozen dolphins fly by on the lip of the bow wave. The water in front of us was alive with wet flying mammals, and they sliced the surface and disappeared into the clear, dark water. My boat responded in kind and surfed down the edge of a short Atlantic roller. And then, just as soon as they came, they were gone. I stared at the swells and hoped that they would reappear, but they disappeared without a trace. Another moment of instant magic vanished into the vast open ocean.

I ducked below and searched for better reception on the radio. The broadcast was scratchy, the way I like it. It reminded me that I was at sea where the news happens to other people. We were in our own world out there, and the feasts and famines of other parts of the planet had little effect on us. Marine forecasts and squalls on the radar were our news. The commentator announced an impending drought in Somalia, and then continued, "The famous French sailor, Mr. Eric Tabarly, has apparently been lost at sea off the coast of Wales. Mr. Tabarly was well known for his successes in single-handed yacht races in the 1970s, and was a veteran of a number of Whitbread Round the World Races."

I stared at the radio in disbelief. Tabarly, that great icon of French sailors, was gone. Lost at sea. Three short words that no sailor ever wants written after their name. I couldn't believe what I had just heard. The commentator continued:

"According to the local authorities, Mr. Tabarly was sailing aboard his yacht, the *Pen Duick*, and fell into the water while changing sails. He was not seen again. Attempts to get help were hampered by a faulty radio, and it was only when an Australian yacht passing by was hailed that the news was passed on to authorities. Search operations have been called off for the night, but will resume in the morning. Local officials are calling the drowning accidental, and are certain that he will not be able to survive the night in freezing temperatures. They hope to recover the body in daylight." I stared at the radio for a moment longer and then flicked it off. I was not interested in the cricket scores.

"Damn," I said to myself, "Tabarly's been lost at sea. Gone forever." The thought sobered me.

Eric Tabarly paved the way for single-handed sailors, and was in a small way responsible for the passage I was now making. I first met him during the 1981 Whitbread Race, and saw him many more times after that. At any big sailing event, Tabarly was there with his ubiquitous Gauloise dangling from his mouth, and twinkling eyes taking in the scene. He inspired legions of young French sailors, many of whom rose to the top of the game to win all of the single-handed around the world races. Those sailors, in turn, inspired me to join the world of solo sailing, and there I was en route to the Azores aboard my own boat.

For the ride over I had crew. For the trip back I would enter Tabarly's world. It was be my first ocean crossing alone. In order to qualify for the Around Alone, competitors are required to cross an ocean single-handed. The trip up from Florida was not enough, and I was looking forward to the challenge, despite the news about Tabarly.

I stared at the radio for a long time. From my nav seat I could see the wind instruments at the top of the mast. A small light illuminated the wand and I saw that the wind was just aft of the beam. The motion of the boat was gentle as it rose and fell on each wave. There was a continual creaking from the halyards, and an audible moan from the autopilot. They were comforting sounds. My instrument panel was like an airplane's and I could monitor just about everything from my seat. I glanced at the radar and it swept a clean scan. The GPS blinked a speed over the ground of nine knots, and put our ETA in Flores at forty-four hours. I noted the details in the log and checked the screen one more time. Speed was up and our ETA jumped forward five hours. We were still way out in the Atlantic with a long way to go. A lot could happen so I disregarded our arrival time. I tilted my seat back and shut my eyes. The news of Tabarly's death stung. One of sailing's best had been lost at sea. If it could happen to him, it could happen to just about any of us, but I already knew that. I squeezed my eyes together and tried to remember his face and the last time I saw him. It was in Uruguay, five years earlier, racing another Whitbread.

Tabarly can be summed up in one story. I was sure that there would be many more told at his memorial service in Paris the next week, but I remember him most from an encounter in England the day before the start of the 1989 Whitbread. That was the year I raced with the Russians aboard *Fazisi*. I was down below stowing my gear when I heard a quiet tap on the hull and a voice with a thick Dutch accent called out. I went on deck to be greeted by Connie Van Rietschoten, the venerable Dutch sailor and winner of two Whitbread races. Connie had upped the ante when he came onto the Whitbread scene, and poured money and organization into his campaigns. They became a benchmark for future winners.

"Can I please come on board for a look around?" he asked. I held out my hand and he jumped the lifeline with an ease that belied his age. I scrambled down the aft companionway and waited in the nav area. Connie slid down the stairs, ducked to fit below, and shook his head in disbelief. His yachts had been finished by expert craftsmen, and a liberal use of teak added to the look of quality. He stared at the dull gray interior, not uttering a word. Clearly life on this Russian yacht was not for him. He stared for a long while, shaking his head, and then left. I watched him walk down the quay. He stopped to talk to someone, and I saw him point towards *Fazisi*. He was still shaking his head. I smiled to myself and returned below to finish unpacking.

A few minutes later there was another knock on the hull, and a French voice called out for permission to board. I went on deck to see Tabarly clambering over the lifelines. He shook my hand, tossed his Gauloise in the water, and asked my permission to go below. I followed him and watched his face light up when he saw the interior.

"Oui, très simple, c'est bon," was all he said, but coming from Tabarly it was tantamount to a blessing. He beamed at me, clearly impressed by the basic layout. He was a man whose spirit truly flourished when surrounded by simplicity. A man true to himself and his profession. The sailing community and the world in general would be worse off without his twinkling grin and sparkling eyes.

My own tendency falls on the side of Tabarly. I prefer simple and functional over ornate and impractical. *Great Circle* is most definitely simple and functional. The boat was built for speed, and as a bonus she rides the ocean with ease and deliberation. That night on the open sea two thousand miles from Marblehead, my home away from home was flying through the dark night, silent as a ghost. The only trace she left was a sparkle of florescence that bubbled in our wake. A trickle of water on the hull hummed as we accelerated, and the autopilot moaned in response. If all went well we would make Flores, the westernmost island in the Azores group, in a passage of less than ten days. I could almost smell the flowers.

My crew jumped ship in Flores. The lure of life on land and the pressing need to attend to daily business quickly snuffed any thoughts of continuing on to Horta. They took a small commuter jet to Punta Delgado, and in moments were back in the traffic and jams of the real world. I was left to my own thoughts, tied to the quay while a front passed overhead. The wind whipped through the rigging and volcanic grit from the dock splattered the hull while I holed up in my bunk reading, waiting for a break in the weather. Every hour or so I climbed ashore and clawed my way to the edge of the breakwater to gaze at the waves crashing into the concrete pylons. I would rather have been riding out the storm far out to sea, but once tied to the quay I was reluctant to leave. Some boats simply do better away from land, and *Great Circle* is definitely one of those yachts.

By early evening the front was showing signs of easing and a short walk beyond the breakwater to a high point on the island confirmed that the sky was brightening to the west. I did not want to spend another night listening to the dock-lines tugging at the cleats, so I readied ship for departure. It took only a few minutes to secure below and crank up my outboard, and I left Flores as dusk descended on the island. I was anxious to be away.

The sea was still lumpy and confused, but the wind had definitely dropped. Black rain squalls lashed the higher elevations. To the west puffy pink clouds reflected the last light of day. The storm was over. Feeling a bit seasick and lonely I hoisted the main to the second reef and dialed in a course for Horta, 132 miles away. "I'll be there before dark tomorrow," I thought, but I had forgotten that islands create their own weather. I was going to pay for my impatience before this trip was over.

I spent a restless night scouting the horizon for ships and feeling the boat wallow with too little sail up. I did not have the energy to hoist the main all the way, and we flopped around with two reefs and a jib until a cloudy dawn rousted me from my lethargy. I set a full main and washed the decks to get rid of the grit. A large, even swell was running in from the southwest bumping up against the new wind from the east, and the slop and chop left me feeling queasy. With the end of the passage in sight, I was thinking about beer and hot food in Peter's Café Sport in Horta. I could almost taste dinner.

The afternoon wore lazily on as the wind came and went. I ran the outboard a few times. It was my only engine, but it made no difference against the slop and I resigned myself to missing closing time at Café Sport. The breeze, or what there was of it, was coming right from the direction I was heading. I fell asleep while my carbon-fiber home bounced around until I could just make out Horta on the radar. It was shrouded in fog, not visible from the deck. The air was still and moist. The radar hummed while I watched the blip of land remain steady at ten miles. Suddenly, on the opposite end of the screen, another blip appeared as the scan found a disturbance on the water. A squall I thought, and went up on deck to investigate.

The western horizon was black with low storm clouds marching in formation. It was a solid wall. The radar screen confirmed my visual, but I was not concerned. We were close to getting in and I was ready for some rest. We plodded along with the autopilot driving, barely making three knots. I grabbed my foul weather gear and made a cup of coffee. The line marched closer; suddenly it was upon us. I felt the first fingers of wind whip the jib and the boat heel gently in response. There was a light rain, and I was pulling up my foul weather bib when the front hit. It slammed us with all the might of a moisture-laden army and in a second we were rail down and spinning out. The autopilot alarm screeched a warning as I hit the standby button.

"This is all I need now," I thought. We were so close to land, so close to getting in—then I looked at the radar again. The screen was a solid mass of interference. Whatever had been behind was now directly overhead and here to stay. The autopilot alarm screamed with more intensity and refused to relinquish the wheel. I jabbed at the buttons while water broke over the side of the boat, but the pilot held fast and I was unable to alter course. I jumped down the companionway and scrambled aft to the switchboard to hit the circuit breaker. I could feel the yacht lurching and moaning under the load. I snapped the switch off and the alarm stopped.

I grabbed my harness and shot back on deck, grabbing the helm. It was still frozen. The pilot was off and the alarm was silent, but the helm remained jammed. "Oh, Christ," I thought, "now what?" We were knocked flat on our side with the mainsail sheeted in and the jib still pulling. I released the jib halyard and heard the sail let go. It flapped loudly, but the force of the wind prevented it from dropping to the deck. I would have to drag it down. The deck was at eighty degrees and I inched my way forward bracing against the side of the cabin. I grabbed handfuls of sail and the sail came down easily. I lashed it with a tie and inched my way aft to the cockpit again. I still had to deal with the mainsail.

By now the wind was blowing over forty knots. I removed the mainsheet from the winch where it was fastened, and eased it out. The pressure came off the sail and the boat came upright. It wallowed for a second with the sails flapping, and then the autopilot had a change of heart. Its small, computerized brain decided that it wanted a different course, and I watched the wheel slowly turn to port. The first fingers of fear tickled the base of my spine.

"Oh Christ, no, please don't do that," I said out loud. I watched the wheel turn in slow motion, and felt the boat lumber in response. The bow dropped away and the boat came upright. We took off on a reach, the wind on our beam. I hung onto the side of the cockpit trying to stop the wheel from turning, but it was no use. I watched as the boat continued to turn and the world started to spin a little slower. The wind died, the noise of the knockdown replaced by a more gentle whistling in the rigging and the scream of water flying past the hull. I clung to the cockpit side in horror as the boat took off down a wave and the speedo topped sixteen knots.

"Oh fuck, oh please no!" I yelled into the wind and then flung myself onto the cockpit floor. I watched the speed climb to eighteen knots while the wheel continued its slow turn, and then with all the force of a five-ton yacht on the lip of wave, we gybed. White water screamed past the boat, the boom flicked into the air, and then it swept the deck. It whistled over my head as I crouched in the cockpit, and with a huge crash slammed into the leeward rigging. There was no way the boat could withstand the impact. Either the mast, the boom, or the rigging would have to break, and if the rigging broke, the mast would soon follow.

In a split second we were back over on our other side and rounded up into the wind. I saw that the mast was still in one piece just as it dipped below the surface of the water. We had capsized, and to make things worse, the autopilot still had the wheel in a tight grip. To my huge surprise, nothing was broken. I unclipped my harness and climbed below. Spaghetti from the stove was plastered on the bulkhead and loose gear had fallen into the bilge. I dragged myself through the narrow alley that separates the main cabin from the back of the boat, and found the steering quadrant. It was dark and wet and almost upside down, but I knew where the autopilot ram was connected, and searched for the nut that held it to the quadrant. The nut was loose, and in a second it was off. I hit the ram and it came away easily. The wheel was now free from the autopliot and I scrambled on deck to figure out what to do next.

The mast was still slapping the surface of the water, but at least it was in one piece. The noise of the wind was ripping through the rigging and waves crashed over the boat. I looked up at the sky hoping Tabarly was up there watching me.

"Come on, Eric," I shouted. "You've been here, give me a break," but my words were lost in the wind. Tabarly was still a newcomer up there and probably did not carry any clout.

I scrambled down to the leeward side to release the part of the rigging that was causing the boat to remain pinned on its side when I noticed that the rope cover had ripped. Before I could get the boat to come upright, I was going to have to cut the cover away. I crawled below again and found my sharpest knife laying in the bilge. I grabbed it, and on the way back stopped by the nav station and opened my laptop to check my course. The electronic chart was blaring a warning. Our projected course was heading directly for land, five miles to leeward. A lee shore in a full gale. We were drifting at two knots.

I felt surprisingly calm. All I needed to do was cut the cover, ease the mainsail until the boat came upright, drop the sails, set a storm jib and alter course away from land. It was simple to see, but looked impossible. I wrapped myself around a winch that was half under water, and slowly cut away at the cover. Inch by inch it came free. Bits of spectra yarn littered the cockpit, but were soon washed away by the rain and waves. The knife was big and sharp, but I wished I had a pair of scissors on board. It would have been easier with scissors. Raindrops pelted the water and the mast continued to tap dance with the waves. It was a precarious situation, but surprisingly under control. Then we were broadsided by a large wave.

I heard it an instant before it hit us. The wave came with a low growl slamming into the side of the boat, tossing us over like a tiny cork. I saw the mast disappear below the waves again, and grabbed a winch feeling a sharp sting on my thumb. I waited while the boat lurched under the load and then slowly the mast came back out of the water. It labored under the weight of water on the sails and I was sure it would break, but the boat just shook and shuddered and tried to come back upright. The wind kept slamming us over. The water around me was tinged red, and I looked down at the bare bone of my thumb. The knife had slit it cleanly open and the skin peeled back to reveal a stark white bone.

I cursed out loud. I could not feel any pain, but the blood was making a mess of an already messy situation. I was skidding around trying to brace myself so that I could finish removing the cover. Inch by inch I cut it away, and then finally it was gone and I was able to ease the sails out. The boat slowly came upright and the mainsail started to flap violently in the wind. I saw that the battens were broken and protruding from the sail. The mainsail flogging was tearing at the mast while the whole rig shook and shuddered. My nerves were screaming for relief.

"Okay, okay, Hancock," I said to myself. "Just get the damn thing down and you can get out of here." I climbed below again and checked the chart. We were still drifting towards land, now less than four miles away. "Jesus," I muttered. "A lee shore in a full gale without an engine." Blood was still pouring from my hand and I felt light-headed. I wondered if it was from lack of blood, or from a massive rush of adrenaline. Either way I felt like puking. The bulkhead was smeared with blood and my foul weather gear was stained crimson.

"Come on, Eric, help me," I yelled. The sky above was black and angry. It was time to drop the mainsail. I wrapped the halyard around a winch, carefully flaking it so that it would run freely, and then eased it out. I felt the boat shake as the load came off the sail, and saw the front of the sail drop a few feet. I eased the halyard some more and the sail dropped another foot. I took a wrap off the winch and paid it out some more, but this time the sail did not come down.

"Now what?" I yelled. The halyard was free and the top ten feet of the sail was loose, but it appeared as if one of the slides that attach the sail to the mast was hanging up. It was hard to see in the fading light, but I was sure that something was caught. I wrapped the halyard around the winch again and wound it back up a few feet. The rain and gray skies had visibility reduced to zero. From the base of the mast I looked aloft and could just make out the head of a bolt sticking out from the mainsail track.

"Oh man, now I'm in trouble." It was definitely the head of a bolt. The track is bolted to the mast and with all the shaking and banging one of the bolts had backed out. Its head was projecting out less than a quarter of an inch, but that was enough to stop any of the sail attachments from passing by.

For a moment my legs felt weak, and I slumped onto the cockpit floor to think. The rig was still in the boat, the boat was upright and despite the flogging and broken battens, the mainsail seemed to be in reasonable condition. The only major problem was land. Hard, rocky land. I have never had to call for help and I was reluctant to do so now, but what were my options? If I could not drop the sail I would drift slowly towards the beach and sometime in the middle of the night we would be wrecked. I had no energy to do anything. Blood was still pooling on the deck. It mixed with the salt water, turning everything a soft crimson.

My other worry was insurance, or more to the point, lack of insurance. Every single asset I had accumulated in forty years of living was right under me, bobbing towards the beach, and I was not sure how to save it, or for that matter, how to save myself. I shook my head trying to think clearly and realized that I had no safety net. I was going to have to save my own skin.

Spurred by the thought of hitting the bricks, I went back to the mast and looked up. It was almost dark and I could no longer see the bolt protruding from the track, but the sail was still hung up and I knew that one way or another, I was going to have to get it down. Back in the cockpit I loaded a reefing line onto a winch and started to wind it tight. The line ran to a reef point on the front of the sail. The wraps snugged up on the winch and the reef line went taut. I kept on winding, feeling the load, desperate to get the sail down. There was loud bang and bits of black plastic from the disintegrating sail slide fell to the deck. The reef line went slack and the sail dropped a few feet, then stopped. Next problem. This one was a ball-bearing car at the inboard end of a batten. I felt it snug up against the bolt as I wound as hard as I could on the reef line until it was strung taut like a guitar string, but it still held fast. I re-led the line to my biggest winch. With all my weight, powered by a spurt of adrenaline, I cranked the handle. There was a ripping sound, then a shower of ball-bearings. The line went slack and the sail dropped another few feet. Another grunt, another grind, and another shower of plastic.

It was completely dark by the time the sail was down. I took a knife to the last few feet and lashed it to the boom. It was strangely quiet without the flogging. Below deck the lights cast a pale glow on the interior. It was a mess. Spaghetti sauce everywhere, and the bulkhead smeared with dried blood. I looked at my thumb and the wound lay open. It had stopped bleeding, and for the first time since cutting myself I started to feel pain. A slow throb at first, followed by a searing hot pain running up my arm. First the storm jib, and then I would bandage the cut. We were still drifting towards the island of Faial, now under two miles to leeward. Its mass was clearly visible on radar. From the deck I could make out an occasional light on land.

The storm jib was buried under a pile of sails and spilled vegetables. I found the bag and threw it out the fore-hatch. Attaching the sail was easy compared to the rest of the afternoon's activities, and in a few minutes I had it up and drawing. I eased the helm down, bore away and gybed. For the first time in four hours my course was leading me away from land. Away from danger, but also away from rest. With the autopilot broken, I would have to remain at the wheel until we docked in Horta. I lashed the helm riding a course away from the island, and went below to tend to my hand and make some soup. My body was shivering violently despite the warm night air. I wished there was rum on board, but we had finished the last bottle in Flores. Maybe it was better that way, I thought. The rum would only dull my senses at a time when I needed them most. I found a bandage, wrapped it around my thumb, and tried to decide what to do next.

My first impulse was to sail as far away from land as possible, away from danger, but getting back without a mainsail would be a problem. *Great Circle* does not sail very well into the wind with only a jib. I could not motor because the boat was only powered by a small outboard engine. My batteries were low and I was tired. The autopilot was broken, and my sails were ripped. Making Horta would be a relief, but sailing along the coast at night with only a storm jib was not smart. I was close enough to see lights clearly despite the rain. I gybed again and aimed at the narrow strip of water between Faial and the big island of Pico. My course was a close reach to the channel, and then a short beat up to the harbor of Horta. "Go for it," I thought. If something goes wrong I could always bail out and get clear of land. I was too tired to make rational choices, and the pull of land was strong.

Fortified by the soup and the thought of a safe harbor, I sheeted the storm jib and braced myself at the wheel. My speed over the ground was less than two knots and would diminish as we encountered an adverse current between the islands. *Great Circle* hobbled along the coast, short tacking through a wide arc, making slow progress towards Horta. Sometime after midnight we were abeam of the small airport halfway up the coast, and by four in the morning I could make out the loom of the city and see the lighthouse on the breakwall. My hand throbbed and my body felt like a soft sponge that had been beaten with a stick. It was only the persistent rain that kept me awake.

The faint fingers of a gray dawn were filtering through rain squalls as I made the breakwater. My outboard started on the first pull and I dropped the storm jib on deck. It had been nineteen years since I was last in the Azores and my memory of the place had faded. I recalled that there was a big seawall where all transient sailors painted their names, and the name of their yachts. I had left my mark there aboard a boat called *Battlecry* on a passage between the Caribbean and England, and wondered if it would still be there. A new inner harbor had been built and I could see a forest of masts. The old seawall was empty except for some of the local fishing fleet and a small freighter unloading cargo. I circled once to be sure it was a good place to dock, and then tied up alongside. I felt exhaustion seep through my body. A lee shore in a full gale with no insurance was every sailor's nightmare. And then I remembered Tabarly. "Thank you, Eric," I said quietly.

The squalls were moving out to sea and the sky to the west was clearing. The sun hit the whitewashed buildings, and the green fields above Horta were rinsed clean, their fragrance carrying over to me. I could smell cows and hear sheep bleating in the distance. Down below was a mess, but I crawled into my bunk, flicked the light off, and dreamed of a cabin in the mountains, far, far away from the ocean.

CHAPTER 15
A DATE WITH A WALL

"Follow in my wake, you've not that much at stake, for I have plowed the seas, and smoothed the troubled waters. Come along let's have some fun, the hard work has been done, we'll barrel roll into the sun, just for starters."

—*Jimmy Buffett*

I watched the tall peak of Pico slip silently into the haze behind me. For a while I could make out a dim outline, and then it was gone. I was alone again. Bermuda was two thousand miles away and would be my next landfall, but between my bow and that distant island lay open ocean. I said a silent prayer for a safe passage, and then set about organizing my stores and plotting a course. The past few days had been busy and I was glad to be off. I listened for the slap of the waves on the hull and quickly settled into the rhythm of life on board.

My stay in Horta had been hectic. There was much to do to repair the damage done by the knockdown, and a team of volunteers lent a helping hand. The mainsail was my biggest concern. It had taken a pounding and needed a lot of attention.

It was now patched and I hoped it would hold together until Bermuda. The autopilot head had been replaced and was working fine. I could hear its moan as the hydraulic arm tugged at the steering quadrant, and I felt the boat respond to the course dialed into the computer. *Great Circle* heeled to the breeze and sliced through the clear water. It felt good to be back at sea again. Fortunately, one can't see too far into the future. If I could have I might have remained in the Azores.

As the day faded into night I sat alone on the deck and watched the water trickle in my wake. I had set a course that would take us south for three hundred miles, before slowly turning to the west. I needed to skirt the Azores High, and a direct course for Bermuda would have taken me straight through the windless zone. So far my tactics seemed to be working. The wind was on my beam and blew warm and soft. It was the same temperature as my skin and I could not feel where my skin ended and the air began. In the east a full moon rose slowly from the ocean. It shed its silver light onto the dancing water and sparkled in my wake. It was a night of pure magic.

And then suddenly I remembered. I had forgotten to paint my name on the wall. The old seawall, the new seawall, the docks and the jetty are all covered with paintings, and it is becoming difficult to find a place to leave your mark. The day after I arrived in Horta I searched for the painting I had left behind in 1979. It took hours to find and was faded and chipped, but the red spinnaker with a white cross was still visible, as was the name *Battlecry*, painted below. I had wanted to leave *Great Circle's* logo for all to see, but in my haste to leave, I had forgotten. While I am not superstitious, legend has it that it is bad luck to leave Horta without leaving your mark. I gazed at the water rushing by and hoped that my luck would hold, at least until I made it safely across the Atlantic.

I remained awake all night keeping a lookout for ships, and as dawn lit the sky I crept into my bunk and slipped into a deep sleep. My radar was alarmed to warn me if anything came within range, and I had set my alarm clock to roust me in an hour. I hoped shipping was keeping a good lookout. The memory of almost being hit by the freighter off Cape Hatteras was still fresh in my mind.

The sun rose early. It pounded down on the boat and I woke in a pool of sweat. I lay in my bunk thinking about the day. It was going to be hot. It was already too hot to be below so I climbed onto my nav seat and dug through the nav station looking for sunscreen, but could not find any. I searched my stores. No luck. I searched everywhere and eventually gave up. I knew that I had brought some with me, but could not find it. Two weeks in the Tropics and no sun protection—I hoped I could find the toilet paper. The wind had swung aft with the new day, and I dropped the big Genoa and set a spinnaker. We were already two hundred miles from Horta and I was enjoying the passage. So far, so good.

A few days after my arrival in the Azores, I had returned to the US. The knockdown had banged an important lesson into my brain—you can never let your guard down when you're alone. The ocean is forgiving to a point, but push your luck and you pay dire consequences. I had been lucky, but then I was born under a lucky star. I left the boat on a mooring in

Horta harbor and flew back to Marblehead. Sigrun and I (yes, I had eventually persuaded her into a relationship) planned to spend some quiet time together before the Around Alone, before our lives got caught up in a media frenzy. It was just before July 4th and the town was decorated with banners and bunting. Marblehead is one of those perfect New England towns that responds to patriotism, and with flower boxes blooming and flags flying high, it looked postcard perfect. Without hesitating I asked Sigrun to marry me while the town was still decorated, and she agreed. A day later, with a Justice of the Peace presiding and Marblehead harbor as a backdrop, we tied the knot in a simple ceremony. A honeymoon would have to wait; I still had an ocean to cross and a world to circumnavigate.

A week after returning to the States I woke in the middle of the night in a cold sweat. I had been dreaming that the dockmaster in Horta was calling me and telling me to come and get my boat. I lay quietly with my heart pounding, trying to recall my dream. The dockmaster had been yelling into the phone that there was danger coming. I had to move my boat, he said. I glanced at the clock next to my bed and saw that it was two in the morning. After a long while I went back to sleep. It was not restful and when the sun came up I opened the curtains and flicked on the television. The lead story was about an earthquake that had hit the Azores. The town of Horta had been woken just after dawn to a tremor that destroyed much of the island. The quake had happened at two in the morning, US east coast time. When I returned to the Azores I was amazed to see the damage. One third of the rural buildings were demolished. Roads were damaged and bridges had collapsed. There was not much damage in Horta, and people in the marina had only felt their rigging shake. They said it sounded like a low-flying jet passing overhead. *Great Circle* was safe on its mooring.

Three days after leaving the Azores I found the Trade Winds. I felt that luck was running my way and dismissed the sunscreen as a simple oversight—until I tried to start the generator. It was dead. I bled the system and cranked the engine; still nothing. I changed the fuel pump and tried one more time; still dead. It would take me over a week to figure out the problem, until which time I ran on no power. There was no chance of turning back. The start of the Around Alone was rapidly approaching. Instead, I shut off all lights, alarms, instruments and stereo, and used the solar panels to power the autopilot. I started to wish I had painted my name on the wall.

The days blended into nights and back into days as we slowly inched our way across the chart. The wind remained aft of the beam, and other than the intense heat and lack of sun protection, it was turning out to be a fine passage. I caught a few fish and made sushi. The Portuguese cheese and olives were good, and a healthy dose of fresh air made a world of difference to my temperament. The knockdown off Horta was fading to a distant memory. Life was good and so far being married was great! It took me a week to get the generator working again, and once I had the batteries charged I fired up the stereo and plugged in a disk, but soon shut it off. The silence had become addictive and the commercial sounds of normal life seemed intrusive. I preferred the noise of water rushing by the hull, and wind whistling in the rigging. All was right with the world except that there was no sea life. Nothing. No birds, no dolphins, no whales, no flying fish—nothing. Every so often I would see some piece of garbage float past, but that was all. I was disgusted by the pollution and saddened by the lack of living things. After two weeks we approached land.

My chart showed a thin line snaking towards a small island far out in the Atlantic. Bermuda was drawing closer, and suddenly we were there. I made landfall on St. George's light and sailed right into the harbor. There were a few boats at anchor, but most had headed for safer waters with hurricane season approaching. I tied up alongside the Customs building and felt a deep sense of accomplishment. I had been lucky with the weather and guessed that other than misplacing the sunscreen and generator problems, my luck was holding. I still wished that I had painted the wall, though. My luck would soon run out.

I left Bermuda at the same time Hurricane *Bonnie* was flirting with the Gulf Stream east of Miami. Forecasters were predicting that the storm would either track across Florida, or turn north and pass between the US mainland and Bermuda. It was a few days from my location and I reasoned that I would have plenty of time to turn around and go back if the storm came my way. I was anxious to get back to the United States, and cast my lines ashore.

I sailed out of St. George's harbor just before midnight, and by the following morning was one hundred miles closer to home. *Bonnie* had stalled and was sucking up the warm waters of the Gulf Stream, and intensifying. I was getting nervous. It had become a Category Three hurricane—not the deadliest kind, but enough to make my life miserable. The storm was packing hundred-mile-an-hour winds and there was a distinct possibility it might head north. There was no use pressing my luck. I had pushed it far enough just by leaving, so I turned *Great Circle* around and headed back to Bermuda. The afternoon air was still and moist, and the wind died away to a passing zephyr. I motored, and as the sun dropped into the ocean behind I grilled a steak on the barbecue. It was a spectacular sunset—I hoped to be back on land before midnight.

Approaching Bermuda from the west is much trickier than coming in from the east. The northwest side of the island is bordered by a huge reef, but it is well lit. I called Bermuda Harbor Radio and asked for the coordinates of the lights on the reef and noted them in my log. My chart was for the entire Atlantic Ocean and did not show details of the approach to Bermuda. I programmed my GPS and made landfall on the first light at two minutes past ten. The lights of Bermuda twinkled in the distance and St. George's lighthouse cast its beam far out to sea. I sailed right up to the light so that I could check my GPS, and then altered course for the second light. It was less than a mile away.

A dim red glow from the night lights illuminated the interior and the green radar screen showed a mass of land off to starboard. I could see the light I was heading towards on my screen, directly ahead. The waves slapped their familiar rhythm on the hull as we heeled gently in the dying breeze. And then we hit.

The noise of carbon being wrenched from the hull by the sharp edges of coral still rings in my head. The forward fin hit first and ripped out of the boat, leaving a gaping hole. I felt the keel hit as I ran up the companionway and grabbed the wheel. I swung the boat away from land and we hit again. This time I could feel the rudder jerk in my hands. It was a dark night and the water was still. We had been sailing at four knots on a calm sea. There was nothing around us. Ahead I could see the light we had been sailing towards, and behind me the dim glow of the one we had just come from. Frantic, I gybed the boat in towards the reef and we spun in a tight circle. The boom came across and miraculously we found open water and I sailed away from danger. Below, the water was flowing swiftly. It was already up to just below my knees and filling fast. I slammed the watertight bulkhead closed to contain the leak in the forepeak, and started the bilge pump. *Great Circle* wallowed and I wept for my stupidity. Later when I looked at a chart I saw that the reef sticks out beyond the straight line. You cannot sail directly between the lights. It was nearly a fatal error.

With the watertight bulkhead containing the leak, the forepeak filled until the level inside matched the sea outside, and then it stopped. I dropped my sails and started my outboard, and once I was certain that we were not going to sink, I motored slowly, and painfully, back to Bermuda. My dream of sailing around the world alone had come to an end. The boat was not damaged beyond repair, but fixing it would take more than I had left, both emotionally and financially. My respect for superstition and legend had grown. I vowed to return to the Azores to paint my name on the wall.

The following winter was one of the worst of my life. Perhaps I made too much of the grounding. To non-sailors it was just a simple mistake, but to me it was everything. I had spent two decades learning my craft and was proud of my record as a professional sailor. Running aground and nearly sinking was about as bad a thing as I could imagine happening. I floundered without direction, struggling to shake a mood of melancholy that had settled on me. I repaired the boat in Bermuda, and the day it was relaunched, I watched with dismay as the Around Alone fleet sailed from Charleston towards South Africa. I had worked for two years to be a part of that great adventure, but it was not to be. The boat was fixed and I was soon back sailing, but remained afloat in a sea of self doubt. My pride wounded, my psyche damaged, my confidence in the dumper. I kept wondering if the wall had something to do with it.

By spring, the Around Alone fleet was already on its last leg back to the US. Cape Horn and the Southern Ocean were behind them and they were headed for the finish and fame. I was still floundering, but had decided that it was time to return to the Azores to splash some paint on concrete. It had to be done. I had to break the curse and the only way I could think of was to return to the Azores and paint my boat's name on the wall. A friend called and told me of a skipper who needed a hand for a trip from Newport to Horta, and I signed on for the passage. There would be two of us on board, and we would sail a well-appointed forty-six-foot yacht back across the Atlantic. It was a nice boat, but it resembled floating furniture, as I like to call yachts that look like a bungalow in *House Beautiful*. I barely gave a moment's thought to the trip other than to pack some paints, paintbrush, and a toothbrush, and think about what kind of design I would do when we got there. We left Newport on a starlit night in early June.

By the second day we were pounding into steep seas and strong headwinds. I looked at the pilot chart for the North Atlantic and it showed a two percent chance of easterly winds for the month; none of them should blow more than 12 knots. The strange strong wind continued for another day and then died. I was glad to get my two percent out of the way early in the passage. But then the trouble really started.

My shipmate woke me in the night to announce that he had dropped the fuel separator for the main engine overboard, and did not have a spare. It was potentially a serious problem, but we found a plastic glass in the galley that could be modified to fit the fuel filter. We epoxied the two and set the jury-rig aside until morning. I wanted to be sure that the epoxy set properly before we ran diesel through it. We would run on the power we had and use the generator to charge batteries in the morning, but something was draining them, and before dawn they were flat and useless. We cranked up the generator, but it would not charge. My bad luck with engines was returning and by noon that day we did not have enough power to light up the compass light—and that was the least of our problems.

Modern sailboats are designed to consume electricity and provide all the conveniences of home. The winches turn effortlessly at the push of a button. The autopilot keeps the boat on a course straight and true. The drinks are cooled with crisp chunks of ice, and the frozen steaks are thawed before grilling. Lose power and you lose it all. I was most concerned about having to hand steer the rest of the way. We took up a watch system of helming two hours on, and two off, twenty-four hours a day, and spent the off-time trying to bypass the systems on the boat that needed power to operate them. The gas stove has sensors to make them safe, but no power means no sensor, and no sensor means no gas. There was no running water, no lights and worst of all, the food went bad. And then the wind swung back into the east and a gale started blowing. I thought long and hard about superstition and legend and we talked about turning back, but I was adamant about pressing on—I had a date with a wall.

The wind gusted over forty knots and the seas on the edge of the Gulf Stream were big and confused. We were able to rig the helm so that the boat sailed itself while we sat below and watched as the waves crashed over the deck. We could feel an occasional weightlessness as the boat plunged from wave crest to bottomless trough, but the boat soldiered on and we were safe and dry. Until the boom separated from the mast.

The fitting that attaches the boom to the mast had ripped in two and the reefed mainsail was flogging frantically while the aluminum boom thrashed about trying to wrench the rig to pieces. We managed to lash it and effect a temporary repair. The boat wallowed and lurched from gust to gust as sheets of rain blew horizontally. Spindrift laced the gray water. There was no sign of an end to the storm, and as I made my way below I felt my back let go. There was a sharp pain in my lower back and then a searing hot pain throughout my body. My battle with back pain was back. For those who know the pain of a problem back, imagine how it feels when the boat is lurching from wave crest to trough.

I made it to a quarterberth and wedged myself in with cushions, trying vainly to lie still. Any movement of the boat was painful, and in an easterly gale there was a lot of movement. I gazed blankly at the overhead and wondered what else we were in for. Two days passed before the wind subsided, along with the pain. I crept tenderly behind the wheel to steer while my shipmate gratefully found his bunk—he had been at it for forty-eight hours without a break.

After a week at sea the wind slowly came aft and the sun

came out. All we needed was power, and life would be back to normal. Well, some food would have been nice. We were reduced to eating pasta and cans of tuna, but at least we were not starving. If we lost the wind completely we would be in trouble. Life settled into a rhythm. Families back home became increasingly worried. There was nothing we could do other than plod on towards Horta. And then the wind died.

We were twelve days into the trip and the ocean was flat and featureless. It did not resemble the sea we had been looking at for so long. The steep gray waves were now gently rolling turquoise. The sails slatted incessantly in the dying wind and filled with the occasional zephyr, but mostly we drifted in circles while our ETA on the hand-held GPS showed us arriving in Horta in mid-September. I wondered how many cans of tuna we had on board and guessed it would not be enough.

As the sun set on our thirteenth day, dolphins joined us to watch the spectacle. The air was heavy with squalls reflecting the evening light. I watched a small rain cloud on our beam and thought I noticed a hard edge to it. The edge grew more distinct until the bridge of a ship appeared. A ship with food, and perhaps an emergency battery charger. We had saved the hand-held VHF radio for just such an emergency, and a scratchy call had us in touch with the *Crown Topaz*, a Chinese freighter bound for Miami. The captain did not speak much English, but for some reason he did understand the words "jump-start." Perhaps he drove an old car. Whatever the case I saw them alter course and head in our direction.

We inflated the dinghy and got ready to launch it. I called the captain again and explained that I would be in the dinghy and they should drop a battery down to me so that we could use it to start our engine. I did not think it was a good idea to have the ship come alongside, and the captain agreed, or at least he seemed to. As the light faded I set off and rowed in the direction of the ship. Our boat bobbed in the slop and looked small and vulnerable. The ship was drifting slowly and I intercepted it at the bow.

From my vantage it looked massive. The sides were sheer and steep steel. I scraped down the hull fending off with an oar, and halfway down looked up at the smiling faces of the Chinese crew. They were dangling a battery at the end of a line with the idea of dropping it into my boat. I thought about what might happen if fifty pounds of battery landed in my rubber raft and hoped they were kidding. They weren't, but fortunately the ship was moving too fast. I skidded past the drop site, ducking to miss the battery that remained dangling at the end of the rope, and drifted aft towards the propeller. I was desperately attempting to row away from the ship, but the wash sucked me back in and I was headed right for the prop. By luck, or by chance, the captain had shut the engines down, and as I was spat out the back I passed the huge propeller, missing it by two feet. The blades were motionless—they were knife sharp and reflecting dully in the fast fading light. The ship kept on drifting, and I was left bobbing in its wake. And then it started to rain. The tropical water poured down, reducing visibility to zero, while the water all around the dinghy was churned white by the torrent. Both the boat and the ship were lost from sight. I spun the dinghy around and started to row towards where I thought they might be.

After a while I could just make out the ship. It was maneuvering alongside the boat, and my shipmate was vainly attempting to hang fenders over the side. They were a long way off and our yacht looked pathetic and small alongside the freighter. Even the freighter was dwarfed by the vast ocean. I pulled on the oars and slowly gained on them until I could see the battery on deck and a small Chinese man scrambling down a rope ladder. The crew on the freighter rigged spotlights to help out and the boat rocked gently in the lee of the ship. My shipmate and the engineer were below fiddling with jumper cables and the battery.

 I scrambled on board in time to see a garbage bag of food land on the foredeck, followed by another filled with drinks. I gave a thumbs up as the engine roared to life, and watched as the small engineer climbed back on board his ship. The *Crown Topaz* pulled away and sailed into the dark night. Her stern light faded with the arrival of a slim moon. The spirit of seamen was alive and well and I thanked the captain and thanked the gods. We would make Horta before September. Then the wind picked up and swung back into the east.

 We beat through the night, eating cheese sandwiches and listening to the sound of the autopilot groaning aft. The next morning the wind had picked up to gale force and we slammed and slogged towards Horta. I thought of my trip across a year earlier—it might as well have been a different ocean. The dolphins had given us luck, but it was paint on the wall that would change it for good. Horta was still two days' hard sailing away.

 Dawn on day sixteen broke wet and windy. The green hills of Faial were laced with lashing rain and the tall peak of Pico was shrouded in a low fog. The wind funneled between the two islands as we plowed our way up the coast. The weather was not going to give us a break. I remembered creeping towards Horta a year before with ripped sails and a heavy heart, and thought about all that had happened since. It had been an eventful year, not all good, most of it interesting, some of it challenging.

It was time to paint the wall and head home. My plane was scheduled to leave for Lisbon right after lunch. We tied up alongside and I felt a weight lift from my shoulders. There was just enough time to clean the boat, have lunch at Café Sport, and then do a bit of painting.

The wind died and the sun came out, drying the concrete pavement. I found a small spot without a boat name, and left my mark. It said *Great Circle*, 1999, and in the top right-hand corner, I wrote my name.

EPILOGUE
A WARRIOR SPIRIT

"Well I've been to the mountain and I have been in the wind. I've been in and out of happiness. I have dined with kings, I've been offered wings and I've never been too impressed."

—*Bob Dylan*

The cold waters of Newfoundland are a good place to think, and in the spring of 2000 I needed time to think. I was traveling down the dark side of my mind, where doubts fed upon themselves and grew in my imagination. It was not a good place to be, but the mood of melancholy that had settled on me after the grounding was unshakable. I had naively thought that painting the wall in Horta would kick the curse and I would regain my confidence as a sailor, but it wasn't to be. I returned home and started to piece my life back together, confident that I could repay the debts that had accumulated while I trained for the Around Alone. Instead I floundered without direction. My campaign had given me focus and being focused is a wonderful way to live. It seemed strange to me to be feeling this way, but perhaps I had underestimated how much failure would impact me. I didn't feel like a failure, but no matter what I told myself, I was still having a hard time coming to terms with the grounding.

I thought about seeking professional help, but instead opted for an old-fashioned cure. The Australians have a term for it. They call it going "walkabout." I needed to go walkabout. I needed to spend time where the world was uncluttered and unspoiled. Being in the wilderness has always allowed me to think clearly. Just as I had traveled to Tierra del Fuego after my marriage to Erin ended, I traveled this time to Newfoundland to join friends for a passage along the north coast of the Canadian province.

I flew to Nova Scotia and connected with a small four-seater plane that would take me to St. Anthony on the northern peninsula of Newfoundland. We took off and flew low along the coast, looking down on rugged, windswept countryside. There were fjords and remote anchorages, reminding me a little of Tierra del Fuego, especially when I saw the first iceberg. It was bright white, the billions of compacted snow crystals reflecting the afternoon sunshine. As I watched the berg disappear under the wing of the plane, I knew that I was heading in the right direction, and as we touched down at the small airstrip I was sure I had done the right thing by getting away. The air was cool and clean. I breathed deeply and felt tension drain from my body. By the time I stepped on board the boat an hour later, the familiar surroundings of a well-appointed yacht were a little like coming home. The warm teak trim and comforting slap of water on the hull were old friends. I cherished the feeling and as I looked around the small Newfoundland fishing village, I knew that I was on the right track.

We would sail the rugged northeast coast, slowly making our way towards the capital city of St. John's on the east coast, and then passage across the Grand Banks to Nova Scotia. It was then a short hop from Halifax to the boat's home base of Dark Harbor, Maine. As night fell I heard the clear mournful lilt of a loon. It reflected my mood perfectly.

We left St. Anthony right after dawn and sailed smack into iceberg alley. On the horizon ahead a massive tabular berg was drifting slowly south. There were smaller bergs floating closer and we set sail for an angular chunk that lay directly in our path to our evening anchorage. The bergs had been spawned from the Arctic icepack three years earlier. The icepack calves virgin bergs into Greenland Sea, where they are picked up by the Labrador Current and swept south. The ice sails in the cold water, traverses from the Greenland shore to the Canadian coast, and converges at the Straits of Belle Isle. When they pass St. Anthony, their steep sides show deep striations where warmer weather and relentless, pounding seas have taken their toll. They balance precariously on an eroded underside and capsize with regularity.

We approached our berg like typical tourists, launching the dingy for a closer inspection. We were just approaching the ice when the side sheared off and crashed into the sea. The berg listed heavily, and for a moment it rocked gently, threatening to capsize, but just as quickly it settled back on its axis as we scurried for the relative security of the boat. We were learning the ways of temperamental ice and gaining respect for its timeless beauty. The grounding off Bermuda was starting to seem like a far-off memory, and when a bald eagle buzzed us, I knew that I was on the mend.

I have always been attracted to remote places, and the steep-sided fjords and rugged coastline of Newfoundland have long held a fascination. So too have the people that inhabit the island. I have tremendous respect for the qualities that bind people together, especially those who live in an uncompromising environment, and the spirit and generosity of the people we met along the way were a true testament to their nature. A week into the trip we found ourselves wedged up a fjord in an anchorage off a small fishing village. The water was still and the colorful cottages reflected gaily in the fading light. As the last rays of day seeped from the sky we heard clear voices singing out to us. Two young girls from the village had walked to the water's edge, and were singing traditional Newfoundland songs. Their voices carried across the calm water and amplified on the steep sides of the fjord. They sang until it was dark, and we sat and listened to songs of love and life drift gently on the evening air.

The next day the wind was honking from the south and we sailed close-hauled along the coast. Arctic terns and Atlantic puffins kept us company. We laughed at the frantic flight of the puffins — their frenzied flapping barely kept them airborne. Humpback whales blew fishy air while they cruised slowly past the boat, each following an ancient calling. It was cold, and layers of warm fiber-pile kept the chill from my bones. For the first time in a long time I felt as if my life was back on track. I sat and watched the spray from the bow wave wash the foredeck and thought about how lucky I had been since leaving South Africa more than two decades earlier. I had lived a blessed life, full of fun and adventure. That simple dream I had had while taking the train across the Karoo, a plan to leave South Africa to sail for a living, had all come true. I had not succeeded in my attempt to sail around the world alone, but I had succeeded in many other areas. I was healthy and strong with beautiful children. I had stories to tell my grandchildren, and most of all I had not wasted a moment of my life.

We left our final anchorage in Newfoundland in the early morning. There was a low mist drifting across the bay and wisps of cloud hung in the trees. A small boy rowed his skiff out to watch us leave. He reminded me of myself — a boy with dreams in his heart. As the anchor came up and we slowly motored away, I turned to wave goodbye, but the boy just stared after the boat. He too was traveling, his own thoughts taking him to faraway places. Finally, almost as an afterthought, he waved back and seconds later was swallowed up by the mist.

We hoisted the sails and set a course for Nova Scotia. I was looking forward to seeing my family again. Bermuda and the grounding seemed like a lifetime ago. The sound of carbon being ripped from the hull and the feel of warm water around my ankles had become just another experience. I had replaced those bad memories with better ones: memories of a beautiful land with caring people, of wild animals and spectacular scenery, and of open spaces and clean air. Getting away to enjoy the simple things in life, like trolling a line for dinner, had put life itself into perspective.

While I sat daydreaming a chilly wind picked up, and the new waves slapped on the hull. The rhythm resonated through the rigging and carried back to me at the helm. I watched the land sink slowly into the sea behind as we sailed away, and I felt like the luckiest person alive. The horizon ahead was curved in a wide arc like outstretched arms. The future was fresh and new and full of possibility.

The next day we made landfall on the north coast of Nova Scotia and found another perfect anchorage tucked in behind a steep cliff. We rowed ashore to a small beach littered with driftwood and made a bonfire. A full moon rose behind a forest of birch casting its bright light on the still water. As I watched it slowly transit the sky I remembered a poem that I had once been given. The words rang true.

Some say the young boy became a sailor.
That his warrior spirit carried him to distant shores . . .
I remember seeing him once on the southern shore of Africa
His eyes caressing the canvas . . .
I heard him whisper his dreams to the southwest wind.